CHANGING
THE EDUCATIONAL
LANDSCAPE

CHANGING THE EDUCATIONAL LANDSCAPE

~

Philosophy, Women, and Curriculum

JANE ROLAND MARTIN

ROUTLEDGE NEW YORK LONDON

Published in 1994 by

Routledge
29 West 35th Street
New York, NY 10001

Published in Great Britain by

Routledge
11 New Fetter Lane
London EC4P 4EE

Library of Congress Cataloging-in-Publication Data

    Martin, Jane Roland, 1929–
    Changing the educational landscape : philosophy, women, and curriculum / Jane Roland Martin.
      p.   cm.
    Includes bibliographical references (p.   ) and index.
    ISBN 0-415-90794-2.   ISBN 0-415-90795-0 (pbk.)
    1. Education—Philosophy. 2. Feminism and education. 3. Education—Curricula.   4. Educational change. I. Title.
LB885.M26C47 1993   93-26612
370'.1—dc20   CIP

British Library Cataloguing-in-Publication Data also available

To the past and present members
of PHAEDRA

Ann, Susan, Nancy, Barbara,
Susie, Beebe, Jennifer and Janet
with gratitude for their critical readings
and constant encouragement

CONTENTS

One Woman's Odyssey:
To Philosophy and Back Again

I. Education/Philosophy, Round Trip

"I was in my fiftieth year when I began this book: for me a time of flowering," Carolyn Heilbrun wrote in the preface to *Reinventing Womanhood*.[1] I was fifty-one when my flowering occurred and it happened at the same place. When I arrived at the Bunting Institute of Radcliffe College in September 1980 I had taught my university's course on Philosophy and Feminism but had done no scholarly work of my own on women. When I left the following June, I had written four papers on the place of women in educational thought and was drafting an outline for a book. But that is the least of it. My year at the Bunting changed my research and my life.

Legitimizing subject matter that I had never thought to explore—that no one so far as I knew had explored—the study of women removed the veil that had kept me in ignorance of my forerunners. Opening up new avenues of inquiry, suggesting questions that I would not previously have dreamed of asking, it also put me as a philosopher in touch with the world as I knew it. After hearing me respond to a public attack on the papers I wrote at the Bunting, a man I had known for years said: "You are a different person. What's happened to you?" I looked at him and wondered if I should list my new feminist scholar-friends and explain that because I was now writing about education in relation to marriage, childcare, daily domesticity, sex role stereotypes, a gender based division of labor, and women's double-binds, I was at long last able to identify with my subject matter. "I finally know what I am saying," I replied.

One unexpected benefit of my study of women was that it allowed me to develop a voice of my own. Another boon was that it brought my scholarship into close connection with my everyday life. My research into women's education and "place" illuminated what happened at home and in my classrooms and what occurred in those arenas was grist for my mill. Perhaps the most important windfall, however, was that it changed the way I thought and wrote about education, thus hastening the day when I could keep the promises I had made when I left school teaching to study philosophy.

My mother was a teacher and so were many of her friends. Anxious to know if I would one day join their ranks, they periodically inquired if Jane was planning to teach. "I don't know," my mother would say. "You'll have to ask her." Jane, who at a very early age must have internalized the culture's denigration of her mother's profession, would respond when asked, "A teacher? Never!" It was with a good deal of embarrassment, therefore, that within a year of graduating from college, having by then discovered how few options were open to me, I had a change of heart.

Except for being the mother of two sons, nothing I have done since has been so difficult as school teaching. Yet I loved working with fifth and sixth graders and I might have stayed in the classroom for as many years as my own mother did, had I not gone back to school part-time to earn a master's degree. There is no doubt about it: my immediate motivation was the desire for higher pay, not a love of learning. In the event, however, a late afternoon course about research on teaching opened my eyes to a world of scholarship that I had not known existed. Another introduced me to the study of philosophy.

I still remember where I was sitting the day I realized that some people actually spend their lives doing research on teaching, and I can recall my excitement. I also know that when I tried to picture myself running experiments, collecting data, doing statistical analyses, my imagination failed. Analytic philosophy as taught by Israel Scheffler was a different story. If I could not quite see myself in the role of philosopher, neither could I escape its spell.

My move into philosophy was accelerated by the fact that I was then, of my own accord and in solitary splendor, spending weekends and holidays critiquing my school's curriculum. The 1950s are sometimes represented as one of education's golden ages but my experience of having to teach children long lists of isolated, unconnected facts and tell eager fifth graders that the sixth grade course of study was out of bounds to them belies the myth. When I tried to design better curricula, I was brought up short, however, by the arbitrariness of my attempts. What justified my thinking that this social studies curriculum was better than the one in place, I wondered. How did a person rationally decide what content to include and when? Once I discovered analytic philosophy, I knew that to answer my own questions I would have to continue my studies.

The trouble was that the further I traveled into philosophy, the more distant seemed the problems that had once so exercized me. Before long, debates about the structure of explanation loomed larger on my horizon than discussions of the school curriculum.[2] Insofar as I thought about education at all, definitions of teaching and learning commanded my attention. When I left the classroom I did not dream that it would take far longer to return to those original issues than it did to leave them behind. No one ever told me it would be much more difficult to discover how to apply the philosophical proficiencies I acquired in the academy to the real life problems of education than to gain that expertise in the first place. No one informed me that the way back was not well charted.

My trip home from the land of pure philosophy began in the late 1960s. The student protests about the irrelevance of the university curriculum, set as they were against the backdrop of the Vietnam War, struck a sympathetic chord in one who, from childhood, had been taught that no hard and fast lines should be drawn between school and world. In a period when some of my colleagues were inclined to protect philosophy's good name by denying the validity of the criticisms, I grew determined to bring my chosen field into closer connection with educational practice.

That I was slow to embark on this journey, and did so only at the urging of students, is a measure of the academy's success in transforming a school teacher, whose questions about educational practice had sent her on a quest for illumination, into a member of the philosophical profession. By the time I left graduate school in 1961 I had thoroughly internalized the lesson that the greater one's distance from one's object of study, the better one can understand it. I had become convinced that, intellectually speaking, there was no higher good than clarity. I had been persuaded that philosophers *qua* philosophers were not qualified to make value judgments. And I had learned to view with suspicion those few philosophers who wrote and spoke in a language that everyone could understand.

From the vantage point of the 1990s my ready acceptance of an ideology of disconnection may seem inexplicable. Feminist critiques of science have revealed the gendered assumptions of methodologies that presuppose a radical separation of subject and object and the uncoupling of knowledge and its uses.[3] In addition, the ideal of accessible scholarship was subscribed to by the second wave of feminism from the beginning, even if it has often been celebrated in the breach. But I absorbed these lessons when analytic philosophy was in its heyday, analytic philosophy of education was just coming into its own, and feminism was on hardly anyone's mind. Nobody deliberately taught me these doctrines. As a conscientious student I simply imbibed the background assumptions of my professors along with their daily lectures.

Besides, the years of my apprenticeship were a heady time for the philosophy of education. I spent my evenings at the very first meeting of the field's professional organization I attended sitting on the floor in the rooms of the analytically trained colleagues I had only just met, zealously reading and discussing papers that the organization had not allowed on its official program. Seldom since have I seen people so intellectually excited and so willing to learn from one another. I doubt that anyone there dreamed that our brand of philosophy would one day dominate the field, as it eventually did. Yet much as I felt I was joining the vanguard of a revolution in scholarship when I began my work on women, I then saw myself as part of an underground movement.

My belief that philosophy of education bears more or less automatically on the real world also caused the delay. The misapprehension was understandable. When its subject matter is compared to that of logic and metaphysics, the area seems positively mundane. Besides, philosophy of education has never been considered "pure" philosophy. Still, had it occurred to me to question the presuppositions of the philosophical approach I was using, I would have realized that it could shed little light on actual educational practice.

The philosophy of education that I was becoming adept at was aptly termed a "second-order" activity. Its objects of study were not phenomena in the real world but *talk about* such phenomena; for instance, about the verbs "to teach" and "to learn" or, alternately, about the concepts of teaching and learning. At best, then, its findings were a step removed from education itself. The relationship between philosophy and education was further strained by a methodology that detached phenomena from their historical, cultural, and socio-economic contexts. Lorraine Code has pointed out that philosophers of knowledge "commonly treat 'the knower' as a featureless abstraction. Sometimes, indeed, she or he is merely a place holder in the proposition 'S knows that p'."[4] For analytic philosophers of education, both teachers and students were featureless abstractions: place holders in, for instance, the proposition "X teaches Y to Z." The connection to real world issues was made even more tenuous by my adopted field's self-referential focus. One did not so much write about the term "to teach" or the concept of explanation as about another philosopher's analysis of that term or concept. As language was interposed between philosopher and world, some extant analysis of language was inserted between language and philosopher.

My first published paper, "On 'Knowing How' and 'Knowing That'," is an example of what was really a third or even a fourth-order activity. It is about someone else's critique of Gilbert Ryle's analysis of the verb "to know."[5] When I was invited to revise it for inclusion in the anthology *Language and Concepts in Education*,[6] and one of the editors asked me to make its relevance to education clear, I scarcely knew how to proceed.

Reflecting on the direction analytic philosophy of education was taking, Abraham Edel said of that revised paper: "Here Martin the analyst profits from Martin the educator and the analytic products are steered precisely along those distinctions that are important to educational experience. Martin is less applying analytic distinctions than setting them up to be useful to what the lessons of educational experience have shown to be important."[7] Arguing that in "Basic Actions and Education," written some ten years later, I also assumed the "double role" of philosopher and educator, he remarked: "Gradually Martin the educator begins to call the tune."[8]

"Note the implications of such a study," Edel said. "It calls for a two-way interaction of educational problems and experience and analytic process and products."[9] This call would be repeated in virtually all my work. I sounded it in "The Disciplines and the Curriculum," first published in 1969, and in the introduction to a section of my 1970 anthology *Readings in the Philosophy of Education: A Study of Curriculum*, when I said that the street between curriculum planner and epistemologist is two-way.[10] A decade later it could be heard in the chapter I wrote for a National Society of the Study of Education Yearbook on Philosophy and Education, "Needed: A New Paradigm of Liberal Education." And an echo is even discernible in "Curriculum and the Mirror of Knowledge," an essay written in the 1990s.

If Edel was right that in my "knowing how" paper "the lessons of educational experience break in—even if only surreptitiously—upon the analytic process,"[11] then I exaggerate when I now say that I lost all sight of education as I traveled into philosophy. It is not the same, however, to introduce an educational standpoint into one's philosophical analyses—as I did consciously in the case of action and perhaps unconsciously in the case of knowing—and to bring philosophy to bear on the pressing educational issues of our times. Even if my analyses were "education laden" from the outset, in those early days I was not interested in applying my newly acquired analytic methods to the educational problems crying out for solution. Clarification was my business, not the guidance of practice.

Mind you, the educational discourse of the time desperately called for clarification. A site of vagueness and ambiguity with policies smuggled into definitions of human nature and slogans and metaphors masquerading as arguments, it needed what analytic philosophy had to offer. My objection is not to the search for clarity, which I still consider a great good, but to the assumption that it is the sole or even the primary task of philosophy of education. "There are two sorts of things that go by the name of philosophy of education today, one traditional and one newish," William Frankena wrote in 1966. The newish kind is analytic philosophy, he explained. The other "is what educational philosophers have done historically and what some of them still do."[12] In the fashion of the day he called this latter "normative philosophy of education." For awhile the "newish" kind of philosophy of education so bedazzled me that I did not know I was mistaking a part for the whole. I did not see that for clarity's sake I was turning a means into an end, a process into a product.

In reflecting on the great gap between analytic philosophy and education I find myself reiterating the argument of "The Disciplines and the Curriculum." Rejecting the assumption, popular in the mid 1960s, that the traditional disciplines should be granted a monopoly on curriculum space, I maintained that we have no reason to believe that the various fields of intellectual inquiry will illuminate life's important issues—war and peace, for instance, or even marriage and divorce. I also pointed out that even if the intellectual disciplines do speak to the full range of topics that children should study in school, the ways in which they relate to them would have to be made plain to students, for they are not self-evident. And I said that practice in applying them to everyday affairs would have to be given.

I am not at all sure that, at the time, I saw the relevance of my thesis to my own situation. Did I have in mind the curriculum questions my former teaching self had asked when I wrote that because the concerns of philosophy are so general, one wonders if that field can directly illuminate particular problems and issues? Was I assuming that philosophy of education was exempt from my criticisms or was I finally discarding the assumption that the problem of relevance would take care of itself in my chosen area of philosophy? I frankly cannot say. I do know, however, that in the late 1960s my reasons for doing philosophical analysis began to change and my focus gradually shifted from the level of language back to that of practice. I did not stop—I have never stopped—analyzing terms or concepts. But in a seminar I taught during that period on the role of discovery in teaching and learning and in several papers I then wrote,[13] I began to explore questions of what could and should be done in education. I also know that the pace of the journey back from the far reaches of philosophy picked up when in 1980 I began to work on the place of women in educational thought.

My immediate reason for applying for a Bunting Institute fellowship was time off from university teaching and an office of my own in which to write the presidential address I was scheduled to deliver to the Philosophy of Education Society in April 1981. Intent on raising my colleagues' consciousness about the status of women in the theories and narratives of our field, I needed uninterrupted time to do the requisite research. What I originally intended to be a short-term study soon turned, however, into a major research program that would occupy me for years to come. The question I took to the Bunting was: What is the place of women in educational thought? As Carol Gilligan—the feminist scholar-friend whose work on women had an enormous influence on my own thinking and whose enthusiasm and unfailing support gave me the courage to proceed—liked to point out, the question I left with was: What happens to educational thought when women are brought into it?

It did not take long to answer my original question. The discovery of our absence from the texts and anthologies of the field and the androcentric bias of the prevailing analyses and interpretations was depressing but not unexpected. The surprise was that if one lifted the veil of ignorance and began to see women as both the subjects and objects of educational thought, the field would be transformed.

Little did I dream when I sat down to write a paper about Rousseau that "Sophie and Emile: A Case Study of Sex Bias in the History of Educational Thought" would be a case study of the transformative potential of scholarship on women. As I pored over Book V of *Emile* and immersed myself in commentaries on it, I began to understand just how deeply dependent on his philosophy of girls' education was Rousseau's philosophy of boys' education. Then, sitting at my desk on the Institute's top floor one Friday afternoon, I was electrified by the thought that if Sophie is brought into the equation, the standard interpretation of Rousseau's philosophy of education is proven wrong.

Here then was my first inkling that when girls and women enter the scene, educational thought itself changes. That hypothesis was confirmed when, in writing "The Ideal of the Educated Person," I discovered that if the education of women is taken seriously, the ways in which our culture's concept of what it is to be an educated person must be redefined. It was further elaborated in "Excluding Women from the Educational Realm," the last essay I wrote at the Bunting Institute. I put the case more strongly still in *Reclaiming a Conversation*, the book that grew out of my work at the Bunting Institute, and have continued to make it whenever and wherever I could.[14]

As my research questions began to change, so did my methods. Looking back, I discover that in a commentary on a paper presented at the 1979 meeting of the Philosophy of Education Society I rejected philosophical distinctions and analyses that allowed my colleagues and me to detach curriculum theory from empirical fact and from social and political philosophy.[15] A short while later I was acting on those methodological musings. Finding it unproductive to talk about the education of Sophie or even the female guardians in Plato's Just State without also discussing the societal roles that Plato and Rousseau assigned women, I gave up the analytic practice of abstracting educational phenomena from their contexts. Judging it impossible to determine the extent and import of the androcentric bias in education's controlling definitions and governing ideals if I ignored the harm it did women, I discarded the analytic strategy of ignoring empirical issues.

The response to "The Ideal of the Educated Person," my Presidential Address to the Philosophy of Education Society, documents my departure from my field's methodological norms. In that paper I deliberately brought one of the dominant analyses in my field into contact with the real world. Announcing that "any writing produced in a reformist spirit is no longer philosophy, it is advocacy,"[16] one critic placed me in the class of practitioners who "have yielded to the human temptation to be relevant for practice, and have thereby wandered some distance from the philosophical fold."[17] Acknowledging the truth of my finding that the overarching ideal of education put women in a painful double-bind but going on the assumption that a philosophical analysis need take no account of the facts, a speaker at the 1983 meeting of the Philosophy of Education Society took a different tack. He exonerated the philosopher who had formulated the ideal, saying that the qualities built into it were genderized by society, not by R.S. Peters.[18]

It is, of course, ludicrous to say that writing about education produced in a spirit of reform is no longer philosophy. According to this criterion, Rousseau, John Dewey, and probably even Plato would be driven from the fold. It is equally absurd to say that I deemed it Peters's fault that rationality, analytical acuity, objectivity are evaluated positively in our culture when possessed by males[19] and negatively when possessed by females. The question my research raised was whether Peters should have proceeded as if the facts were none of his business. Or, if the facts I adduced in 1981 were not known to him when he constructed his analysis, the question is whether others, once informed, should have been defending an analysis that neglected these facts.[20]

In 1993 I have to remind myself that I once sang the praises of philosophical irrelevance; that I too claimed that a philosopher of education should have no truck with the ways of the world. My excuse—and I do not say it is a good one—is that I did so before I knew how much harm abstract ideals can do, before I remembered that the guidance of practice was the business of the great historical philosophers of education, before I recollected my reasons for entering the field of philosophy of education in the first place.

This "accomplished, tough-minded philosopher of education"[21] who presumably lost her way when she undertook the study of women was already writing in a reformist spirit when she arrived at the Bunting Institute. If, as commentators on "Needed" claimed, I said nothing there that Dewey had not said,[22] I took a giant step in the course of writing "The Ideal of the Educated Person" in a direction that Dewey had not gone. It was easy enough to show that the governing educational ideal incorporated traits that are culturally and historically associated with men while excluding those that are thought to belong to women. To move beyond the usual attributions of sex bias was far more difficult. Thus, for me it was another red letter day when I first saw with startling clarity that the conception of liberal education upon which the accepted ideal of an educated person rests is informed by the desire to prepare people for the public world of work and citizenship and not for the world of the private home—or, as I chose to say, defining the key concepts very broadly, for carrying out society's productive processes and not its reproductive ones. If this is now a commonplace, in 1981 no one, to my knowledge, had pointed it out.

In making my way across a terrain that Dewey did not traverse, I learned that the problems of education that exercised him—for instance, the split of mind from body and of reason from feeling and emotion; the devaluation of experience and of social cooperation—have gendered roots. On a path that might look like a detour but in fact pointed me in the direction of home, I also discovered that it is self-defeating to try to change the education of girls and women without radically revising the education of boys and men.

Perhaps, as the mother of two sons I was especially attuned to the issue of boys' education. Certainly, were I to draw a single conclusion from my research on women's education it would be that so long as women and men live in the world together, their educations must be designed and continually redesigned together. The education Rousseau prescribed for Emile made sense only in relation to the orders he wrote for Sophie. Do what we do now: extend Emile's education to Sophie without changing his education so as to incorporate what is valuable in hers, teach both Sophie and Emile to carry out society's productive processes but not its reproductive ones, and there is bound to be trouble. His expectations will be dashed and so will hers. Worse still, society's reproductive tasks themselves will be put at risk and with them the care, concern, and connection that make up what Gilligan has called the ethic of care.[23]

In my Presidential Address I said that an adequate ideal of the educated person must give the reproductive processes of society their due and I repeated the point in *Reclaiming a Conversation*, adding that education would have to be redefined to achieve this.[24] Some readers could not believe that I was talking about the education of girls *and* boys. Many of those who did asked what "giving the reproductive processes their due" entailed and were barely satisfied when I answered that, at the very least, it meant bringing the 3Cs of care, concern, and connection into the education of both sexes. "We need to know more than that," they said. "Give me time," I replied. "I still have to work it all out."

It took time and, when I did work it out, my answer was a surprise even to me. The last thing I expected when I left the Bunting Institute was another period of flowering. My second blooming happened the year of my Guggenheim Fellowship when, as a Visiting Scholar at Radcliffe College, I found myself in a secluded office as grand as the earlier one had been spartan. It began the day I realized that Maria Montessori had, in effect, formulated an idea of school as a surrogate home for children.

I think it fair to say that, from 1969 on, my research tended toward a new concept of curriculum.[25] My work on women pointed me, in turn, toward a revised conception of an educated person. Oddly enough, however, even though I assigned Dewey's *The School and Society* in my philosophy of education courses, until the autumn of 1987 it never once occurred to me that, as a philosopher, I could rethink the very idea of school.

They say that discoveries require a prepared mind. Having barred Montessori from the conversational circle in *Reclaiming a Conversation* on the grounds that she had developed a philosophy of education without reference to sex or gender, on first reading I did not see in *The Montessori Method* the germ of what I was seeking: a concept of school that gave the reproductive processes of society their due. Luckily, the work I did the year before I settled into my new Radcliffe office came to my rescue.

Becoming increasingly concerned about the poverty, the plight of the homeless, the violence in American society in that period, I suddenly remembered that the framers of the U.S. Constitution included domestic tranquillity in the Preamble's list of goods to be insured. Upon reaching the conclusion that it was important to increase our vision of the domestic sphere to match theirs, yet equally essential to enlarge their understanding of tranquillity to meet present realities, I began to work out the implications of making domestic tranquillity an overarching aim of education.[26] How can I be sure that my conceptualization of the nation as a domestic realm was the catalyst that allowed me to understand just how relevant Montessori's idea of school was for today's world? I simply speculate that without it I might never have seen the Casa dei Bambini in a new light.

In "Romanticism Domesticated: Maria Montessori and the Casa dei Bambini," a paper I wrote for a fall 1988 conference on the Romantic Legacy in Education, I put forth my new reading of Montessori's work. When, some months after finishing that essay, I realized that the Casa dei Bambini could be considered a moral equivalent of home, I knew that my own arrival home was at hand. Dismayed by the steady stream of books and articles on education that ignored my country's changed and changing social realities, I had been growing more determined daily to develop an educational philosophy that fit the occasion but I was still not clear what shape it would take. When it suddenly dawned on me that if ever such a moral equivalent was needed it was now, I was able to proceed.

Here finally was my chance to bring philosophy to bear on educational practice. Not, to be sure, on minute to minute or even day to day life in classrooms. I could not write a "how to" manual if I tried. Not on administration and finance or on learning disabilities and career counseling, either. I had no expertise in these areas and, besides, my interests lay elsewhere. The aims of education, the structure of curriculum and its underlying assumptions, the boundaries this culture has drawn between home and school and also home and world: these would be my concerns. My touchstones would be my awareness of the great changes in both the structure of "the" American home and family and the composition of the United States population and my consternation about the violence in U.S. culture.

It took several years to write *The Schoolhome: Rethinking Schools for Changing Families*[27] for I had to clarify my relationship to Montessori, grasp the connections between the idea of school I was formulating and my rereading of the domestic tranquillity clause, explain why the issues of home and domesticity that I wanted to highlight had been for so long ignored, and develop a concept of curriculum sufficiently inclusive to take into account race, class, gender, ethnicity, and other markers of human diversity. I also had to figure out how to make my experiment in imagination accessible to readers.

Had anyone told me when I reprinted Frankena's essay about the two kinds of philosophy of education in my book of readings on curriculum that some two decades later I would be practicing traditional philosophy of education, I would have rejected the suggestion and have felt insulted, to boot. Yet I do not now think it far-fetched to say that this is what I did in *The Schoolhome*. Focusing on problems that I would once have ruled out of court, moving into the background the philosophical analysis that used to stand in the very center of my work so that it would *inform* what I had to say about education rather than *be* what I had to say, putting forward the kind of value judgments about education that I had come to think were beyond a philosopher's scope, and all the while employing a far different style from the academic one that in graduate school I had finally made my own, I wrote a book that, in Frankena's words, "makes normative statements about what education, educators, and the schools should do or not do, about what the aims, content, methods, etc., of education should be or not be."[28]

The Schoolhome did double-duty for me. It answered the question that *Reclaiming a Conversation* left open of how to give the reproductive processes of society their due and also brought me back to the institution I had left behind some thirty-five years earlier. I was, of course, a different person on my return and school was a different place. American society is different too. But though both the world and I have changed, in my most recent book I addressed the questions about aims and content and about what education and schools should do that were on my mind long ago. Still, the fact remains that *The Schoolhome* did not quite deliver me back to my starting point. As *Reclaiming a Conversation* left hanging the question of how to give the reproductive processes of society their due in the education of both sexes, its sequel left unanswered the question of what to do about the superabundance of subject matter to teach. This is where I came in. When I was singlehandedly trying to rewrite my school's social studies curriculum, this was the issue that sent me on my quest. And it is the issue to which I will turn my attention as soon as this collection of essays goes to press.

II. Travels with Girls and Women

For that master's degree I aspired to as a school teacher I took a course in the history of educational thought. I can still recall how eager I was to know what the great minds of the past had thought about education and how disappointing my meetings with them turned out to be. At the time, I attributed my disillusionment with both course and content to the speed with which we covered three thousand years of educational wisdom, but I now suspect that my dissatisfaction was in large part a measure of my inability to see my mother, my friends, and myself in the ideas under discussion. I even wonder if the seeds of "Excluding Women from the Educational Realm," the opening essay in this volume, were not sown then and there.

Although some of the men whose philosophies fall into the category of "educational wisdom" wrote about the education of girls and women, my professor managed to steer clear of the topic. To wit: Plato and Rousseau were well represented in that historical overview but neither Book V of the *Republic* nor Book V of *Emile* was on the syllabus. Gertrude, Pestalozzi's model of a good teacher, made an appearance in our readings, but she was missing from the lectures. The instructor also sailed successfully past those theories of the last three millennia whose authors happened to be female. The likes of Mary Wollstonecraft, Catharine Beecher, Charlotte Perkins Gilman, and Montessori were nowhere to be seen in the course materials.

I do not wish to do that eminent scholar an injustice. It is quite unlikely that in the early 1950s he would have known about the life and works of any of these people save Montessori. Yet one cannot be sure that my teacher would have introduced Wollstonecraft, Beecher, Gilman into his narrative had he known of them. There certainly was no rush to correct the oversight when in 1982 I documented their absence from the standard texts and anthologies.

If anything, I wrote cautiously in "Excluding Women from the Educational Realm." Never questioning the practice of canonizing philosophers and their works, I went so far as to say that the writings of the excluded women would have to be studied and their significance determined before one could be sure that they warranted inclusion. I was also unduly sanguine. I fully expected that philosophers of education would want to be introduced to those women and would welcome them into the canon at least conditionally; or, if that step seemed a bit rash, that they would encourage interested students and scholars to do the necessary analytic and evaluative work and give those efforts their full support. But instead of withholding judgment until such inquiries were undertaken, they ignored the women whose acquaintance I was beginning to make or else dismissed without cause their claims to inclusion. The speaker at the 1983 meeting of the Philosophy of Education Society even made it clear that if he had any say in the matter, it would not be easy for women to enter the educational realm.

Calling Montessori my "best case," that critic of my Bunting Institute research on women summarily rejected my application for her admission into the canon. "According to standard criteria such as quality of argument, connection with a certain literature, etc., Montessori's works would not count as examples of philosophy of education," he said without referring to her works or documenting their deficiencies.[29] Judging the credentials of the other female candidates to be weaker than Montessori's but never putting their writings to the test, he then shifted the burden of proof. Before anyone could dream of admitting my nominees, I would have to formulate the field's criteria of relevance and significance.

Women's absence as authors of educational thought was one of several troubling issues I took up in "Excluding Women from the Educational Realm." Another was that we are missing as its objects, a topic I explored first in a paper on Plato's philosophy of women's education,[30] and then in two essays included here: "Sophie and Emile: A Case Study in the History of Educational Thought" and "The Ideal of the Educated Person."

Deciding somewhat uncharacteristically to start at the beginning, as soon as I settled into my office at the Bunting Institute I wrote an essay on Book V of the *Republic*. After sending it off to the editor of a projected anthology, I opened an unabridged edition of Rousseau's *Emile*—again to Book V—and started to read.

Women are a clear presence in Rousseau's educational philosophy. Yet when I first encountered Sophie, she—and by extension we—had been rendered invisible by the received interpretations of his thought. So hidden were we that although I had been discussing *Emile* in my own philosophy of education courses, I had no more included Book V on the syllabus than my professors had on theirs. It pains me to think that in the 1970s I could have been working through Rousseau's discussion of the education of Sophie with my students but instead fluctuated between evading the topic of girls and women altogether and telling students to assume that what Rousseau had to say about the education of males applied also to females. The second essay in this collection was halfway done before I admitted to myself that what I had considered mere laziness on my part was in fact a form of intellectual dishonesty.

As its title indicates, the focus of my paper on Rousseau is not his sex bias but that of his interpreters. When I came to the study of *Emile*, Rousseau's misogyny was well known. What was not recognized was that the standard interpretation of a central work in the history of Western thought was deeply flawed. Rousseau prescribed different educations for boys and girls. But in attributing to him two separate and opposite philosophies of education, feminist commentaries left intact the interpretation of *Emile* as a story of the natural growth and development of an autonomous man. Even they did not pay heed to his utter dependence on Sophie. On the afternoon in 1980 when the parts of my paper fell into place like the pieces in a kaleidoscope, I saw Sophie and Emile standing together. In this relational configration I discerned a single philosophy that yielded different educational recommendations for the two because of their different societal roles. I also perceived that the favored reading of Emile's education owed its plausibility to Sophie's disappearance from the scene.

One would think that this rendering of Sophie's case would convince scholars that the exclusion of women as the objects of educational thought is a dangerous policy. You might imagine that once they were shown—as they were in "The Ideal of the Educated Person"—that the inadequacies in the reigning ideal of an educated person derived from its failure to take women into account, philosophers of education would try to rectify the situation. As it happened, bewildered female graduate students began writing and telephoning and even traveling to Boston to tell me about the dissertations they wanted to write on topics having to do with girls and women and about the obstacles their male mentors were putting in the way. Meanwhile, outspoken critics called for more criteria, this time to determine if a subject "is or is not a bona fide concern of philosophy of education;"[31] they challenged the distinction between two kinds of societal processes I had introduced to illuminate the boundaries of the educational realm; and they charged me with essentialism.

Even as I wrote the phrase "truly feminine qualities" in "The Ideal of the Educated Person" I knew that the genderization of traits was an artifact of culture, not a fact of nature. Yet I did write those words and I certainly lived to rue the day. To my dismay, commentators were a lot quicker to express their indignation about this lapse of mine than about said bias.[32] An acquaintance with the existing disciplines of knowledge—not idealized versions of them—and a tendency or propensity to look at the world in their terms was built into the accepted definition of an educated person. People in the philosophy of education seemed to be far more outraged by those three words, however, than by the discovery that these fields were systematically biased against women; in fact, most of them were relatively unmoved by my report that a controlling paradigm of analytic philosophy of education was riddled with gender bias.

In that Presidential Address I placed on record the new findings about the representation of women in the disciplines of knowledge, pointed out the gendered status of the traits that an educated person was supposed to possess, and outlined the double bind that the ideal created for women. When writing that paper, however, I considered its most important contribution to be its functional analysis. If there was one aspect of liberal education about which there then was general agreement it was that it did not constitute preparation *for* anything. Once I read Lorenne Clark's account of politics[33] and saw the analogy between the political and the educational realms, I realized that this was a myth.

I owe Clark, a traveling companion I have never actually met, a great debt. Her demonstration that political thought defined its subject matter in relation to the world of work and politics while relegating home and family to the "ontological basement," helped me understand that, like it or not, women travel with heavy baggage. It caused me to see that if we are missing from the theories and narratives, interpretations and analyses of education, then the tasks, duties, personal traits, societal roles and institutions that are culturally and historically associated with us are missing too. How did educational thought effect the exclusion of what Clark—defining the term broadly to include childrearing, homemaking, nursing, care for the elderly—called society's "reproductive" processes? As in the case of politics, it was done by fiat. So quietly was it accomplished that although analytic philosophers of education had been mapping the "logical geography" of education since the 1960s, no cartographer had ever noticed that, in general, the reproductive processes of society fell outside the boundaries of the realm of education.

In "Excluding Women from the Educational Realm" I showed in some detail how the contemporary philosophical analyses of the concepts of education, liberal education, and teaching placed society's reproductive processes, broadly defined, beyond education's borders. In "The Ideal of the Educated Person," which I wrote first, I made the case that once society's productive processes are understood to include political, social, and cultural as well as economic activities, one can clearly see that liberal education does after all serve a function outside itself. Just as vocational education is intended to prepare people to carry out one set of society's productive processes, liberal education and the closely related ideal of an educated person are designed with the performance of another set of productive processes in mind.

It took me a while to grasp the larger implications of women's exclusion from the educational realm and even longer to decide to follow Clark's use of the productive/reproductive distinction and her non-Marxist definitions. One reason I did follow her in this was that the other available distinctions—for instance between public and private realms—had serious problems of their own. Another was that I saw the need for a conceptual framework capable of distinguishing not just between "spheres" or "realms" but between the activities and processes our society associated with the civic or public or work "sphere" or "realm," on the one hand, and the private or domestic or home "sphere" or "realm" on the other. Take, for instance, the case of Plato's guardians. Without this theoretical apparatus one might not notice—or, if one noticed, one might not think it important or might not know how to say—that although the private or domestic arena is removed from people's lives, the activities and processes traditionally housed there still have to be carried out.

Because I had some misgivings about Clark's language, I urged readers to substitute their own labels if they did not like mine. Approving my labels but not my redefinitions of them, a pair of critics, citing established educational scholars who relied on the standard Marxist interpretation of the productive/reproductive distinction, objected in print to my "idiosyncratic" notion of reproduction.[34] My analysis would have been far more acceptable had I embraced the same Marxist framework, they implied, never mentioning that the men they held up to me as model traveling companions had not even noticed the exclusion of women and the functions and tasks associated with us from the realm of education.

Rejecting my labels but offering no replacements, a non-Marxist charged me, in turn, with "generating confusion" by using terms "that belong to a different domain of discourse."[35] Yet theory building in any field, not just in the philosophy of education, would be in sad straights if terms used in one domain could not be introduced into others and reinterpreted in the process. I do not see how Marx himself could have employed the productive/reproductive distinction had he operated on the principle that a domain's terminology is its private property, for despite my critic's assumption that this language belongs to economics, "reproductive" has strong biological connections.

My own and other people's qualms notwithstanding, the productive/reproductive distinction was initially illuminating. It proved an especially valuable conceptual tool when I took up the gauntlet in *Reclaiming a Conversation* and, while exploring differing philosophies of women's education, sought to demonstrate that Wollstonecraft, Beecher, and Gilman were bona fide educational thinkers by treating them as such and seeing if they lived up to expectations. Why then did I drop that distinction in *The Schoolhome*? As I approached home, what had earlier struck me as appropriate terminology began to sound unduly dry and technical. Besides, I could no longer ignore the many readers who by then were telling me privately that they found the biological connotations of "reproductive" troubling.

It is perhaps no accident that in the late 1980s esoteric language made me increasingly uncomfortable for that is when I met up with two women working outside the academy whose writings profoundly affected my own—Montessori and Virginia Woolf. When upon completion of *Reclaiming a Conversation* Montessori's *Education for Peace* all but jumped off the shelf into my hands, I had no idea that the man who had called her my best case was right. Nor did I make this discovery when I celebrated our having been introduced by writing a paper in which I compared Montessori's vision of peace to those of Gilman and William James.[36] It was only when I outlined an essay that would treat four historical theories of home and school, and this time started my research not at the beginning but with the woman on the scene, that I learned how important Montessori's contribution to that chapter of educational history was.

William Heard Kilpatrick, one of Dewey's disciples, said in the early part of this century: "they are ill advised who put Madam Montessori among the significant contributors to educational theory. Stimulating she is; a contributor to our theory, hardly if at all."[37] Demonstrating how ill-advised his assessment was, "Romanticism Domesticated: Maria Montessori and the Casa dei Bambini," the fourth essay in Part One of this book, offers further confirmation of the hypothesis that when women appear on the landscape, educational thought changes. Montessori's idea of school as a surrogate home not only casts doubt on the standard interpretation of the "Romantic" label, it challenges the accepted dogmas about the relationship of school to both home and world.

I was outraged when I first came across Kilpatrick's commentary but I am now able to read it as a cautionary tale. Calling to mind Thomas Kuhn's thesis that, in science, "novelty emerges only with difficulty, manifested by resistance,"[38] it reminds me that those who swear by existing modes of thought may find cold comfort in women's transformative potential.

For every philosopher of education who has been disquieted by what I discovered on my travels with women, however, there have been scholars and teachers around the world who have accepted my invitation to readers of *Reclaiming a Conversation* to enter the book's conversational circle. Moreover, many of these have taken steps to expand the original group. Thus, for example, Inga Elgqvist-Saltzman and her students at the University of Umeå have brought in women educators and activists from earlier periods of Swedish history.[39] In The Netherlands, Mineke van Essen, Mieke Lunenberg, and their colleagues have made Dutch women teachers and professors of pedagogy parties to the discussion.[40] In Canada, David MacGregor has included Hegel and the fascinating, but little known, Theodor Gottlieb von Hippel in the group.[41] In the United States, Susan Laird has brought Louisa May Alcott into it;[42] participants in a forum at Guilford College organized by Robert Roemer have extended membership to Margaret Fuller, Charlotte Bronte, and other luminaries;[43] and Mary Ann Connors, a student at the University of Massachusetts has added the collective voice of the American Association of University Women.[44]

The anomalous in the educational realm—girls and women—may not yet be the expected. But because, to use Kuhn's language, the discoveries about my female traveling companions and myself which continue to be documented and elaborated in greater and greater detail "penetrate existing knowledge to the core," there is good reason to think that we are the very kind of anomaly that leads to paradigm change.[45]

Yet I would not want it thought that one who in her travels joins forces with women cannot also make common cause with men. In the paper I wrote for the 1987 Guilford College Forum I stressed our anomalous status, something John Stuart Mill had made plain one and a quarter centuries earlier. Regretting almost as soon as I completed *Reclaiming a Conversation* that I had not included a discussion of Mill's ideas, in "The Contradiction of the Educated Woman" I assigned a leading role to the man whose *System of Logic* I read in that analytic philosophy course I took for my master's degree. In a companion piece written for the Fall 1988 inauguration of the Project on the Study of Gender and Education, I then placed Virginia Woolf's voice in counterpoint with his.

Woolf's bridge "which connects the private house with the world of public life"[46] fig-ures prominently in *The Schoolhome* but I first used this metaphor in "The Contradiction and the Challenge of the Educated Woman," reprinted here. Elaborating the geograph-ical dimension of her imagery, in this paper I sketched the landscape that women enter when they walk across the bridge each morning. The question Woolf posed in 1938 was whether we should join the procession of men on the bridge. Half a century later I asked what challenges educated women face when they enter the world of work and the pro-fessions and what ones their entrance into that realm pose for educators.

I took up the same subject in "A Professorship and Office of One's Own," also included in this volume. Upon receiving an invitation to participate in a symposium on Women Doing Philosophy of Education, I thought not of *Three Guineas*, however, but of Woolf's response to a request to speak on the topic of women writing fiction. Like her, I had a lot to say about my assigned subject and I also wondered how to speak my mind with-out sounding at war with my lot. Of Charlotte Bronte, Woolf remarked in *A Room of One's Own*: "She will write in a rage where she should write calmly. She will write fool-ishly where she should write wisely."[47] Because in 1991 I did not want to leave my story "to attend to some personal grievance,"[48] I looked to Woolf for guidance.

"Was your contribution to the symposium fact or fiction?" members of the audi-ence asked me. The log of a day in the life of a female philosopher of education, "A Professorship and Office of One's Own" transmuted the one into the other and then concluded with a call for "newly cut turf." Since I ended "Excluding Women from the Educational Realm" and "The Ideal of the Educated Woman" on this same note, it is fair to ask if the educational landscape had not changed since the day in 1981 when, as President of the Philosophy of Education Society, I received a bouquet with its enclosed card addressed to Dr. James Martin.

In 1991 the educational terrain was still inhospitable to me and my traveling com-panions in some salient ways. Nevertheless, both the composition of the symposium audience and its responses reassure me that some livable, breathable space for women has been created. There are many more women philosophers of education than there were, a number of us are now doing research on women and gender, and more men in the field than ever before appear to be interested in this work and willing to take the plight of girls and women to heart.

The educational scene was not the only thing that changed during the brief span of time represented by the papers in Part One of this volume. In 1981 the subject for fem-inist scholars in the United States was women. By the time I sat down to write "A Professorship and an Office of One's Own," doing research on women was considered risky business. After my spring 1981 speech on "The Ideal of the Educated Woman," a philosopher of education confided to me that he could never have "gone out on a limb like that." In 1991 a feminist who spoke or wrote about women would be out on a limb not because her male colleagues might look askance at her research and even try to disown her and it, but because feminist scholars themselves might do this.

The titles of the books on my shelves indicate that by the mid-1980s the subject for feminist scholars was shifting from women to gender. At decade's end both of these had become suspect categories and she who persisted in their use did so at her own risk. For one who had been trying for years to bring her research into closer touch with educational realities and who felt that in her research on women she was finally succeeding, this postmodern turn posed a difficult dilemma. Here was I, still thinking and writing about the education of women and girls and daily discovering more reasons why from a practical standpoint it was important to do so. And there were some of my relatively new traveling companions saying that this kind of project was methodologically mistaken and in all likelihood morally misguided.

When, in celebration of the twentieth anniversary of undergraduate coeducation at Princeton University, I was asked to participate in a symposium entitled "The Gendered Voice in the Classroom," the dilemma became quite real for me. Because I wanted to discuss the classroom quartet consisting of student, instructor, text, and disciplinary voices, the first thing I did after accepting the invitation was to change my title from "*The* Gendered Voice in the Classroom" to "Gendered *Voices* in the Classroom." The next thing I did was worry about the trouble I would be in if I then went on to speak about "the" gendered voice. By the summer of 1989 I had read too many books and articles by women accusing other women of essentialism and false generalization to want to draw these criticisms. Besides, scholars whose opinions I valued would not listen to my message were I to fall into one or another of these traps.

From my reading of present day feminist theory I knew that one good way to avoid the charges would be to shift my attention from the world—in this case the world of the ivory tower—to language and to deconstruct the symposium's title. Methodologically speaking, I would then be above reproach. However my belief that girls and women students in the United States are at risk today,[49] in combination with my conviction that it is my responsibility as a philosopher of education to address "real world" issues and my longstanding desire to improve educational practice, kept me from adopting this strategy. Although my methodology might pass muster if I focused on the symposium title instead of on the problems women face in college classrooms, I would in effect be shirking my duty.

The policy I finally adopted for the Princeton symposium was to proceed with my plea for a balanced quartet of gendered classroom voices, but to preface it with a brief discussion of the very real pitfalls that a party to a meeting on "the" gendered anything must try to avoid and a description of several opposite and equally dangerous traps. I also promised myself to explore these issues more fully another time. The symposium on Women Doing Philosophy of Education was not the right occasion to keep that pledge, but I soon had the chance to do so.

I will not repeat here the arguments of the long essay on feminist methodology I wrote for a conference on Interdisciplinary Approaches to Knowledge and Gender.[50] The question of whether in investigating the place of women in educational thought I have all along been assuming an essential female nature, is certainly germane, however. My answer—and I realize that a philosopher of education is not necessarily her own most perceptive critic—is that despite my linguistic lapse, even in my earliest work on women and education I said repeatedly that I was not making claims about what women were like "by nature" and was not resorting to one or another form of biological determinism.[51] Besides, my personal history did not allow me these luxuries for my analytic training left me with an abiding distrust of essence talk.

The question remains if in using the label "women" in my research I have masked diversity. To this let me say that insofar as I was focusing on differences in 1981 they were between women and men and were not our differences from one another. By 1984, however, the importance of attending to women's diversity was on my mind and in the last chapter of *Reclaiming a Conversation* I listed some of the differences arising within gender categories—race, ethnicity, economic status, sexual orientation—that still needed to be addressed. By 1988, students in the feminist theory course I taught, as well as my sister scholars and theorists, had made me keenly alive to the racism and classism implicit in writing as if all women were, like me, white and middle class.

But why, if I perceive the dangers of generalizing falsely from my own experience or else from the standpoint of my race and socio-economic class, have I continued to use those suspect "universalist categories," girls and women?[52] And why have I used the word "women" in both the subtitle and a section heading of this book? I have gone out on a limb because I see grave peril in a retreat from research that looks for similarities across differences.

There are by now enough studies of schoolrooms, playgrounds, college classrooms and extracurricular activities in the United States to lead me, at least, to the discomforting conclusion that a hidden curriculum in misogyny flourishes in our educational landscape. Both it and the hidden curriculum in anti-domesticity that I have found there create an environment that does untold harm to girls and women from just about all backgrounds.[53] Different sorts of girls and women are affected differently and studies of these differences will definitely enrich our understanding of both women and education. But the fact is that, whatever other categories they also fall into, those people our culture calls girls and women undergo some terrible experiences in the course of being educated in the United States. It defies the imagination that the multifaceted violence they experience in school is not implicated in the violence in their homes, on our streets, and in the workplace.[54] It is to me unthinkable that the attitudes toward them and toward what even now is considered their work, which are transmitted as much by the silences of school's curriculum as by any overt lessons, have no bearing on the unequal gender distribution of domestic labor and responsibilities.

Had I stayed in the far reaches of philosophy, or had I not traveled back in the company of women, I might not know what actually happens to girls and women in America's schools and universities. If I did know, I would not consider it a philosopher's business. But I did not stay and I do know. Where I now stand I see the elimination of "girls" and "women" from my research vocabulary as an act of betrayal to parents, teachers, citizens, and children of all ages. For me, the methodological problem is not how to avoid the categories and language that as a philosopher I only began to employ in 1980—ones that many people in my field have never yet used—but how to discover ways of factoring in the incredible variability they cover. The practical problem is how to make the educational landscape one in which girls and women can live and breathe well.

III. Adventures in Curriculum

It has taken me some twenty-five years to figure out the ways in which the educational landscape can and should be changed and I am still learning. It is only in writing this introduction, however, that I have come to realize why the educational reformers I have encountered since I left school teaching to study philosophy have been so loath to redraw the boundaries of the educational realm, rethink education's function, redefine its goals, reexamine the relationship between knowledge and curriculum.

In *Deschooling Society*, Ivan Illich maintained that schooling perpetuates itself through its hidden curriculum in dependency on schools. Confusing process and substance, it successfully teaches the lesson that to get an education you must go to school.[55] Well, education perpetuates itself too. I am not saying that educated people become addicted to education, although this may be true. Rather, they are indoctrinated into the educational ideology of their culture. For most people who have been educated, fundamental educational change is practically unthinkable. "But this is what education is," an educated person will say when the structure of the traditional liberal curriculum is questioned or the received ideal of an educated person is challenged. "Change this and you will no longer have education," is his or her response to calls for newly cut turf.

In educational circles the label "Essentialist" was in the past applied to those who claimed that the school curriculum should always and everywhere be composed of the "traditional" subjects—the 3Rs, history, literature, mathematics, etc. But the fact is that both educational Essentialists with a capital E and those reformers who welcome the inclusion in the curriculum of untraditional studies are "lower case" essentialists. Assuming that the goals and functions, definitions and boundaries of education that now exist are immutable givens, they treat these as eternal and immutable features of the landscape. Never dreaming that there might be alternatives to what they take for granted, they cannot even see the possibilities that exist.

I did not perceive them when I began my research in the philosophy of curriculum. When I now read "The Disciplines and the Curriculum," the first paper in Part Two of this collection and my earliest venture in that area, I find confirmation of my recollection that in 1968 the upheavals in the universities were forcing me to reconsider my own assumptions about the value of maintaining distance. Yet I marvel that I did not question sooner the underlying presuppositions of the curriculum movement that had been dictating the country's educational discourse for almost a decade. The delay is especially interesting because the school I attended when young was a prime example of what was then called Progressive Education. If anyone knew that education did not have to be and should not be narrowly intellectualistic, my schoolmates and I did.

As an adult my encounters with reform movements began when in 1957 the Soviet Union launched Sputnik, the first artificial Earth satellite. At the time, the surprise for

Americans was not the technological strides the U.S.S.R. had taken since World War II, but how far behind its rival the United States had fallen. Later on, the mystery to me was that a Soviet satellite could have launched a thousand U.S. curriculum projects. Yet it did approximately this. Just as twenty-five years afterwards the announcement that the economy was lagging behind Japan's was followed by massive criticism of American schools and repeated calls for excellence in education, the question of how the Soviet Union could possibly have been the first to launch a satellite was answered by blaming education and then funding the development of what came to be called the New Curricula.

Had I still been teaching fifth and sixth graders when the New Math and Science, and eventually the New Social Studies, sprang into being, I would undoubtedly have welcomed these alternatives to presenting every subject as a series of unrelated facts that students should commit to memory. Authored mainly by imaginative and dedicated academicians according to principles the psychologist Jerome Bruner summarized and elaborated in *The Process of Education*,[56] the New Curricula celebrated the importance of understanding mathematics, physics, biology, chemistry, history, the social sciences. Elementary and secondary school girls and boys would be taught each subject's fundamental ideas. They would be led to view the intellectual disciplines as creative human endeavors rather than God-given bodies of knowledge. And, above all, they would be treated as active learners: as young discoverers rather than passive receptacles of information. As it was, I declined invitations to engage in curriculum development, preferring in good philosophical fashion to observe the excitement from afar.

Rereading "The Disciplines and the Curriculum," my critique of some of the underlying assumptions of the curriculum movement that Sputnik launched, I deplore its systematic use of the masculine pronoun, notice how condescending the royal "let us" can be, and wonder what I could have done to make the discussion more accessible to readers. At the same time I am gratified to see that although I purposely focused on a specific curriculum movement, I found a way to treat topics of lasting concern and, in so doing, to question what education implicitly teaches us to take for granted. The hierarchical relationship between the disciplines of knowledge and the school curriculum is one of those "givens" of the educational landscape. So is the spectator stance toward most of life's activities. My recommendation that students get outside the disciplines of knowledge and inside the activities of life is as relevant now as it ever was, and as subversive of education's reigning ideology. My argument that the disciplines do not have the last word—or even the first—in curriculum matters also challenges education's basic presuppositions.

This essay is noteworthy for its initial formulations of analytic points that I would later develop more fully. But perhaps more important are its intimations of the normative philosophy of education I developed in *The Schoolhome*. In a 1979 discussion of United States history textbooks, Frances FitzGerald distinguished three groups in American society—progressives, fundamentalists, and mandarins.[57] "The Disciplines and the Curriculum" was my first try at showing that mandarin theories of general and liberal education—ones developed by those who, in her words, believe "in the power of the intellect, and in the value of science and the cultural tradition"[58]—are much too narrow in scope. Insofar as I proposed alternatives that embrace ways of acting and forms of living as well as fields of knowledge, it also represented my first real break with the analytic lessons of my past and contained my first sketches of a reshaped turf.

It is hardly surprising that the academy based curriculum movement that wanted children to get inside the intellectual disciplines in order to understand them displayed little interest in bringing other modes of acting and being into education. As if to compensate for the deficiency, its successor, the Radical School Reform Movement, tried to make education relevant to children's lives. It also placed the spotlight on the lessons in mindless obedience and conformity that are taught by a school's rules and regulations, its architectural design, its administrative hierarchy, its tracking system; a classroom's atmosphere, its daily rituals, its furnishing, its seating plan; a teacher's linguistic practices, motivational strategies, and disciplinary measures.

One quarter of a century later it is not easy to convey the sense of excitement generated by the positive program of this expression of progressivism. Those who could, went to Great Britain to observe "open classrooms" with their "integrated days" in order to determine what they could import back to the United States. Experienced teachers, inspired by the reports from abroad and rejuvenated by the movement's faith in their competence and creativity, combed city streets and ocean beaches for new kinds of educational materials. Young college graduates founded schools where they could put their ideals of individual autonomy, free choice, and respect for children into practice. Meanwhile, one best seller after another bewailed the state of schooling in America and promised a better future.

In light of my own schooling, one would have expected me from the start to have been that quite unusual being: a philosopher of education temperamentally in tune with this new incarnation of progressivism. But my college career had quite literally turned me against the education of my youth and my graduate training had reinforced the about-face. It took the Vietnam War and the student protests to convince me to end my brief love affair with traditional schooling. Even then, while I cheered the Radical School Reform Movement's critique of schooling from my philosophical seat on the sidelines, I did not automatically applaud its positive recommendations. My next two ventures in the philosophy of curriculum reflected this ambivalence. In "Choice, Chance, and Curriculum," my 1975 Boyd H. Bode Memorial Lecture at The Ohio State University, I tested the limits of the free student choice plank of the reform program.[59] Then in "What Should We Do with a Hidden Curriculum When We Find One?" I attempted to clear up misunderstandings surrounding the concept of a hidden curriculum and to lay out alternative courses of action.

Like the first essay in Part Two of this collection, the second speaks to the "real world" of education. It is true that whereas I bracketed the definition of the term "discipline" in "The Disciplines and the Curriculum" in order to address more substantive concerns, in "What Should We Do with a Hidden Curriculum When We Find One?" I gave an extended analysis of the concept of a hidden curriculum. Yet my decision to take seriously the close descriptions and evaluations of schooling provided by the radical reformers and to forego discussion of the views of other philosophers signifies that I was in fact trying to achieve clarity without altogether removing myself from actual educational practice. My extended discussion of what should be done with a hidden curriculum reflects the same intention.

I wanted to clarify this pivotal concept because I had discovered in the school reform literature a tendency to conflate the *concept* of a hidden curriculum and *one* particular hidden curriculum, namely that of American schools. So far as I could determine, the false equation was preventing people from realizing that hidden curricula other than the ones the reformers talked about might even then be in place. It was also keeping them from seeing that the measures they favored carried hidden curricula of their own. The assumption that school was the only bearer of a hidden curriculum was troubling too, for it allowed school critics of that period to extol out-of-school learning environments without asking what hidden messages these might be transmitting.

Interestingly enough, whereas the hidden curriculum represented a gap in the texts of the New Curricula, curriculum proper was the gap in the Radical School Reform Movement text. Compared to that of their predecessors, the scope of the radical reformers was broad. Upon discovering school's hidden curriculum in docility, obedience to authority, competitiveness, self-hatred, and learning how to fail, they proposed alternative school structures, classroom environments, teaching methods, and learning activities. But they never worried about subjects and subject matter. They seemed to think that once their ideas were adopted, these would simply fade away.

In "Needed: A New Paradigm for Liberal Education" and "Two Dogmas of Curriculum," both of which are reprinted here, I expressed my conviction that curriculum proper would not take care of itself. These undertakings in the philosophy of curriculum bear traces of my disappointment that those who so successfully deconstructed schooling did not turn their radical imaginations onto school subjects. I did not realize when I wrote them that to have done as I wished, the reformers would have had to raise to consciousness the hidden curriculum concerning education's logical geography that they themselves had unconsciously absorbed in the process of becoming educated.

If these essays look back with some regret upon an educational movement many of whose impulses I shared, they are primarily responses to yet another a curriculum movement, one that tried to undo what the radical reformers had accomplished and to discredit what they had said. FitzGerald's categories serve as reminders that those who join ranks in opposition to an educational reform movement may have dissimilar agendas. Although the most outspoken members of the Back to Basics Movement were prime examples of her fundamentalism, the movement had two factions. United in opposition to the "romanticism" of the Radical School Reformers—to its perceived idealization of "the child" along Rousseau-like lines and its apparent dismissal of subject matter—each built an edifice on this common ground that the other could not comfortably inhabit. The more vocal group—the one usually identified with the basics—would have reduced the school curriculum proper to the 3Rs. In its opinion, everything else was a frill.[60] The other, a direct descendent of the 1950s Council for Basic Education and a forerunner of the 1980s "Restorationists," wanted schools to teach science, mathematics, history, literature, foreign languages in addition to the 3Rs. The frills of this clear case of FitzGerald's mandarinism were dance and driver education.

In taking issue with the mandarin position in "Needed" I chose to discuss the British philosopher Paul Hirst's formulation rather than one of the many indigenous varieties. His theory of liberal education was the one to which English-speaking philosophers of education then gave allegiance. Besides, Hirst's was an extremely sophisticated defense of the kind of curriculum I had already criticized in "The Disciplines and the Curriculum." I reasoned that if I could show that the best philosophical foundations a philosopher could give to the mandarin construct were shaky and could begin sketching plans for a plausible alternative, my case for a more inclusive curriculum would be strengthened.

Readers may find it hard to believe that "The Ideal of the Educated Person" and "Needed" were published the same year. I certainly do. The latter makes no reference to women. It ignores the gender bias in the very forms of knowledge that Hirst claimed were essential to the development of rational mind. It posits the development of persons, instead of minds, as the goal of liberal education without asking if, historically, attributes culturally associated with women had ever been included in the concept of a person. And it suffers from a lack of attention to both the context of education and the consequences of philosophizing.[61]

In point of fact I finished this "gender insensitive" paper some months before I began my research on women but the disparity between it and my subsequent writing underscores the profound effects that my new traveling companions had on me and my work. Indeed, the changes were so dramatic that I am tempted to think of my later writings as breaking radically with my earlier scholarship. Yet I know this view of the matter magnifies the extent of the rupture. A careful reader of that work cannot help but notice that I was bothered by the absence from general and liberal education of topics such as love, friendship, marriage, divorce, childrearing, and family living and disturbed that students were not taught to feel connected to one another and to the natural environment. Besides, although the new inquiries introduced a dimension into my thinking that was ultimately transformative, the main themes of my "pre-feminist" writings, as a colleague and friend calls the first four papers in Part Two of this collection, recur in my later work. One of these is that liberal education as defined by our culture is overly narrow and intellectualistic. Another is that adequate alternatives need to unite mind and body, thought and action, reason and emotion. A third theme, discernible in all my essays but especially prominent in "Two Dogmas of Curriculum" and "The Radical Future of Gender Enrichment," is that more decisions enter into curriculum development than meet the eye.

Guided by an interest that on the face of it seems to conflict with my professed desire to get back in touch with the practice of education, in the 1970s I became increasingly engrossed in a challenging and exhilarating, albeit highly abstract, enterprise. Having mapped some important but neglected curriculum decision points in both "The Disciplines and the Curriculum" and "What Should We Do with a Hidden Curriculum When We Find One?," I set out to find more. In "The Anatomy of Subjects," one of the few published reports of this analytic adventure, I described several that educators blithely ignore in debating what to teach because they think of school subjects as somehow beyond human control. Concentrating on questions internal to school subjects, I left open there the issue of what things can be subjects.

As "Needed" carried forward the discussion of "The Disciplines and the Curriculum," "Two Dogmas of Curriculum"—published after my term at the Bunting Institute ended but based on this earlier research—is the sequel to "The Anatomy of Subjects." Can anything at all be a subject or are there only a few qualified candidates? In my disciplines paper I distinguished subjects from subject matter. Differentiating in this essay between both of these and what I called a "subject-entity"—the thing, be it the science physics, the language French, the activity of driving, that provides the raison d'être for a subject—I took up this issue. I also treated its special case, the question of what things qualify as educational basics.

Although the Back to Basics Movement dominated the educational landscape in the mid to late 1970s as surely as the Radical School Reform movement had in the preceding decade, it held no attractions for me. Once I judged the mandarin position too narrow, I could scarcely embrace the even more limited fundamentalist stance. Besides, the latter's commitment to drill, espousal of dress codes, and conviction that learning and pain are indissolubly linked were anathemas to one who had attended a school that refused to honor the distinction between work and play, whose fifth and sixth graders had learned most when they approached their studies indirectly, and whose own children were daily demonstrating the joys of learning. An inquiry into the concept of the basics had its fascinations, however. Why, I wondered, were some subjects thought by their very nature to be basic while others were considered frills? And why was it assumed that if a subject is basic, a central place for it in the school curriculum is assured? Exploring areas of curriculum in "Two Dogmas of Curriculum" that philosophers of education had rarely entered, and equipped with maps prepared by philosophers of action for quite a different purpose, I tried to figure out what it means to say that a subject such as reading or physics is or is not basic. Walking over ground that curriculum theorists seldom surveyed, I finally satisfied myself that the basics of education, like other subjects, are the products of human decision, not the givens of nature or the gifts of gods.

Once I turned my attention to the subject of women I had little time to spend on the search for uncharted curriculum decision points. It took me awhile, moreover, to realize that the esoteric knowledge I had gained on that analytic endeavor could inform my new investigations. Granted, in "Two Dogmas of Curriculum" I defended Women's Studies against the charge that it was not "really" a subject made by those who wanted to bar it from the college and university curriculum. But "Becoming Educated: A Journey of Alienation or Integration?," included here, is the first paper in which I consciously tried to connect the two projects.

By the mid-1980s I had become acutely aware of how easy it would be—and how unsatisfactory—to design curricula that met the letter but not the spirit of my dictum that the reproductive processes of society should be given their due. I did not yet know exactly how to translate that spirit into educational practice. Still, the need for at least two caveats was evident. In "Becoming Educated" I thus made it clear that it was not necessary to put courses in the 3Cs of caring, concern and connection into the curriculum. Instead of turning these components of the ethic of care into school subjects, they could easily be made to serve as general curricular goals. In addition, I argued that it would be a terrible mistake to replicate the societal split between productive and reproductive processes in the school curriculum by creating a split between two kinds of subjects with two quite different functions.

"Becoming Educated" was a new adventure for me in another way, too, for in it I took the education of a minority man, rather than a woman, as my starting point and then worked my way into a discussion of gender. In "Needed" I called the products of the sort of education that philosophers like Hirst and Peters advocated "ivory tower" people. The self-portrait that Richard Rodriguez drew in his educational autobiography, *Hunger of Memory*, was of just such a person.[62] That his narrative unwittingly revealed the workings of gender in educational thought made it doubly interesting. In addition, his attitudes toward domesticity made me more keenly aware than I had ever been that to attempt to give the reproductive processes of society their educational due without addressing the cultural value hierarchy that denigrated them and their constituent tasks, traits, and functions would be a futile exercise.

Rodriguez wrote the saga that struck me as a profound but very sad commentary on this culture's educational ideals during a period of renewed criticism of American education and incessant demands for excellence, this time in response to Japan's economic feats. I have called the school and university critics of the 1980s Restorationists because their main object was to reinstate the curriculum of an earlier time.[63] Deploring the very real gaps in young people's knowledge of history and literature, science and mathematics, reading and composition, they maintained that only the course of study of their own youth could adequately transmit the cultural heritage that young people were no longer acquiring. Appropriating the language of integration and cohesion, they adamantly opposed proposals to give Women's Studies, African-American Studies, Asian Studies, and the like curriculum space. Restricting curriculum to the content that they themselves had been required to learn, they portrayed the traditional Western curriculum as the one and only integrated—in the sense of unified—course of study.

The Restorationist Movement was spearheaded by academicians who once again had no knowledge of or interest in the context of schooling and who compounded the error by ignoring the United States's changed and changing social realities. This time, even if I had wished to, I could not simply watch from the sidelines. Restorationism was a direct answer to the increasing presence in higher education of Women's Studies, Black Studies, Gay and Lesbian Studies and the other new interdisciplinary "multicultural" subjects. As someone who did research on women and who taught Women's Studies courses, I was a player in the scene: an advocate of the curriculum the Restorationists scorned and a contributor to the knowledge they spurned.

In "Curriculum and the Mirror of Knowledge," reprinted in this collection, I challenged both the inward gaze of the Restorationists and their presumption that the curriculum of yore was worthy of everyone's devotion. In the course of explicating the metaphor of curriculum as mirror I pointed out that the unity of that old time course of study, such as it was, derived from the fact that every subject partook of the white man's perspective on nature and the world. I also drew on my earlier explorations of curriculum decision points to demonstrate that valid inclusionary alternatives could be constructed. In addition, whereas my own inclusionary impulses had in the past been directed primarily to bringing the lives, works, experiences, and voices of women into the curriculum, I tried to make this essay a living demonstration of my belief that the available curriculum space must also be filled with the lives, works, experiences, and voices of nonwhite men.

When I wrote "Curriculum and the Mirror of Knowledge" I was only too conscious that I was turning the spotlight on but one of the Restorationist program's many flaws—its exclusionary agenda. Other supporters of Women's Studies, African-American Studies, and the like who have challenged the validity of "the" canon in Western literature, art, philosophy that the Restorationists extol, as well as the universality of those intellectual disciplines whose praises they sing, do not seem to have been troubled by the intellectualistic presuppositions of this mainly mandarin movement. Many of these "New Radicals" have tried to change the curriculum proper, but I have not heard them fault the other aspects of the Restorationist position. Wanting to break the white man's monopolistic hold on curriculum space, they would, if they could, substitute inclusionary versions of the intellectual disciplines for the exclusionary ones now in place. But suppose they accomplished this difficult feat. From what they have said—or rather, from what they have not said—they would seem to be content to perpetuate the form of education that Western culture misleadingly calls "liberal."

Thinking back over the curriculum movements I have encountered as an adult, I realize that few people besides the Radical School Reformers have thought of students as flesh and blood human beings. Hence, it has rarely been considered necessary to connect curriculum either to the here and now or to the future of their lives. The Radical School Reformers did not pay nearly enough attention to the issues of diversity that in the 1980s began to engage the Women's Studies Movement and that have in the 1990s become so pressing in the United States. As a matter of fact, at the very time when research on girls and women was beginning to uncover school's hidden curriculum in sex role stereotypes, the Radical School Reformers made little or no effort to give even gender its due. Still, they resisted the temptation to which even many New Radicals succumb. The earlier radicals were frequently accused of romanticizing children. Instead of repairing the fault by viewing girls and boys in all their incredible variety, their critics and the critics' successors fell back into the habit of treating them as "featureless abstractions."

Forget about the placeholder Z in the proposition "X teaches Y to Z" and the importance of transforming curriculum's goals will be overlooked. Fail to see the need for newly cut turf—especially for redefinitions of the function of education and of an educated person—and proposals concerning those goals will in any case be inadequate.

"The Radical Future of Gender Enrichment," the paper with which this volume closes, was not intended as a sequel to "Curriculum and the Mirror of Knowledge," but in counting the ways in which the traditional curriculum is inadequate, it can be read as such. One thing I wanted to do in writing this paper was to challenge the assumption made by many scholars today—even many feminist scholars—that, from an educational standpoint, it is enough to include the lives, works, and experiences of women in the curriculum. I did not also explicitly question this tenet as it relates to nonwhite men because the paper was designed for a volume on gender and curriculum, but my point can certainly be generalized. My second object was to summarize my findings to date about the myriad ways in which curriculum can be changed. My third was to specify what changes are both suggested and vindicated by the study of gender. Bringing my analytic work in the philosophy of curriculum and my research on women into closer connection than ever before, by incremental steps I tried to show that these changes, when taken together, add up to a much more significant curricular transformation than most of the New Radicals have envisioned.

When I ask myself why so many colleagues in philosophy of education have been resistant to the idea of women entering the scene, I of course think that they want to protect their own turf.[64] They are also subject to the understandable, and I would say quite realistic, fear that this already devalued territory will lose status if women are allowed in. If you stop to think about it, the academy operates on a principle of guilt by association. A scholar has only as much status as does his or her discipline. This latter, in turn, has only as much status as does the field's subject matter—or rather, its subject-entity. Given the standing in the culture's value hierarchy of both women and the cultural baggage we carry, if the philosophy of education welcomes us into the landscape, its practitioners may well be perceived as even less important than we now are.

When I ask myself why scholars across the range of new studies do not notice the need for newly cut turf, I again see the principle of guilt by association at work. As both the "products" and "transmitters" of liberal education, they do not question this culture's underlying educational presuppositions. One unanticipated outcome of my philosophical adventures in curriculum has been an ever increasing respect on my part for how deeply embedded in our cultural consciousness are some very questionable assumptions about education. Another is the growing suspicion that, because of education's self-serving hidden messages, people in the academy are singularly ill-equipped to redesign the landscape. Trained to interrogate the works of white men, to problematize the idea of a canon, to historicize the concepts of gender and race, and to treat even the human body as a social construct, we are simultaneously indoctrinated in the belief that the present configuration of education is one of this world's brute facts.

Since society's reproductive processes are at issue here, one might expect feminist scholars to demand a brand new educational landscape, yet even those most interested in curriculum seldom do. Granted, some still blame women's subordination on the tasks and functions, institutions and virtues to which we continue to be culturally linked. In their eyes, to bring these into education would be to perpetuate our oppression. But, as I discovered when I was roundly applauded at the

1990 meeting of the National Women's Studies Association for saying that the challenge now is to make domesticity everyone's business, many, many feminists now think otherwise. They believe, as I do, that girls and women suffer today because boys and men are not taught to shoulder their fair share of society's emotional labor and domestic responsibilities.

It is one thing to agree with this assessment, however, and quite another to call for new curricular definitions, functions, ideals. Lest we forget, education is one of those subject-entities that falls beyond the pale of liberal education. Judging it to have no redeeming value and perhaps afraid of being contaminated by the study of it, feminist theorists and researchers have been loath to explore the logical geography of education for themselves or even to keep abreast of the relevant chartings of others. When in 1981 I was wondering whether to send the papers I had just written to an education journal or to one of the relatively new feminist ones, a member of the small group of women scholars with whom I have shared my work for over twenty years advised me to try first an educational journal. She said, and I agreed with her, that feminist scholars were so starved for information about women that they would find these papers wherever they were published, whereas educators would never read a feminist journal. Neither of us realized then that even feminists have their limits. The hunger for new material might send them across disciplinary boundaries but it would not drive them across the accepted borders of liberal study itself.[65]

For any number of reasons, many of which are made clear in the essays in this collection, the education gap in the feminist texts is self-defeating. Here let me just add that the great social and political thinkers of the Western tradition, both male and female, knew that a vision of a better society is incomplete if it does not include a design for an education that will help create and maintain it. Sad to say, end-of-twentieth-century feminists have developed new and sometimes inspired visions of peace, justice, politics, better science that would all founder, if they could miraculously be translated into action, because they implicitly rely on old paradigms of education.

On the first page of *Reclaiming a Conversation* I asked why the construction of an adequate philosophy of women's education is seldom seen as part of the task of developing feminist theory. I still want to know, although today I would prefer to ask why the construction of an adequate philosophy of education *for all* is not seen in that light. Can it be that even feminist theorists mistake tradition for necessity and thereby overlook the possibilities for change that there really are? One last theme that connects the early and later writings in Part Two of this volume is that curriculum development is a genuinely creative human endeavor. No one knows better than feminist scholars and other New Radicals that there are no ready-made bundles of subject matter out there waiting to be found. We make them. They above all know that there is no preordained set of school subjects. We select them. This is merely the beginning of the story, however. There is also no preexisting short list of the basics. We choose them. Nor are there any pre-determined goals. We set them. The intellectual disciplines have no natural right to curriculum space. We decide how to allot it. There is no one natural societal function that education serves. We determine this.

But I have said more than enough about the intellectual challenges presented by the philosophical study of curriculum and about the imaginative feats required of those who would transform the educational landscape. In my Bunting Institute essays I asked my colleagues in the philosophy of education to welcome women into our field. It did not then occur to me to ask my colleagues in feminist research and theory to welcome the philosophical study of education into theirs. I do this now. My hope is that as I go out in search of new adventures in curriculum, I will be traveling in the company of both sets of friends.

Notes

1. Carolyn G. Heilbrun, *Reinventing Womanhood* (New York: W.W. Norton & Co., 1979) p. 15.

2. The structure of historical explanation was the subject of my doctoral dissertation, "Explaining, Understanding, and Teaching History: A Philosophical Analysis." cf. Jane R. Martin, *Explaining, Understanding, and Teaching* (New York: McGraw-Hill, 1970).

3. See, e.g., Evelyn Fox Keller, *Reflections on Gender and Science* (New Haven: Yale University Press, 1985); Sandra Harding, *The Science Question in Feminism* (Ithaca: Cornell University Press, 1986).

4. Lorraine Code, *What Can She Know?* (Ithaca: Cornell University Press, 1991), p. 1.

5. Jane Roland, "On 'Knowing How' and 'Knowing That'," *The Philosophical Review LXVII* (1959), pp. 379–388.

6. Jane Roland, "On the Reduction of 'Knowing That' to 'Knowing How'," in B. Othanel Smith and Robert H. Ennis (eds.) *Language and Concepts of Education* (Chicago: Rand McNally & Co., 1961), pp. 59–71.

7. Abraham Edel, "Analytic Philosophy of Education at the Crossroads," in James F. Doyle (ed.) *Educational Judgments* (London: Routledge & Kegan Paul, 1973), p. 239.

8. Ibid, p. 240.

9. Ibid.

10. Jane R. Martin (ed.) *Readings in the Philosophy of Education: A Study of Curriculum* (Boston: Allyn and Bacon, 1970), pp. 154–155.

11. *Op. cit.,* p. 238.

12. William K. Frankena, "A Model for Analyzing a Philosophy of Education," in Martin (ed.) *op. cit.,* p. 15.

13. See, e.g., "What Should We Do with a Hidden Curriculum When We Find One?," Chapter 8 in this volume.

14. For example, in the paper I wrote for the 1987 Guilford College Forum on The Educated Woman, Jane Roland Martin, "The Contradiction of the Educated Woman," *Forum for Honors XVII* (1987), pp. 3–20, reprinted in Joyce Antler and Sari Knopp Biklen

(eds.) *Changing Education* (Albany: State University of New York Press, 1990), pp. 13–31; and in "The Contradiction and Challenge of the Educated Woman," Chapter 5 in this volume.

15. Jane Roland Martin, "Response to Roemer," Jerrold R. Coombs (ed.) *Philosophy of Education 1979* (Normal, Ill.: Philosophy of Education Society, 1980), pp. 190–194.

16. D.C. Phillips, "Philosophy of Education: In Extremis?," *Educational Studies, 14* (1983), p. 22.

17. Ibid, p. 25.

18. Harvey Siegel, "Genderized Cognitive Perspective and the Redefinition of Philosophy of Education," in Robert E. Roemer (ed.) *Philosophy of Education 1983* (Normal, Ill.: Philosophy of Education Society, 1984), pp. 39–41.

19. I should have said, by white, middle class males.

20. I should point out that these facts were known by some of Peters's predecessors, e.g. Rousseau.

21. Phillips, *op. cit.*, p. 22.

22. Decker F. Walker, "Comments of a Curriculum Specialist on the Eightieth Yearbook," *Educational Theory 31* (1981), p.24; Foster McMurray, "Animadversions on the Eightieth Yearbook of NSSE," p. 75.

23. Carol Gilligan, *In a Different Voice* (Cambridge: Harvard University Press, 1982); cf. Nel Noddings, *Caring* (Berkeley: University of California Press, 1984).

24. Jane Roland Martin, *Reclaiming a Conversation* (New Haven: Yale University Press, 1985), p. 187.

25. See, e.g., "The Anatomy of Subjects," *Educational Theory 27* (1977), pp. 85–95; as well as "The Disciplines and the Curriculum," "What Should We Do with a Hidden Curriculum When We Find One?," "Needed: A New Paradigm of Liberal Education," "Two Dogmas of Curriculum," "Becoming Educated: A Journey of Alienation or Integration?," Chapters 7–11 in this volume.

26. See, e.g., "To Insure Domestic Tranquillity: Liberal Education and the Moral Life." Working Paper Series, No. 8. (Cambridge: Radcliffe College Project on Interdependence, 1988).

27. Jane Roland Martin, *The Schoolhome* (Cambridge: Harvard University Press, 1992).

28. Frankena, *op. cit.*, p. 15.

29. Siegel, *op. cit.*, p. 50.

30. Jane Roland Martin, "Sex Equality and Education: A Case Study," in Mary Vetterling-Braggin (ed.) *"Femininity," "Masculinity," and "Androgyny"* (Totowa: Littlefield, Adams & Co., 1982), pp. 279–300.

31. Siegel, *op. cit.*, p. 42.

32. J.C. Walker and M.A. O'Loughlin, "The Ideal of the Educated Woman: Jane Roland Martin on Education and Gender," *Educational Theory 34* (1984), pp. 333–334; Siegel, *op. cit.*, p. 40.

33. Lorenne Clark, "The Rights of Women: The Theory and Practice of the Ideology of Male

Supremacy," in William R. Shea and John King-Farlow (eds.) *Contemporary Issues in Political Philosophy* (New York: Science History Publications, 1976), pp. 49–65.

34. J.C. Walker and M.A. O'Loughlin, *op. cit.*, p. 330.

35. Nel Noddings, "Educating Moral People," in Mary M. Brabeck (ed.) *Who Cares?* (New York: Praeger, 1989), p. 224; *Women and Evil* (Berkeley: University of California Press, 1989), p. 108.

36. Jane Roland Martin, "Martial Virtues or Capital Vices?: William James' Moral Equivalent of War Revisited," *Journal of Thought 22* (1987), pp. 32–44.

37. William Heard Kilpatrick, *The Montessori System Examined* (New York: Arno Press & The New York Times, 1971), p. 66.

38. Thomas S. Kuhn, *The Structure of Scientific Revolution* (Chicago: University of Chicago Press, 1970, Second Ed.), p. 64.

39. See, e.g., Inga Elgqvist-Saltzman, "Research on Gender and Education—What is Going On at Umeå?," in Elgqvist-Saltzman (ed.) *Education and the Construction of Gender*, Kvinnovetenskapligt Forums Rapportserie, NR 2, 1991.

40. See, e.g., Mieke Lunenberg, "Emily and Sarah: The Significance of Role Models in History and Today. The Dutch Case," lecture delivered at Alice in Wonderland: First International Conference on Girls and Girlhood, Amsterdam, June 1992; Mineke van Essen, "Schoolgirls and Femininity. Girlhood in the Netherlands in the 19th and 20th Century," unpublished paper.

41. David MacGregor, *Hegel, Marx, and the English State* (Boulder: Westview Press, 1992), Ch. 5.

42. Susan Laird, "The Ideal of the Educated Teacher: 'Reclaiming a Conversation' with Louisa May Alcott," *Curriculum Inquiry 21* (1991), pp. 271–297; cf. "Teaching in a Different Sense: Alcott's Marmee," presented at the 49th Annual Meeting of the Philosophy of Education Society, New Orleans, March 19, 1993.

43. See, e.g., Meg McGavran Murray, "Beyond Anomaly: The Educated Woman, Past and Present," *Forum for Honors XVII* (1987), pp. 37–51 and Brenda J. Powell, "The Voice of the Educated Woman," pp. 3–13. These are but two of the many papers written in response to my "The Contradiction of the Educated Woman," and to Barbara Miller Solomon's "The Educated Woman and Professional Identity: The First Phase," both of which were written for the Guilford College Forum, sponsored by the National Collegiate Honors Council, and were published in *Forum for Honors XVII* (1987).

44. In a paper in Kevin Grennan's course on Contemporary Philosophy of Education. Although this list is not meant to be exhaustive, I would like to add that students of Averil McClelland at Kent State University enacted and filmed a "Meeting of the Minds" symposium on ideals of the educated woman; while at Aquinas College in Grand Rapids, Michigan, men and women in James Garofolo's classes stepped into the discussion to give moving accounts of themselves in relation to the ideals put forth by the members of the original circle.

45. Kuhn, *op. cit.*, p. 65.

46. Virginia Woolf, *Three Guineas* (New York: Harcourt Brace Jovanovich, 1938), p. 18.

47. Virginia Woolf, *A Room of One's Own* (New York: Harcourt Brace Jovanovich, 1929), p. 72.

48. Ibid, p. 76.

49. For a discussion of this risk see Martin, *The Schoolhome, op. cit.*

50. Jane Roland Martin, "Methodological Essentialism, False Difference, and Other Dangerous Traps," *Signs* 19 (Spring 1994) forthcoming .

51. See, e.g. Martin, "Sex Equality and Education: A Case Study," *op. cit.*, esp. notes 27 and 29.

52. cf. Judith Stacey, "On Resistance, Ambivalence and Feminist Theory: A Response to Carol Gilligan," *Michigan Quarterly Review XXIX* (1990), pp. 537–546.

53. Cf. Martin, *The Schoolhome, op. cit.*

54. Of course the causal influence travels in the other direction too.

55. Ivan Illich, *Deschooling Society* (New York: Harper & Row, 1972).

56. Jerome S. Bruner, *The Process of Education* (Cambridge: Harvard University Press, 1960).

57. Frances FitzGerald, *America Revised* (New York: Vintage Books, 1980).

58. Ibid, p.199.

59. Jane Roland Martin, "Choice, Chance, and Curriculum," Boyd H. Bode Memorial Lectures, No. 3, College of Education, The Ohio State University, 1975.

60. I hasten to add that many of them, however, had a full agenda for school's hidden curriculum.

61. On this issue see Barbara Arnstine, "To Whom It May Concern? A Review of Philosophy and Education: Eightieth Yearbook of the National Society for the Study of Education," *Educational Theory* (1981), pp. 17–22; Patricia Albjerg Graham, "Comment on Philosophy and Education," pp. 29–30.

62. Richard Rodriguez, *Hunger of Memory* (Boston: David R. Godine, 1982).

63. In Martin, *The Schoolhome.* I suppose that they could equally well be called New Essentialists.

64. For the record, *Reclaiming a Conversation* was not reviewed in *Educational Theory*, the journal that calls itself "A Medium of Expression for . . . the Philosophy of Education Society." Nor was it the topic of a Philosophy of Education Society symposium, as so many other books in the field have been.

65. This may explain why the bibliography of books on feminism and philosophy, published in the April 1988 issue of the American Philosophical Association *Newsletter* did not include *Reclaiming a Conversation*.

PART I

When Women Enter the Scene

CHAPTER 1

Excluding Women from the Educational Realm

When as a fellow at the Mary Ingraham Bunting Institute of Radcliffe College I sat down to write about the place of women in the narratives and theories of philosophy of education, I thought I was composing the first section of my Presidential Address to the Philosophy of Education Society. However, my material soon outran the space I assigned it and took on a life of its own. I open this collection with the essay that I then fashioned, although in so doing I break with strict chronological order, because "Excluding Women from the Educational Realm" surveys the ground covered by the papers in Part One. Situating the two studies that predate it, it demonstrates the need for the ones that came after. This paper also introduces one of the book's recurring themes: the importance of redrawing the boundaries of education. That in predicting enrichment for a field which welcomes women it sets the stage for the discussion at volume's end of the far more radical goal of transformation, is again a reason for putting it first.

In recent years a literature has developed which documents the ways in which intellectual disciplines such as history and psychology, literature and the fine arts, sociology and biology are biased according to sex. The feminist criticism contained in this literature reveals that the disciplines fall short of the ideal of epistemological equality, that is, equality of representation and treatment of women in academic knowledge itself—for example, in scientific theories, historical narratives, and literary interpretations. The disciplines exclude women from their subject matter; they distort the female according to the male image of her; and they deny the feminine by forcing women into a masculine mold. While certain aspects of philosophy have been subjected to feminist scrutiny,[1] the status of women in the subject matter of philosophy of education has not yet been studied. This is unfortunate, for philosophy of education has more than theoretical significance; in dealing with prescriptive questions of education which touch all our lives, it has great practical significance. Furthermore, as a consequence of state teacher certification requirements and the fact that public school teaching is primarily a women's occupation, a large proportion of philosophy of education students are women. It is important to understand, therefore, that, although throughout history women have reared and taught the young and have themselves been educated, they are excluded both as the subjects and objects of educational thought from the standard texts and anthologies: as subjects, their philosophical works on education are ignored; as objects, works by men about their education and also their role as educators of the young are largely neglected. Moreover, the very definition of education and the educational realm adopted implicitly by the standard texts, and made explicit by contemporary analytic philosophers of education, excludes women.

Invisible Women

In an earlier essay I argued that the common interpretation of Rousseau's educational thought cannot explain what he has to say about the education of Sophie, the prototype of woman.[2] Rather than admit to the inadequacy of the accepted interpretation, the standard texts either ignore Rousseau's account of the education of Sophie or treat it as an aberration in his thought.

Rousseau's account of the education of girls and women is no aberration; on the contrary, it is integral to his philosophy of education. Nor is Plato's account of the education of women in Book V of the *Republic* an aberration; yet a number of the standard texts and anthologies omit all references to Book V. Others neither anthologize nor comment on those sections containing Plato's proposal that both males and females can be rulers of the Just State and that all those who are suited to rule should, regardless of sex, be given the same education.[3] Moreover, the texts which mention Plato's views on the education of women do so in passing or with significant distortion.[4]

A study done by Christine Pierce has shown that translators and commentators have consistently misinterpreted Book V of Plato's *Republic;* they have been unable to comprehend that such a great philosopher sanctioned the equality of the sexes.[5] Few writers of the standard texts in the history of educational philosophy seem able to grasp this either. Other scholars, for example John Dewey and Thomas Henry Huxley, have also treated women's education seriously.[6] Nonetheless, only one standard text lists girls and women in its index.[7] The others do not perceive sex or gender to be an educational category, even though many of the philosophers whose thought constitutes their subject matter did.

The standard texts have also ignored what philosophers of education have said about the educative role of women as mothers. In his classic pedagogical work, *Leonard and Gertrude,* Johann Heinrich Pestalozzi presents Gertrude neither—to use his biographer's words—"as the sweetheart of some man nor, in the first place, as the wife of her husband but as the mother of her child."[8] As such, Pestalozzi presents her as the model of the good educator. When the nobleman Arner and his aide visit Cotton Meyer in Gertrude's village, Meyer describes Gertrude as one who understands how to establish schools which stand in close connection with the life of the home, instead of in contradiction to it.[9] They visit Gertrude and closely observe her teaching methods. Arner's aide is so impressed by Gertrude that he resolves to become the village schoolmaster. When he finally opens a school, it is based on principles of education extracted from Gertrude's practice.

Pestalozzi is not discussed in as many of the standard texts as are Plato and Rousseau. Insofar as the texts do include his thought, however, they scarcely acknowledge that he thinks Gertrude's character and activities "set the example for a new order."[10] Pestalozzi's insight that mothers are educators of their children and that we can learn from their methods has been largely ignored in educational philosophy.

Just as the exclusion of women as objects of educational thought by historians of educational philosophy is easily seen from a glance at the indexes of the standard texts, their exclusion as subjects is evident from a glance at the tables of contents in which the works of women philosophers of education have been overlooked. The one exception is Maria Montessori, whose work is discussed at length by Robert Rusk.[11] However, she is neither mentioned nor anthologized in the other texts I have surveyed, including Robert Ulich's massive anthology, *Three Thousand Years of Educational Wisdom*.

Montessori's claim to inclusion in the standard texts and anthologies is apparent, for her philosophical works on the education of children are widely known. She is not, however, the only woman in history to have developed a systematic theory of education. Many women have been particularly concerned with the education of their own sex. For example, in *A Vindication of the Rights of Woman*, Mary Wollstonecraft challenged Rousseau's theory of the education of girls and developed her own theory.[12] Wollstonecraft, in turn, was influenced by the writings on education and society of Catherine Macaulay, in particular her *Letters on Education*.[13] In numerous books and articles Catharine Beecher set forth a philosophy of education of girls and women which presents interesting contrasts to Wollstonecraft's;[14] and the utopian novel *Herland*, written by Charlotte Perkins Gilman, rests on a well-developed educational philosophy for women.[15]

While Montessori's work was certainly familiar to the authors and editors of the standard texts and anthologies, it is doubtful that Macaulay, Wollstonecraft, Beecher, and Gilman were even known to these men, let alone that they were perceived as educational philosophers. It is possible to cite them here because feminist research in the last decade has uncovered the lives and works of many women who have thought systematically about education. The works of these women must be studied and their significance determined before one can be sure that they should be included in the standard texts and anthologies. This analytic and evaluative endeavor remains to be done.

It should not be supposed, however, that all the men whose educational thought has been preserved for us by the standard texts are of the stature of Plato and Rousseau or that all the works represented in the anthologies are as important as the *Republic* and *Emile*. On the contrary, a reader of these books will find writings of considerable educational significance by otherwise unknown thinkers, and writings of questionable educational value by some of the great figures of Western philosophy. Thus, while criteria do have to be satisfied before Macaulay, Wollstonecraft, Beecher, Gilman, and others are given a place in the history of educational thought, they cannot in fairness be excluded simply for being regarded as less profound thinkers than Plato.

The question remains whether the women cited here can be excluded because their overriding interest is the education of their own sex. In view of the fate of Sophie, Gertrude, and Plato's female guardians as objects of educational thought, one can only assume that, had the works of these women been known to exist, they also would have been ignored by the standard texts and anthologies of the field. From the standpoint of the history of educational thought, women thinkers are in double jeopardy: they are penalized for their interest in the education of their own sex because that topic falls outside the field; and, as the case of Montessori makes clear, those who have written about education in general are penalized simply for being women.

Defining the Educational Realm

Lorenne Clark has shown that, from the standpoint of political theory, women, children, and the family dwell in the "ontological basement," outside and underneath the political structure.[16] This apolitical status is due not to historical accident or necessity but to arbitrary definition. The reproductive processes of society—processes in which Clark includes creation and birth and the rearing of children to "more or less independence"—are by fiat excluded from the political domain, which is defined in relation to the public world of productive processes. Since the subject matter of political theory is politics, and since reproductive processes have been traditionally assigned to women and have taken place within the family, it follows that women and the family are excluded from the very subject matter of the discipline.

The analogy between political theory and educational philosophy is striking. Despite the fact that the reproductive processes of society, broadly understood, are largely devoted to childrearing and include the transmission of skills, beliefs, feelings, emotions, values, and even world views, they are not considered to belong to the educational realm. Thus, education, like politics, is defined in relation to the productive processes of society, and the status of women and the family are "a-educational" as well as apolitical. It is not surprising, then, that Pestalozzi's insight about Gertrude is overlooked by historians of educational philosophy; for in performing her maternal role, Gertrude participates in reproductive processes which are by definition excluded from the educational domain. If Gertrude is outside the educational realm, so is Sophie, for the training Rousseau intends for her aims at fitting her to be a good wife and mother, that is, to carry on the reproductive processes of society.[17] Yet, the exclusion of these processes from education does not in itself entail the exclusion of training *for* them;

people could be prepared to carry on reproductive processes through bona fide educational activities even if the processes themselves are outside of education. However, since educational philosophy defines its subject matter only in terms of productive processes, even this preparation is excluded.

We can see the boundaries of the educational realm in the distinction commonly made between liberal and vocational education. Vocational education is clearly intended to prepare people to carry on the productive processes of society.[18] Liberal education, on the other hand, is not seen as preparation for carrying on its reproductive processes. Even though disagreements abound over which intellectual disciplines are proper to liberal education and the way they are to be organized, no one conceives of liberal education as education in childrearing and family life. The distinction between liberal and vocational education corresponds not to a distinction between the two kinds of societal processes but to one between head and hand *within* productive processes. Liberal education is thus preparation for carrying on processes involving the production and consumption of ideas, while vocational education is preparation for processes involving manual labor.

Historians of educational philosophy have no more interest in Sophie than they do in Gertrude, for Rousseau places Sophie in the home and tailors her education to the role he assigns her there. Indeed, educational philosophy has no ready vocabulary to describe the kind of education Rousseau designs for Sophie. It is not a liberal education, for she will learn coquetry and modesty and skill in lacemaking, not science, history, literature, or rational thinking.[19] Like vocational education, her training has narrow and clearly specified ends. Yet vocational education programs prepare their graduates to enter the job market, whereas Sophie's education is designed to keep her out of that arena.[20]

Philosophy of education has no ready classification for the training Rousseau would provide women because it falls outside the educational domain. However, there is a classification for the training Plato would provide the women guardians of his Just State. For Plato, ruling is a matter of knowing the Good, which involves using one's reason to grasp the most abstract, theoretical knowledge possible. Thus, the education he prescribes for the guardian class is a type of liberal education—one which greatly influences educational thought and practice even today. How, then, are we to explain that historians of educational philosophy ignore Plato's theory of the education of women? In a field which excludes the reproductive processes of society from its subject matter and identities women with these processes, Plato's theory is an anomaly. Plato places women in the public world and prescribes for them an education for the productive processes of society. Although their education falls squarely within the educational realm as defined by the field and can be readily classified, the fact that *women* are to receive this education is lost to view. The position of women in the history of educational philosophy is not an enviable one. Excluded from its subject matter insofar as they are commonly tied by theory to the reproductive processes of society, women are denied recognition even when a particular theory such as Plato's detaches their lives and their education from childrearing and the family.

The Analytic Paradigm: Peters's Concept of Education

Contemporary philosophical analysis has made explicit the boundaries of the educational realm assumed by the standard texts in the history of educational philosophy. In *Ethics and Education*, R.S. Peters writes that education is something "we consciously contrive for ourselves or for others" and that "it implies that something worthwhile is being or has been intentionally transmitted in a morally acceptable manner."[21] Peters distinguishes between two senses of the word "education." As an activity, education must fulfill three conditions—intentionality, voluntariness, and comprehension—for it involves the *intentional* transmission of something worthwhile, an element of *voluntariness* on the part of the learner, and some *comprehension* by the learner both of what is being learned and of the standards the learner is expected to attain.[22] As an achievement, education involves also the acquisition of knowledge, understanding, and cognitive perspectives.[23]

The analytic literature in philosophy of education is filled with discussions of Peters's concept of education, and at various points in his career he has elaborated upon and defended it.[24] Over the years he has come to acknowledge that there are two concepts of education: one encompassing "any process of childrearing, bringing up, instructing, etc.," and the other encompassing only those processes directed toward the development of an educated person.[25] Peters considers only the second, narrower concept to have philosophical significance. He has analyzed this concept in one work after another and has traced its implications in his book, *The Logic of Education*. This narrow concept is the basis not only for his own philosophical investigations of education but also for those of his many collaborators, students, and readers.

Peters is no insignificant figure in the philosophy of education. Indeed, his concept of education, which excludes the reproductive processes of society, defines the domain of the now-dominant school of philosophy of education—analytic philosophy of education.[26] Peters has given analytic philosophy of education a research paradigm which defines the types of problems, approaches, and solutions for the field only in terms of the productive processes of society. Thus from its standpoint, when Gertrude teaches her children, she is frequently not engaged in the activity of education. While a good deal of what she does fulfills Peters's condition of intentionality, and although she always acts in a morally acceptable manner, there are many occasions on which the children fail to meet the condition of voluntariness.

At times, however, the children are voluntary learners, as when the neighbor children implore Gertrude to teach them spinning:

> "Can you spin?" she asked.
> "No," they answered.
> "Then you must learn, my dears. My children wouldn't sell their knowledge of it at any price, and are happy enough on Saturday, when they each get their few kreutzers. The year is long my dears, and if we earn something every week at the end of the year there is a lot of money, without our knowing how we came by it."
> "Oh, please teach us!" implored the children, nestling close to the good woman.
> "Willingly," Gertrude replied. "come every day if you like, and you will soon learn."[27]

However, with her own children Gertrude constantly instills manners and proper conduct without their permission:

> "What business was it of yours to tell the Bailiff day before yesterday, that you knew Arner would come soon? Suppose your father had not wished him to know that he knew it, and your chattering had brought him into trouble."
> "I should be very sorry, mother. But neither of you said a word about its being a secret."
> "Very well, I will tell your father when he comes home, whenever we are talking together, we must take care to add after each sentence: 'Lizzie may tell that to the neighbors, and talk about it at the well; but this she must not mention outside the house.' So then you will know precisely what you may chatter about."
> "O mother, forgive me! That was not what I meant."
> Gertrude talked similarly with all the other children about their faults, even saying to little Peggy: "You mustn't be so impatient for your soup, or I shall make you wait longer another time, and give it to one of the others."[28]

There are numerous questions about the transmission of values by the family which philosophy of education could answer: What does "transmit" mean in this context? Which values ought to be transmitted by the family? Should the values transmitted by the family be reinforced by schools or should they be challenged? Do schools have the right to challenge them? Yet as its subject matter is presently defined, philosophy of education cannot ask them, for they are questions about the reproductive processes of society which are inappropriate to raise, let alone to answer.

From the standpoint of contemporary analytic philosophy of education, Gertrude's educational activities and those of mothers in general are irrelevant. Indeed, any account of mothering is considered outside the field. For example, Sara Ruddick's recent innovative account of maternal thought, which gives insights into a kind of thinking associated with the reproductive processes of society, has no more place in the field than Pestalozzi's insights about Gertrude in her capacity as mother.[29]

The kind of maternal thought Ruddick describes and Gertrude embodies is the kind Sophie must exhibit if she is to perform well the traditional female role Rousseau assigned her. As Ruddick makes clear, however, "maternal" is a social, not a biological category: although maternal thought arises out of childrearing practices, men as well as women express it in various ways of working and caring for others.[30] Thus it is something Sophie must learn, not something she is born with. Notice, however, when Sophie learns maternal skills from her mother and in raising her own children, this learning will also fall outside the educational realm. It will lack Peters's voluntariness and intentionality and will be part of the childrearing processes he would have philosophers of education ignore. In sum, the definition of education used by analytic philosophers today excludes the teaching, the training, and the socialization of children for which women throughout history have had prime responsibility.[31]

The Analytic Paradigm: Hirst's Concept of Liberal Education

Yet Sophie's learning would not be admitted to the educational realm even if it were designed in such a way that it met Peters's criteria of an educational process. It would still include unacceptable goals and content. According to Peters, the goal of education is the development of the educated person, who does not simply possess knowledge, but has some understanding of principles for organizing facts and of the "reason why" of things. The educated person's knowledge is not inert, but characterizes the person's way of looking at things and involves "the kind of commitment that comes from getting on the inside of a form of thought and awareness." This involves caring about the standards of evidence implicit in science or the canons of proof inherent in mathematics and possessing cognitive perspective.[32] At the center of Peters's account of education and the educated person is the notion of initiation into worthwhile activities, the impersonal cognitive content and procedures of which are "enshrined in *public traditions.*"[33] Mathematics, science, history, literature, philosophy: these are the activities into which Peters's educated person is initiated. That person is one who has had, and has profited from, a liberal education of the sort outlined by Peters's colleague Paul Hirst in his essay, "Liberal Education and the Nature of Knowledge":

> First, sufficient immersion in the concepts, logic and criteria of the discipline for a person to come to know the distinctive way in which it "works" by pursuing these in particular cases: and then sufficient generalization of these over the whole range of the discipline so that his experience begins to be widely structured in this distinctive manner. It is this coming to look at things in a certain way that is being aimed at, not the ability to work out in minute particulars all the details that can be in fact discerned. It is the ability to recognise empirical assertions or aesthetic judgments for what they are, and to know the kind of considerations on which their validity will depend, that matters.[34]

If Peters's educated person is not in fact Hirst's liberally educated person, he or she is certainly the identical twin.

Hirst's analysis of liberal education has for some time been the accepted one in the field of philosophy of education.[35] In his view, liberal education consists of an initiation into what he takes to be the seven forms of knowledge.[36] Although in his later writings he carefully denies that these forms are themselves intellectual disciplines, it is safe to conclude that his liberally educated people will acquire the conceptual schemes and cognitive perspectives they are supposed to have through a study of mathematics, physical sciences, history, the human sciences, religion, literature and fine arts, and philosophy. These disciplines will not necessarily be studied separately; an interdisciplinary curriculum is compatible with Hirst's analysis. But it is nonetheless their subject matter, their conceptual apparatus, their standards of proof and adequate evidence that must be acquired if the ideal liberal education is to be realized.

In one way or another, then, the intellectual disciplines constitute the content of Peters's curriculum for the educated person. Since the things Rousseau would have Sophie learn—modesty, attentiveness, reserve, sewing, embroidery, lacemaking, keeping house, serving as hostess, bringing up children—are not part of these disciplines and are not enshrined in public traditions, they fall outside the curriculum of the educated person. But this is to say that they fall outside of education itself for, as we have seen, education, in Peters's analysis, is necessarily directed to the development of the educated person. Just as Rousseau's curriculum for Sophie is excluded from the educational realm, curricula in Beecher's domestic economy, Ruddick's maternal thinking, and Nancy Chodorow's mothering capacities would also be excluded.[37] Given the analyses of the concepts of education, the educated person, and liberal education which are accepted in general outline by the field of philosophy of education, no curriculum preparing people for the reproductive processes can belong to a realm which is reserved for the ways of thinking, acting, and feeling involved in *public* traditions. Since girls and women are the ones who traditionally have carried on the reproductive processes of society, it is *their* activities of teaching and learning and *their* curriculum which are excluded from the educational realm. Sophie and Gertrude are as irrelevant to analytic philosophers of education as they are to the writers of texts in the history of educational philosophy.

The Analytic Paradigm: The Rationality Theory of Teaching

I have said that Gertrude teaches her children even though analytic philosophers of education would say she is not educating them. Yet according to Peters, only a fraction of what Gertrude does could be called "teaching." This is because the concept of teaching is so closely linked to the concept of education that, in ruling out so many of Gertrude's activities as instances of education, Peters's analysis also rules them out as instances of teaching.

But quite apart from Peters's criteria, Gertrude fails to qualify as a teacher according to the accepted analysis of the concept of teaching. Perhaps the best brief statement of this analysis—what I have elsewhere called the rationality theory of teaching[38]—is found in a little known essay by Israel Scheffler. Beliefs, Scheffler says,

> can be acquired through mere unthinking contact, propaganda, indoctrination, or brainwashing. Teaching, by contrast, engages the mind, no matter what the subject matter. The teacher is prepared to *explain*, that is, to acknowledge the student's right to ask for reasons and his concomitant right to exercise his judgment on the merits of the case. Teaching is, in this standard sense, an initiation into open rational discussion.[39]

In this passage Scheffler harks back to the original account of teaching he gave in his earlier book *The Language of Education* where he states that to teach "is at some points at least to submit oneself to the understanding and independent judgment of the pupil, to his demand for reasons, to his sense of what constitutes an adequate explanation." And he adds:

> Teaching involves further that, if we try to get the student to believe that such and such is the case, we try also to get him to believe it for reasons that, within the limits of his capacity to grasp, are *our* reasons. Teaching, in this way, requires us to reveal our reasons to the student and, by so doing, to submit them to his evaluation and criticism.[40]

Scheffler is not the only contemporary philosopher of education who has emphasized connections between teaching and rationality. Numerous colleagues and critics in the field have elaborated upon and modified his analysis of teaching, and others have arrived independently at conclusions similar to his.[41] The relevant point for the present inquiry is that, according to this analysis of the concept of teaching, the learner's rationality must be acknowledged in two ways: the manner in which the teacher proceeds and the type of learning to be achieved. Thus, the rationality theory holds that to be teaching one must expose one's reasons to the learner so that the learner can evaluate them, and also that one's aim must be that the learner also have reasons, and attain a level of learning involving understanding.

On some occasions Gertrude does approximate the conception of teaching which the rationality theory embodies. When she tries to get her children to learn that virtue must be its own reward, she cautions them to give away their bread quietly so that no one may see them and reveals to them her reason that "people needn't think you want to show off your generosity."[42] When one son asks her to give him a mouthful of bread for himself since he is giving his portion away, she refuses to do so. He asks for her reason and receives the reply: "So that you needn't imagine we are only to think of the poor after our own hunger is satisfied."[43] Yet one is left wondering what Gertrude would say and do if her children ever questioned the values she instills in them. One suspects that she would quickly resort to appeals to authority, a move of which the rationality theory would not approve.

Consider now the occasion on which Gertrude attempts to transmit her values to some neglected children by washing them, combing their hair, dressing them with care, and scrubbing their house. She neither gives reasons for the values of cleanliness and order in which she so firmly believes nor tries to *acknowledge the rationality* of the children in other ways.[44] And on another occasion when Gertrude invites these children to pray with her own children, and then accompanies them to their house with a "cheery parting, bidding them to come again soon,"[45] the intention is that they acquire good habits, but the mode of acquisition is quite divorced from the giving of explanations and the evaluation of reasons. Gertrude expects that through her kindness, good example, and the efficacy of unconscious imitation, these derelict children will adopt her values. She does not seem to care whether they understand the habits and values they are adopting or have proper backing for the associated beliefs they are acquiring.

It must be made clear, however, that the rationality theory does not function as an account of *good* teaching. It is not meant to be prescriptive; rather its function is to tell us what *constitutes* or *counts as* teaching. If Gertrude's actions do not meet its twofold requirement of rationality in the manner in which the teacher proceeds and in the type of learning to be achieved, adherents of the theory will not judge her teaching to be deficient; they will judge her not to be teaching at all. They will do so, moreover, no matter how reasonable or appropriate her actions may be. That Gertrude's actions are appropriate, given the value she places on cleanliness and godliness, the age of the neighbor children, and their condition, will be evident to readers who know young children. However, the rationality theory is not concerned that teaching be a rational activity in the ordinary sense that the actions constituting it be suited to the ends envisioned. Its sole concern is that the learner's reason be taken into account. Thus there are many contexts in which an activity meeting the requirements of the rationality theory of teaching will not be rational from the standpoint of the demands of the particular context.

In the process of bringing new infants to the point of independence, parents often do things which fit the rationality theory's criteria of teaching. Yet most of the teaching and learning which takes place in relation to the reproductive processes of society do not fit these criteria.[46] Values are transmitted, sex roles are internalized, character traits are developed, skills are acquired, and moral schemes and world views are set in place. Yet, if the teacher's reasons are not revealed or the learner's rationality is not acknowledged, the rationality theory denies the labels of "teacher" and "learner" to the parties involved.

The analysis of teaching which occupies a central position in philosophy of education today embodies a Socratic conception of both teaching and learning. The give and take of Socrates and his friends philosophizing in the marketplace, the Oxford tutor and his tutee, the graduate seminar: these are the intuitively clear cases of teaching and learning on which the analytic paradigm is based. Gertrude teaching her children a song to sing to their father when he returns home or the neighbors to count as they are spinning and sewing, Marmee helping Jo to curb her temper, Mrs. Garth making little Lotty learn her place—the activities and processes of childrearing which have traditionally belonged to women as mothers are at best considered to be peripheral cases of teaching and learning and are more likely not to qualify under these headings at all.[47]

A Servant of Patriarchal Policy

In defining education and the questions that can be asked about it, the analyses of contemporary philosophy of education make women and their activities and experiences invisible. The question naturally arises whether this matters. As long as women can enter the educational realm in practice—as they can and do today—what difference does it make that educational philosophy does not acknowledge gender as a bona fide educational category? As long as Plato and Rousseau discussed the education of girls and women in major works and Pestalozzi recognized the ability of mothers to teach, what difference does it make that the texts in the history of educational philosophy ignore their accounts and that the paradigms of analytic philosophy of education do not apply to Sophie, Gertrude, or women in general?

It matters for many reasons. When the experience of women is neither reflected nor interpreted in the texts and anthologies of the history of educational philosophy, women are given no opportunity to understand and evaluate the range of ideals— from Plato's guardians to Sophie and Gertrude—which the great thinkers of the past have held for them. When Wollstonecraft and Montessori are ignored in these texts, students of both sexes are denied contact with the great female minds of the past;

indeed, they are denied the knowledge that women have ever thought seriously and systematically about education. What is more important is that, when the works of women are excluded from texts and anthologies, the message that women are not capable of significant philosophical reflection is transmitted.

By placing women outside the educational realm or else making them invisible within it, the contemporary paradigms of philosophy of education also contribute to the devaluation of women. Peters's conviction that only the narrow sense of education is worthy of philosophical inquiry keeps us from perceiving the teaching which takes place in childrearing as a serious, significant undertaking; it makes women's traditional activities appear trivial and banal. Similarly, in defining teaching in terms of a very narrow conception of rationality—the giving and understanding of reasons— the rationality theory of teaching makes the educational activities of mothers, and by implication mothers themselves, appear nonrational, if not downright irrational.

In a report on recent contributions to philosophy of education, Scheffler protested that philosophy is not a handmaiden of policy. "Its function is not to facilitate policy," he said, "but rather to enlighten it by pressing its traditional questions of value, virtue, veracity, and validity."[48] Yet by its very definition of its subject matter, philosophy of education facilitates patriarchal policy; for in making females invisible, philosophy of education helps maintain the inequality of the sexes. It reinforces the impression that girls and women are not important human beings and that the activities they have traditionally performed in carrying on the reproductive processes of society are not worthwhile. Furthermore, philosophy's traditional questions of value, virtue, veracity, and validity cannot be asked about the education of females because females are unseen in the educational realm. Thus the enlightenment that philosophy is capable of giving is denied to policies which directly affect girls and women.

I do not know if philosophy can ever be as divorced from policy as Scheffler would have it. But as long as there is no epistemological equality for women in philosophy of education, that discipline will serve patriarchal policy, albeit unintentionally. For when the activities and experiences of females are excluded from the educational realm, those of males provide our norms. Thus, the qualities Socrates displays in his philosophical conversations with his male companions in the marketplace are built into our very definition of teaching even as the ones Gertrude displays in her interactions with her children are overlooked. Similarly, the traditional male activities of science and mathematics, history and philosophy are built into the curriculum of the educated person even as activities traditionally assigned to females are ignored.

Do not misunderstand: I am not suggesting that the curriculum Rousseau prescribed for Sophie should become the norm or that cooking and sewing should be placed on a par with science and history. An education for coquetry and guile is not good for either sex; and, while there is nothing wrong with both sexes learning how to cook and sew, I am not advocating that these skills be incorporated into the liberal curriculum. Nor am I endorsing Pestalozzi's claim that Gertrude's particular mode of teaching should be a model for all to emulate. My point is, rather, that when the activities and experiences traditionally associated with women are excluded from the educational realm and when that realm is defined in terms of male activities and experiences, then these become the educational norms for all human beings.

It has been shown that psychological theories of development have difficulty incorporating findings about females because they are derived from male data.[49] It should now be clear that the paradigms of analytic philosophy of education are also based on male data. The examples which generate the rationality theory of teaching, Peters's concept of education and the educated person, and Hirst's theory of liberal education all derive from male experience. The response of the psychologists to the difficulty presented them by female data is to impose on their female subjects a masculine mold. The response of philosophers of education to female data is similar: Gertrude's teaching is at best defective; education for carrying on the reproductive processes of society is at best illiberal. Thus, the male norms which are implicit in the concepts and theories of philosophy of education today devalue women, and thereby serve patriarchal policy. But this is only part of the story. A corollary of this devaluation of women is that men are denied an education for carrying out the reproductive processes of society. In this way, the traditional sexual division of labor is supported.

Reconstituting the Educational Realm

The exclusion of women from the educational realm harms not only women; the field of philosophy of education itself is adversely affected. As the example of Rousseau's *Emile* illustrates, interpretations of works by major educational thinkers in which the education of both males and females is discussed will be deficient when they are based solely on material concerned with males. My discussion of the rationality theory of teaching—a theory which is quite implausible as an account of the teaching of young children—makes clear that analyses of concepts are likely to be inadequate when the cases which inform them and against which they are tested are derived solely from male experience. Furthermore, when gender is not seen to be a relevant educational category, important questions are begged.

When the educational realm embodies only male norms, it is inevitable that any women participating in it will be forced into a masculine mold. The question of whether such a mold is desirable for females needs to be asked, but it cannot be asked so long as philosophers of education assume that gender is a difference which makes no difference.[50] The question of whether the mold is desirable for males also needs to be asked; yet when our educational concepts and ideals are defined in male terms, we do not think to inquire into their validity for males themselves.

Perhaps the most important concern is that, when the educational realm makes women invisible, philosophy of education cannot provide an adequate answer to the question of what constitutes an educated person. Elsewhere I have argued at some length that Hirst's account of liberal education is seriously deficient—it presupposes a divorce of mind from body, thought from action, and reason from feeling and emotion—and that, since Peters's educated person is for all intents and purposes Hirst's liberally educated person, Peters's conception should be rejected.[51] Simply put, it is far too narrow to serve as an ideal which guides the educational enterprise and to which value is attached: it provides at best an ideal of an educated *mind*, not of an educated *person*, although, to the extent that its concerns are strictly cognitive, even in this sense it leaves much to be desired.

An adequate ideal of the educated person must join thought to action, and reason to feeling and emotion. As I pointed out in an earlier section, however, liberal education is designed to prepare people to carry on the productive processes of society, in particular those involving the production and consumption of ideas. Thus Peters's educated person is intended to inhabit a world in which feelings and emotions such as caring, compassion, empathy, and nurturance have no legitimate role to play. To incorporate these into a conception of the educated person would be to introduce traits which were not merely irrelevant to the desired end, but very likely incompatible with it.

Peters's conception of the educated person is untenable, yet the remedy for its narrow intellectualism is unavailable to philosophers of education as long as the criteria for what falls within the educational realm mirrors the distinction between the productive and the reproductive processes of society. An adequate conception of the educated person must join together what Peters and Hirst have torn asunder: mind and body; thought and action; and reason, feeling, and emotion. To do this the educational realm must be reconstituted to include the reproductive processes of society.

It is important to understand that the exclusion of both women and the reproductive processes of society from the educational realm by philosophy of education is a consequence of the structure of the discipline and not simply due to an oversight which is easily corrected. Thus, philosophical inquiry into the nature of those processes or into the education of women cannot simply be grafted onto philosophy of education as presently constituted. On the contrary, the very subject matter of the field must be redefined.

Such a redefinition ought to be welcomed by practitioners in the field, for there is every reason to believe that it will ultimately enrich the discipline. As the experiences and activities which have traditionally belonged to women come to be included in the educational realm, a host of challenging and important issues and problems will arise. When philosophy of education investigates questions about childrearing and the transmission of values, when it develops accounts of gender education to inform its theories of liberal education, when it explores the forms of thinking, feeling, and acting associated with childrearing, marriage, and the family, when the concept of coeducation and concepts such as mothering and nurturance become subjects for philosophical analysis, philosophy of education will be invigorated.

New questions can be asked when the educational realm is reconstituted, and old questions can be given more adequate answers. When Gertrude, Sophie, and Plato's female guardians are taken seriously by historians of educational thought and when Rousseau's philosophy of education is counterbalanced by those of Wollstonecraft, Beecher, and Gilman, the theories of the great historical figures will be better understood. When analyses of the concept of teaching take childrearing activities to be central, insight into that prime educational process will be increased. When the activities of family living and childrearing fall within the range of worthwhile activities, theories of curriculum will be more complete.

It is of course impossible to know now the precise contours of a reconstituted educational realm, let alone to foresee the exact ways in which the inclusion of women and the reproductive processes of society will enrich the discipline of philosophy of education. Yet the need for a redefinition of its subject matter is imperative if philosophy of education is to cease serving patriarchal policy. The promise of enrichment is real.

Notes

I wish to thank Naomi Chazan, Anne Costain, Ann Diller, Carol Gilligan, Diane Margolis, Michael Martin, Beatrice Nelson, and Janet Farrell Smith for helpful comments on the original draft.

1. See Kathryn Pyne Parsons, "Moral Revolution," in *The Prism of Sex*, ed. Julia A. Sherman and Evelyn Torton Beck (Madison: Univ. of Wisconsin Press. 1979), pp. 189–227; and Lawrence Blum, "Kant's and Hegel's Moral Rationalism: A Feminist Perspective," *Canadian Journal of Philosophy XII* (1982), pp. 287–302.

2. Jane Roland Martin, "Sophie and Emile: A Case Study of Sex Bias in the History of Educational Thought," see Chapter 2 in this volume.

3. See Robert Ulich, ed., *Three Thousand Years of Educational Wisdom* (Cambridge, Mass.: Harvard Univ. Press, 1948) and his *History of Educational Thought* (New York: American Book, 1945); Robert S. Brumbaugh and Nathaniel M. Lawrence, *Philosophers on Education: Six Essays on the Foundations of Western Thought* (Boston: Houghton Mifflin, 1963); Paul Nash, Andreas M. Kazemias, and Henry J. Perkinson, ed., *The Educated Man: Studies in the History of Educational Thought* (New York: Wiley, 1965); Kingsley Price, *Education and Philosophical Thought*, 2nd ed. (Boston: Allyn & Bacon, 1967); Paul Nash, comp., *Models of Man: Explorations in the Western Educational Tradition* (New York: Wiley, 1968); and Steven M. Cahn, comp., *The Philosophical Foundations of Education* (New York: Harper & Row, 1970).

4. For example, although Brumbaugh and Lawrence call Plato "the great educational revolutionist of his time" in part because of his "insistence on the equality of women" (*Philosophers on Education*, p. 38), they say not another word about that insistence. Robert S. Rusk, who presents Plato's position on the education of women in some detail in his anthology, is apparently so distressed by it that he says what any reader of the *Republic* knows to be false, namely, "Plato can only secure the unity of the state *at the cost of sacrificing all differences*" (*The Doctrines of the Great Educators*, rev. 3rd ed. [New York: St. Martin's. 1965], pp. 28–99, emphasis added). Nash comments that Plato's model of the educated person applies "only to those rare men *and rarer women* who are capable of understanding the underlying harmony of the universe," (*Models of Man*, p. 9, emphasis added) without acknowledging that Plato himself never makes a comparative judgment of the ability of males and females in his Just State to grasp The Good.

5. Pierce, "Equality: *Republic* V," *The Monist 57* (1973), pp. 1–11.

6. See, for example, John Dewey, "Is Coeducation Injurious to Girls?," *Ladies' Home Journal* 28 (1911), pp. 60–61; Thomas Henry Huxley, "Emancipation—Black and White," *Lay Sermons, Addresses and Reviews* (New York: Appleton, 1870; rpt. in Nash, pp. 285–288).

7. Nash, *Models of Man.*

8. Kate Silber, *Pestalozzi* (New York: Schocken Books, 1965), p. 42.

9. Johann Heinrich Pestalozzi, *Leonard and Gertrude,* trans. Eva Channing (Boston: Heath, 1885), ch. 22.

10. Silber, p. 42.

11. Rusk, Ch. 12.

12. *A Vindication of the Rights of Woman* (New York: Norton, 1967); see also Mary Wollstonecraft Godwin, *Thoughts on the Education of Daughters* (Clifton. N.J.: Kelley Publishers, 1972).

13. *Letters on Education,* ed. Gina Luria (New York: Garland, 1974). For discussions of Macaulay's life and works, see Florence S. Boos, "Catherine Macaulay's *Letters on Education* (1790): An Early Feminist Polemic," *University of Michigan Papers in Women's Studies 2* (1976), pp. 64–78; Florence Boos and William Boos, "Catherine Macaulay: Historian and Political Reformer," *International Journal of Women's Studies 3* (1980), pp. 49–65.

14. For a list of Beecher's published works, see Kathryn Kish Sklar, *Catharine Beecher: A Study in American Domesticity* (New York: Norton, 1973).

15. *Herland* (New York: Pantheon Books, 1979).

16. "The Rights of Women: The Theory and Practice of the Ideology of Male Supremacy," in *Contemporary Issues in Political Philosophy,* ed. William R. Shea and John King-Farlow (New York: Science History Publications, 1976), pp. 49–65.

17. See Susan Moller Okin, *Women in Western Political Thought* (Princeton: Princeton Univ. Press, 1979), ch. 6; Lynda Lange, "Rousseau: Women and the General Will," in *The Sexism of Social and Political Theory,* ed. Lorenne M.G. Clark and Lynda Lange (Toronto: Univ. of Toronto Press, 1979), pp. 41–52; and Martin, "Sophie and Emile."

18. See Marvin Lazerson and W. Norton Grubb, ed., *American Education and Vocationalism* (New York: Teachers College Press, 1974).

19. Rousseau, Ch. 5. For the account of liberal education which dominates the thinking of philosophers of education today see Paul H. Hirst, "Liberal Education and the Nature of Knowledge," in *Philosophical Analysis and Education,* ed. Reginald D. Archambault (London: Routledge & Kegan Paul, 1965), pp. 113–138; rpt. in Paul H. Hirst, *Knowledge and the Curriculum* (London: Routledge & Kegan Paul, 1974). Page references will be to this volume.

20. I recognize that I have omitted from this discussion all reference to home economics education. Briefly, home economics education has historically been classified as vocational education (see Lazerson and Grubb). However, in the form which is relevant to the present discussion, namely, the preparation of women for their place in the home, it lacks the distinguishing mark of other vocational studies in that it is not intended as training for jobs in the marketplace. Furthermore, contemporary philosophy of education has seldom, if ever, recognized its existence.

21. *Ethics and Education* (Glenview, Ill. : Scott, Foresman, 1967), pp. 2–3.

22. Peters, p. 17.

23. Peters, p. 97.

24. See Peters, "What is an Educational Process?," in *The Concept of Education*, ed. R.S. Peters (London: Routledge & Kegan Paul, 1967); Paul H. Hirst and R. S. Peters, *The Logic of Education* (London: Routledge & Kegan Paul, 1970); R.S. Peters, "Education and the Educated Man," in *A Critique of Current Educational Aims*, ed. R.F. Dearden, Paul H. Hirst, and R.S. Peters (London: Routledge & Kegan Paul, 1972); R.S. Peters, J. Woods, and W.H. Dray, "Aims of Education—A Conceptual Inquiry," in *The Philosophy of Education*, ed. R.S. Peters (London: Oxford Univ. Press, 1973).

25. See, for example, Peters, "Education and the Educated Man," p. 8.

26. In this section and the ones to follow I will only be discussing paradigms of analytic philosophy of education. There are other schools within philosophy of education, but this one dominates the field today as the recent N.S.S.E. Yearbook, *Philosophy and Education*, testifies (ed. Jonas Soltis [Chicago: The National Society for the Study of Education, 1981]).

27. Pestalozzi, pp. 87–88.

28. Pestalozzi, p. 44.

29. "Maternal Thinking," *Feminist Studies 6* (1980), pp. 342–367.

30. Ruddick, p. 346.

31. I do not mean to suggest that these activities have been in the past or are now carried on exclusively by women. On the contrary, both men and women have engaged in them and do now. Our culture assigns women responsibility for them, however.

32. Peters, *Ethics and Education*, p. 8ff.

33. Peters, *Education as Initiation* (London: Evans Brothers, 1964), p. 35, emphasis added.

34. Hirst, "Liberal Education," p. 47.

35. For an extended critique of Hirst's analysis in this respect, see Jane Roland Martin, "Needed: A New Paradigm for Liberal Education," Chapter 9 in this volume.

36. In "Liberal Education," p. 46, Hirst listed the seven as: mathematics, physical sciences, human sciences, history, religion, literature and fine arts, and philosophy.

37. See Ruddick; Chodorow, *The Reproduction of Mothering* (Berkeley: Univ. of California Press, 1978); and Catharine M. Beecher, *Suggestions Respecting Improvement in Education* (Hartford, Conn.: Packard & Butler, 1829).

38. Martin, *Explaining, Understanding, and Teaching* (New York: McGraw-Hill, 1970), Ch. 5.

39. "Concepts of Education: Reflections on the Current Scene," in Israel Scheffler, *Reason and Teaching* (Indianapolis: Bobbs-Merrill, 1975), p. 62.

40. *The Language of Education* (Springfield, Ill.: Thomas, 1960), p. 57.

41. See, for example, Thomas F. Green, "A Topology of the Teaching Concept," *Studies in Philosophy and Education 3* (1964–65), pp. 284–319; and his "Teaching, Acting, and Behaving," *Harvard Educational Review 34* (1964), pp. 507–524.

42. Pestalozzi, p. 55.

43. Pestalozzi, p. 54.

44. Pestalozzi, p. 87.

45. Pestalozzi, pp. 88–89.

46. Philosophy of education is not alone in placing Gertrude and the mothers she represents in the "ontological basement." In ch. 2 of *Worlds Apart* (New York: Basic Books, 1978), Sara Lawrence Lightfoot discusses mothers and teachers but never acknowledges that mothers *qua* mothers teach.

47. These examples of mother-teachers are taken from Louisa May Alcott, *Little Women* (Boston: Little, Brown, 1936); and George Elliot, *Middlemarch* (Boston: Houghton Mifflin, 1956).

48. "Philosophy of Education: Some Recent Contributions," *Harvard Educational Review 50* (1980), pp. 402–406.

49. See Carol Gilligan, "In a Different Voice: Women's Conceptions of Self and Morality," *Harvard Educational Review 47* (1977), pp. 481–517; "Woman's Place in Man's Life Cycle," *Harvard Educational Review 49* (1979), pp. 431–446.

50. Jane Roland Martin, "Sex Equality and Education," in *"Femininity," "Masculinity," and "Androgyny": A Modern Philosophical Discussion*, ed. Mary Vetterling-Braggin (Totowa, N.J.: Littlefield, Adams, 1982).

51. Martin, "Needed: A New Paradigm for Liberal Education," Chapter 9 in this volume, and "The Ideal of the Educated Person," Chapter 3.

CHAPTER 2

Sophie and Emile: A Case Study of Sex Bias in the History of Educational Thought

I originally developed the production model of education that figures so prominently in "Sophie and Emile: A Case Study in the History of Educational Thought" and plays a leading role in Reclaiming a Conversation *as a way of introducing Plato to my philosophy of education students at the University of Massachusetts, Boston. It was only after working out the details for a paper on his theory of female education and then studying Rousseau's* Emile *that I realized the model could illuminate philosophies besides Plato's.*

Written while I was a Fellow at the Mary Ingraham Bunting Institute of Radcliffe College, this paper served as the basis for a colloquium I gave there in March 1981 as well as for the lecture I gave at the Ontario Institute for the Study of Education the month before. That February 1981 speech was the very first occasion on which I publicly presented my research on women.

Standard texts in the history of educational thought teach that Rousseau's philosophy of education emphasizes the concept of nature.[1] These texts tell us that Rousseau proposes an education that follows nature, one that trusts the child's spontaneous impulses and allows for natural development. They tell us that the ideal of the educated person Rousseau embraces is that of natural man, that he stresses the common nature of mankind, and that the objective he sets for education is the liberty and happiness of the individual. Above all, they suggest that Rousseau's guiding metaphor is growth: he conceives of the child as a plant whose course of development is determined by nature, and of the educator as a gardener whose task is to ensure that corrupt society does not interfere with that predetermined pattern of development.

I will argue that Rousseau's many references to nature have misled his interpreters and that the model of education Rousseau adopts is one of production, not growth. In the introduction to his translation of *Emile*, Allan Bloom remarked that of Rousseau's major works *Emile* is the least studied and discussed.[2] He is certainly right that *Emile* deserves closer attention than it now receives from philosophers and political theorists. Historians of educational thought, however, have given the first four books of *Emile*, in which Rousseau discusses the education of boys, their due. Their mistake has been to slight Book V of *Emile* containing Rousseau's account of the education of girls. Had interpreters of his educational philosophy taken seriously what he says there, they might have seen through the language of nature.

Although it is much more than a treatise on education, *Emile* sets forth in loving detail what should constitute the education of Emile, who presumably represents Everyboy, from birth to manhood. That it also sets forth the education of Sophie, Emile's "intended" and presumably Everygirl, is something the standard texts in the field scarcely acknowledge. Some of the best known anthologies of historical philosophers of education present Emile's education as Rousseau's ideal for both sexes, and never mention Book V.[3] The texts that mention the education to be given Sophie do so with embarrassment, stating only that Sophie's education is to be very different from Emile's.[4]

Sophie causes historians of educational thought acute discomfort because their interpretation of Rousseau cannot handle her. The education of Sophie is an anomaly relative to the standard interpretation of *Emile*: her education cannot be explained by an interpretation which abstracts education from societal influences and constraints and which pictures it as a process of natural growth and development. The fundamental assumptions Rousseau makes in *Emile* V constitute *a production model of education*. What Sophie is to become is determined not by her nature, as the standard growth interpretation of *Emile* requires, but by the role she is to play in society. Small wonder that historians of educational thought ignore Sophie or dismiss her as an aberration. Rousseau's account of Sophie's education raises serious questions about the interpretation of *Emile* to which they subscribe.

An adequate interpretation of Rousseau must take into account both Emile and Sophie. Since Rousseau says very different things about their education, there are two distinct approaches to take if one acknowledges the importance of *Emile* V. One approach is to attribute to Rousseau two different, conflicting conceptions of education—a growth or natural model for Emile and a production model for Sophie. The other is to attribute to Rousseau a single conception of education. I argue that Rousseau makes the same fundamental assumptions about the education of Sophie and Emile, and that the standard interpretation of his educational philosophy is not only unable to explain what he says about Sophie, but is inadequate even as an interpretation of his account of Emile.

In her important book, *Women in Western Political Thought*, Susan Moller Okin has devoted several chapters to Rousseau's theories. She claims that Rousseau makes fundamentally different assumptions about the education of Emile and Sophie. Okin exposes the sex bias in Rousseau's account of Sophie, and Lynda Lange, in her essay, "Rousseau: Women and the General Will," reveals the sex bias in his political philosophy.[5] Rousseau's philosophy of education and his political philosophy are closely connected and the sex bias to be found in the one is the counterpart of the sex bias in the other. This essay is only indirectly concerned with Rousseau's own sex bias, however; its primary target is the bias exhibited by the discipline of educational thought in its interpretation of Rousseau's masterpiece. When the discipline of the history of educational thought ignores the writings of one of the few truly significant philosophers who have discussed the education of women, one can only conclude that this issue is not considered an integral part of its subject matter. Sophie and Emile constitute a case study of sex bias, not because historians of educational thought have said hostile things about Sophie, and through her about women generally, but because they have not even considered her important enough to be discussed at all.

Plato's Production Model of Education

Allan Bloom has compared *Emile* to Plato's *Republic*, which Rousseau considered "the most beautiful educational treatise ever written."[6] In that work Plato made fundamental assumptions which, taken together, constitute a production model of education. He arrives at his conception of the Just State through a thought experiment in which Socrates and his companions purport to think away existing institutions and imagine the birth of a city. They start with the principle, enunciated by Socrates, that "not one of us is self-sufficient, but needs many things."[7] Implicit in this principle is the assumption that each person is guided by self-interest and that it is in the self-interest of each to share with others.[8] The question that then arises is whether people will specialize—one person, for example, producing enough food for everyone and another making clothes — or whether they will simply help one another when necessary while remaining as self-sufficient as possible.[9]

At this point in the thought experiment Socrates introduces an assumption about human nature that is basic to his theory of education. Each one of us, Socrates says, is born more apt for one task than another.[10] This "Postulate of Specialized Natures" must not be understood as attributing to each individual at birth the knowledge of how to perform a specific task. We come equipped with an aptitude for one task above all others, but the skill, knowledge, and traits of character required for performing that task must be acquired. While an individual's specific nature can flourish or, alternatively, be stunted, a person cannot in midlife acquire some new aptitude that supplants the original one. Different aptitudes or talents are distributed over the population as a whole, not over an individual's life.

The Postulate of Specialized Natures does not in itself answer the question of whether people will specialize. To it, however, he adds an assumption about efficiency. Both production and quality are improved, he says, when individuals practice the one craft for which they are by nature most suited rather than several.[11] Yet even this assumption does not yield the answer Socrates gives to his own question. He chooses specialization as the recommended mode of production in the Just State because it is, in his view, the most efficient and because he values efficiency.[12]

As it stands, the Postulate of Specialized Natures is purely formal; it does not specify the aptitudes or talents people have at birth. Socrates gives this postulate substance in his thought experiment, not, as one might expect, through a close inspection of human nature, but rather by examining the needs of society. From the beginning a city will need farmers, builders, weavers, cobblers and metal workers, cowherds and shepherds, merchants, and sailors. Eventually it will need also warriors and rulers. Socrates builds up in his imagination a city that constitutes Plato's Just State. Socrates discerns the needs of this Just State and then designs human nature so that it fits them.[13] To suppose that he discerns certain natural talents or aptitudes in people and then designs a state which is to fit them is to get things backwards.

Socrates assumes a one-to-one relationship between human nature and societal roles. This "Postulate of Correspondence" is crucial for Plato's theory of the Just State.[14] He identifies three kinds of jobs to be done in the State—artisan (farmer, builder, and so on), auxiliary (warrior), and ruler—and he defines justice as everyone doing precisely that job for which their nature suits them.

Now, since justice requires that each individual perform one and only one job in society and since Socrates assumes that no person is able to do from birth, or simply by maturing, the task for which that person is naturally suited, the role of education in Plato's Just State becomes apparent. Education must equip people with the knowledge, skill and traits of character that will enable them to perform the societal tasks for which nature suits them.

Plato's conception is a production model of education par excellence. Like all raw material, human beings are malleable, but they do have certain fixed talents or aptitudes set by nature. The task of education is to turn this raw material into a finished product—more precisely, into one of three finished products. The particular product is a matter of discovery for the educator rather than a decision, since it is set by nature. The composition of the raw material is a given and so are the specifications for the three kinds of end product. Though Plato recommends that young children be allowed to play,[15] this concession to freedom should not be interpreted as a denial that the educator's role is to produce certain predetermined individuals. Children move about freely and play so that their true natures will reveal themselves. Once their natures are discovered, the production of artisans, auxiliaries, and rulers can begin.

Plato's conception is not a production model *simpliciter*, however. The task of education is not simply to produce three kinds of people, but to produce people who will fill certain necessary roles in society. There is, in other words, a "Functional Postulate" implicit in the account of education contained in the *Republic*. Education is conceived of as a servant of the state whose function, for justice to prevail, is to equip the individuals born into it to perform their preassigned functions.

While education plays a key role in Plato's Just state, Socrates simplifies the educator's task enormously by assuming that to perform the same task, people must

have the same education (the "Postulate of Identity"), and that to perform different tasks they must have a different education (the "Postulate of Difference").[16] He
directs educators to ignore individual differences, except for the inborn talents which
fit people to one societal role rather than another. These postulates lead to three separate curricula—for artisans, auxiliaries, and rulers—but one, and only one, version
of each.

The Education of Sophie

"It is not good for man to be alone. Emile is a man. We have promised him a
companion. She has to be given to him. That companion is Sophie. In what place is
her abode? Where shall we find her? To find her, it is necessary to know her. Let us
first learn what she is; then we shall better judge what places she inhabits" (p. 357). So
begins *Emile*, Book V.

"Everything that characterizes the fair sex ought to be respected as established by
nature," Rousseau says (p. 363). As Book V proceeds, however, it becomes clear that
in attributing traits to Sophie and calling them "natural," Rousseau is selective. What
exactly are Sophie's characteristics? She has an agreeable and nimble mind (p. 364), a
mind for details rather than general principles (p. 377). She loves adornment (p. 365),
guile is a natural talent of hers (p. 370), and the art of coquetry is born with her (p.
385). Rousseau does not envision these or Sophie's other natural characteristics as
emerging full-blown at birth, though he says that her love of adornment finds expression almost from birth in an attraction to jewels, mirrors, dresses, and dolls to dress
up (p. 367). Like Plato's future guardians (his auxiliaries and rulers), in whom the
traits of fierceness and gentleness develop over time, Sophie's natural qualities are simply aptitudes that require training and education so that they will be neither stunted
nor abused.

In Sophie's case Rousseau clearly embraces the Postulate of Specialized Natures:
Sophie's nature is for him as inborn, fixed, and specific as the natures of the inhabitants of the Just State are for Plato. Rousseau also embraces the Postulate of
Correspondence: Sophie's nature suits her for one and only one role in society, namely,
that of wife and mother.[17] Sophie's proper purpose, Rousseau says, is to produce not
just a few, but many children (p. 362). If this appears to be a biological, rather than a
societal, role for Sophie to play, let it be understood that she must also give the children she bears to her husband; that is to say, she must make it clear to him and the
world through her modesty, attentiveness, reserve, and care for his reputation that
they are his (p. 361). The unfaithful woman, Rousseau says, "dissolves the family and
breaks the bonds of nature. In giving the man children which are not his, she betrays
both" (p. 361). Thus Sophie is destined to be not simply the bearer of children, but
the preserver of family bonds. She is destined also to govern her husband's household
(p. 384), oversee his garden (p. 385), act as his hostess (p. 383), raise his children

(p. 361), and, above all, please him (p. 358). In sum, she is to play the traditional female role in the traditional patriarchal family.

Rousseau speaks the language of nature, but his conception of education is, like Plato's, that of production. For Rousseau, Sophie is raw material to be turned by education into a finished product. The basic structure of Rousseau's account of the education of Sophie is identical to that of Plato's account of the education of artisans, auxiliaries, and rulers. The task of Sophie's education is to equip her for her societal role. "Whether I consider the particular purpose of the fair sex, whether I observe its inclinations, whether I consider its duties, all join equally in indicating to me the form of education that suits it" (p. 364). Thus Rousseau embraces the Functional Postulate as well as the Postulates of Specialized Natures and of Correspondence. And when he says, "Once it is demonstrated that man and woman are not and ought not to be constituted in the same way in either character or temperament, it follows that they ought not to have the same education" (p. 363), it becomes quite clear that he also embraces Plato's Postulates of Identity and Difference. Since for Plato societal roles correspond to people's natures, he ultimately connects educational treatment with people's natures, and that is what Rousseau does when he prescribes different educational treatment for Sophie and Emile.

Rousseau repeatedly refers to nature in Book V of *Emile*, yet if a growth conception of education was implicit in his account of Sophie, he would not devote the attention he does to the possibility of Sophie's acquiring characteristics which he claims are not hers by nature. For one who directs his readers time and again to follow nature, Rousseau is inordinately concerned that Sophie might become something other than the obedient wife and nurturant mother he wants her to be. Will Sophie "be nurse today and warrior tomorrow?" Rousseau asks. "Will she suddenly go from shade, enclosure, and domestic cares to the harshness of the open air, the labors, the fatigues, and the perils of war?" (p. 362). Not if Rousseau has his way, but the very questions acknowledge that she might, were her education not strictly supervised. "To cultivate man's qualities in women and to neglect those which are proper to them is obviously to work to their detriment," he continued (p. 364). In Rousseau's concern to tell mothers not to make men out of their daughters, a production interpretation of his theory of education finds its vindication.

As Rousseau conceives of Sophie, she is born with a wide range of capacities. In attributing certain qualities to her nature, he is selective. The traits he calls natural are those which in his view should be developed, but they are certainly not the only ones which *could* be developed. Because Sophie can acquire any number of traits which Rousseau would rather women not possess, it is not plausible to attribute to him a growth conception of education for women in which the teacher is viewed simply as a gardener. A gardener provides the proper conditions for a plant to flourish. In contrast, Rousseau's educator must attend to every detail of Sophie's education so that the traits inappropriate to the role of wife and mother within a patriarchal context are frustrated. Rousseau appeals to nature, but he does not trust it; on the contrary, he insists that positive steps be taken to shape and form Sophie to meet clearly defined specifications.

The Difference of Sex

Plato set forth his thoughts on the education of women in Book V of the *Republic*. Rousseau set forth his in Book V of *Emile*. Plato argues that being male or female is like being bald or hairy: it is a difference of no consequence in determining whether or not a person belongs to the guardian class in the Just State, and so it makes no difference in determining the education an individual should receive.[18] In *Emile* V Rousseau argues that being male or female is a difference of consequence in determining a person's place in society (p. 357 ff.); indeed, a close reading of Book V suggests that he believes that sex is the only difference which makes a difference. "Sophie ought to be a woman as Emile is a man," Rousseau says. "That is to say, she ought to have everything which suits the constitution of her species and her sex in order to fill her place in the physical and moral order" (p. 357). The implications of this statement are clear: Sophie has one place to fill, Emile another, and their education ought to equip them for their respective places. Since the places of the two sexes are different, it seems evident to Rousseau that the education each is to receive must be different.

The objective of the education Plato would provide women—at least those who by nature are suited to be guardians in his Just State—is to develop reason in order to grasp the most general principles and ultimately discern the Good, so that the individual can rule herself and her fellow citizens. The education Rousseau would provide women could not be more dissimilar. Sophie, the prototype of women, is to be educated not to rule, but to obey. She is to learn to be modest, attentive, and reserved (p. 361); to sew, embroider and make lace (p. 368). Works of genius are out of her reach, Rousseau says (p. 386), nor does she have the precision and attention to succeed at the exact sciences (p. 387).

The question naturally arises of how such radically different accounts of the education of women could be given by philosophers who make the same fundamental assumptions about education. The answer lies in the fact that the postulates of the model of education which Plato and Rousseau both embrace are purely formal and that they give them different content. Plato posits three distinct societal roles and maps them onto human nature by attributing to people at birth the aptitudes for the traits and skills which he associates with each role. In his account of the education of Sophie, Rousseau does the same thing, but instead of singling out for Sophie one of Plato's three roles, he selects the traditional female role in a patriarchal society and imposes its associated traits and skills upon her nature. The education Sophie receives has to be different from that of the future female guardians in Plato's Just State. Their nature suits them to rule the state: Sophie's suits her to obey her husband.

Why do Plato and Rousseau give such radically different content to the postulates of the production model of education? There are two separate, but related, answers to this question. In Book V of the *Republic* Plato abolishes private property and the family and institutes instead communal living and childrearing arrangements.[19] Therefore, there is for him no traditional female role of wife and mother to map onto human nature. Second, Plato argues that sex is not a determinant of a person's nature.[20]

Rousseau consciously rejects both these elements of Plato's philosophy. He argues that if the family is removed from society, the bonds of love which Plato wants to establish among members of the guardian class, as well as the attachment he wants them to have for the state, cannot develop. It is "by means of the small fatherland which is the family that the heart attaches itself to the large one," Rousseau says (p. 363). He also maintains that sex is the determinant of a person's nature.

The Education of Emile for Citizenship

One of Okin's major conclusions about Rousseau is that his definition of Emile's nature is an open-ended one while Sophie "is defined in a totally teleological way, in terms of what is perceived to be her purpose in life."[21] She is certainly right about Sophie. Sophie is made to obey Emile: "To please men, to be useful to them, to make herself loved and honored by them, to raise them when young, to care for them when grown, to counsel them, to console them, to make their lives agreeable and sweet — these are the duties of women at all times, and they ought to be taught from childhood" (p. 365). Rousseau says that Sophie has a place to fill in the "physical and moral order." In truth, the place he assigns her falls squarely within the social order.

Okin's thesis that Rousseau uses a double standard in defining male and female natures explains what appear to be two separate strands in Rousseau's educational philosophy: a production model for Sophie and a growth model for Emile. She points out that scholars have acknowledged that the education Rousseau proposes for women "is based on principles that are in direct and basic conflict with those that underlie his proposals for the education of men."[22]

A dualistic interpretation enables one to understand why Book V of *Emile* has caused discomfort to historians of educational thought. They have treated Rousseau as an educational monist whose underlying model is one of natural growth and development. In relation to this interpretation, the education of Sophie is anomalous. There is, however, an alternative monistic interpretation of Rousseau's educational thought that explains both Sophie's and Emile's education. It has the advantage of being able to show that the differences Rousseau insists on in the education of males and females are matters of detail rather than conflicting or contradictory principles. The unified interpretation I propose is that the production model of education presupposed by Rousseau in his account of the education of Sophie underlies his account of the education of Emile as well.

At the beginning of Book I of *Emile*, Rousseau says that on leaving his hands the pupil will be neither magistrate nor soldier nor priest; rather, he will be a man (pp. 41–42). If we take Rousseau at his word, we must conclude that a narrow, vocational mold is not to be imposed on Emile. It does not follow, however, that Rousseau places no mold on him at all. Despite the imagery of plants and shrubs, Emile's tutor is not to allow each and every aspect of his potential to flourish: Rousseau wants Emile to be a particular sort of man and he would have the tutor arrange every detail of Emile's education toward that end. The person Emile is to be is a morally autonomous individual: a rational man who joins thought and action, whose judgments are objective, and whose beliefs are formed independently of others. Trained early to be as self-sufficient as possible—"Let the child do nothing on anybody's word" (p. 178)—it is no accident that the first book Emile is allowed to read is *Robinson Crusoe* (p. 184).

The mold Rousseau imposes on Emile of the rational, moral, autonomous individual may seem to be quite independent of any role or function Emile is supposed to play in society. In fact, however, it matches Rousseau's definition of the most important role of all, namely that of citizen in his ideal city state. *The Social Contract* enables one to understand how Rousseau solves the problem he posed at the beginning of Emile—of educating Emile to be at one and the same time an autonomous man and a citizen. How can a person be free, Rousseau wants to know, if the person is a member of a civil society and hence subject to its laws? Rousseau's solution to this problem is to be found in his concept of the General Will. In contrast to what Rousseau calls the Will of All, which is simply the sum of the private wills of all citizens and as such disregards the common good, the General Will has the common good as its object. It is the result of independent deliberation by citizens who are rational, impartial, and sufficiently informed about the issues.[23] Individual autonomy and obedience to law are reconciled in Rousseau's ideal state because the laws of that state are expressions of the General Will and because each citizen participates in that Will. The laws that each citizen must obey and that seem to limit individual freedom are enactments of the cool, objective deliberations about the common good. Thus, in obeying the laws of the state, each citizen governs himself. Freedom is therefore preserved even as the state rules its subjects.[24] Moreover, since for Rousseau the General Will is always right, the moral integrity of the individual, as well as the individual's autonomy, is preserved in the state. Small wonder Bloom says that Emile is, in effect, taught *The Social Contract*.[25] In educating Emile to be a man, Rousseau is really equipping him with the traits and skills which a citizen in his ideal state must have in order to participate in the General Will.

The function Rousseau assigns to Sophie is that of wife and mother in a patriarchal society; the function he assigns Emile is that of citizen in an ideal state. It is important in reading *Emile* to distinguish between the role of citizen in the actual states Rousseau knew and that same role in his ideal city state. To be sure, Sophie's function, or role, did exist in the states with which Rousseau was acquainted; however, there is no reason to suppose that he intended it to disappear in the ideal city state of *The Social Contract*. Rousseau's arguments against Plato's abolition of the family are enough by themselves to suggest that Sophie would have the same role to play in that state as she would in Rousseau's own France or Geneva. Moreover, in insisting that she is by nature subordinate to Emile's authority, he makes it both necessary for her to remain in the traditional female role and impossible for her to be a citizen in the ideal state.[26] As Okin has said, Emile is educated to be his own man and Sophie is educated to be his own woman.[27] As his own man Emile can be a citizen and participate in the General Will without sacrificing his freedom. As Emile's own woman, Sophie can be neither a citizen in Rousseau's sense nor free in the sense of being an autonomous person.

Upon recognizing that Emile's education is intended to equip him to participate in the General Will, it becomes clear that the fundamental educational assumptions Rousseau makes in regard to Emile are the same ones he makes in regard to Sophie. Like Sophie, Emile is born with certain aptitudes and capacities, but because he is male the capacities and aptitudes he is born with are quite different from those of Sophie. Whereas Sophie is by nature subordinate, Emile at birth has the potential to be his own legislator, which in turn involves the potential to grasp general principles and to reach independent conclusions. Thus his inborn nature, a direct result of his being male, suits him for the role of citizen in Rousseau's ideal city state. Since Emile's natural talents are not fully developed at birth and do not just emerge at maturity, education is necessary. Emile's education is totally different from Sophie's because his role is to be different from hers. Were their roles to be the same, Rousseau would, without a doubt, propose the same upbringing for them.

The Education of Emile for Patriarchy

Okin is mistaken when she says that Rousseau's definition of Emile's nature is an open-ended one and that Emile "must be free to become whatever he can and will."[28] Just as Sophie must develop attractiveness, Emile must develop strength (p. 365); just as she must endure injustice, he must revolt against it (p. 396). If Emile were really free to become anything at all, he would not need a tutor to control and manipulate his total environment. Rousseau says to Emile's tutor:

> Do you not dispose, with respect to him, of everything which surrounds him? Are you not the master of affecting him as you please? Are not his labors, his games, his pleasures, his pains, all in your hands without his knowing it? Doubtless he ought to do only what he wants: but he ought to want only what you want him to do. He ought not to make a step without your having foreseen it; he ought not to open his mouth without your knowing what he is going to say. (p. 120)

Readers of *Emile* cannot help but notice that Emile's tutor appears to manipulate him. In fact, Rousseau requires the tutor to be a master of that art. It is not that in a corrupt society Emile's nature cannot flourish untended, for he is to be educated in isolation from all society. Manipulation is necessary because Rousseau wants to ensure that only selected aspects of Emile's nature will flourish. A citizen in Rousseau's ideal state is both a person who can transcend private interests and a person of independent judgment who is subservient to none. A range of vices and other weaknesses—from lying (p. 101) to arrogance (p. 86)—are hence denied Emile.[29] The qualities which in Rousseau's view define Sophie's nature also are denied Emile (p. 364). He can no more become a gentle person and acquire Sophie's keen powers of observation than become a thief, for his education must equip him not only to be a participant in the General

Will, but to be head of the family Sophie serves. *Emile* ends when, a few months after the marriage of Emile and Sophie, Emile informs his tutor that he will soon be a father. If Sophie is destined to be wife and mother in a patriarchal family, Emile is destined to be the patriarch.

Both Okin and Lange[30] have delineated clearly the societal role Rousseau assigns to Sophie. Neither one, however, has discussed the significance for Rousseau's educational philosophy of his assigning Emile, as Sophie's husband, the societal role of patriarch. Rousseau's definition of Emile's nature is more open-ended than that of Sophie, only insofar as his dual role of patriarch and citizen is more open-ended. Emile is not free to become anything at all; he is the one who exercises authority in the family, who has the ultimate say in decision making, and who represents the family in its dealings with the outside world. He has no choice in these matters.

I emphasize Emile's patriarchal role here, for while Rousseau never explicitly links Emile's education to the role of participant in the General Will, Book V leaves no room for doubt that Emile will play the dominant role in "the small fatherland which is the family" and that his education must equip him for this task. Thus if proponents of the standard interpretation of *Emile* wish to deny my claim that Emile's tutor is training him to be a citizen in Rousseau's sense of the term, they will still have to contend with Emile's other role as head of family. This role, which they can scarcely deny belongs to Emile, lends credence to a production interpretation of Rousseau's educational thought. One perceptive commentator has said that if Rousseau's child "is to walk the path of nature, it will not be because there is a natural affinity between the child and this path, but because his tutor has led him along it."[31] It is clear that the path along which the tutor leads Emile is defined by Emile's function; indeed, Rousseau maps Emile's function onto his nature as surely as he maps Sophie's function onto hers.

A Unified Interpretation of *Emile*

Whether one takes Rousseau to be determining Emile's nature or to be discovering it, it is important to understand that although Emile's education differs in its specifics from Sophie's, the principles which govern his education govern hers as well.[32] "If I do not want to push a boy to learn to read, a fortiori I do not want to force girls to before making them well aware of what the use of reading is," Rousseau says (p. 368). The principle that experience should precede verbal studies because books teach one to talk about what one does not know (p. 184) is an important one for Rousseau and he clearly intends it to hold for males and females. The fact that he assigns different natures and roles to males and females will mean that the uses to which reading is put will vary for Emile and Sophie, and this in turn may dictate a different choice of books. One can be sure that *Robinson Crusoe* will not be given to Sophie, but the principle that books should be avoided until an age at which second-hand experience will amplify rather than be a substitute for first-hand experience is not thereby affected.

It has been said that Rousseau discovered childhood. He certainly does tell Emile's tutor to respect childhood (p. 107) and to treat Emile according to his age (p. 91). Rousseau understood what modern psychology now tells us, namely, that children have their own way of seeing, thinking, and feeling (p. 90). The principle that education must respect the child's cognitive structures and emotional states is as central to Rousseau's philosophy of education as is the principle of delayed verbal learning. It is not, however, a principle which governs the education of Emile alone. One must take account of what is suitable to both age and sex, he says in Book V (p. 374). The principle that childhood must be respected is to be applied to Sophie's education, in the light of her particular modes of thinking, feeling, and perceiving the world.

Books I–IV of *Emile* contain any number of important educational principles, many of which will sound familiar to those who are acquainted with the open-classroom movement of the late 1960s and early 1970s and with the writings of radical school reformers of that period.[33] Rousseau maintains that educators should discard the distinction between work and play, since Emile's games are his business (p. 161); that education comes to us from nature, men, and things (p. 38); that the teacher's first duty is to be humane and to respect childhood (p. 79); that excessive severity and indulgence are to be avoided (p. 86); that the primary instrument of teaching should be well-regulated freedom (p. 92).

These principles all apply to Sophie's education. Sewing is Sophie's work, but it is also her play, for she wants to sew and learns how to do it in order to adorn her doll (pp. 367–368). She is to be subjected early to constraints Emile never knows, because all their lives girls "will be enslaved to the most continual and most severe of constraints—that of the proprieties" (p. 369). Still, she is not to be subjected to undue severity; she ought not to live like her grandmother, Rousseau says, but rather ought to be "lively, playful, and frolicsome, to sing and dance as much as she pleases, and to taste all the innocent pleasures of her age" (p. 374). The real differences between the education Rousseau proposes for Sophie and for Emile are readily accounted for by the differences Rousseau sees in the societal roles he assigns them. The order to be humane is not countermanded in Sophie's case: her role simply requires that the humanity of her teachers take particular forms. Even the fact that Emile is to be educated in isolation and Sophie is not can be explained without positing a conflict of principles. The role of citizen exists in society only in corrupted form. To prepare Emile for that role in the ideal state Rousseau deems it necessary to remove him from society. Sophie's role, however, exists in at least some segments of society in its pure form, and so there is no need to remove her from family and friends.

The elements of Books I–IV of *Emile* which so many educators have found attractive are compatible with the unified interpretation of *Emile* I am presenting here.[34] The principles of teaching and learning which Rousseau sets forth in those books can be understood as specifying the content of the educational treatment ordered by the Postulates of Identity and Difference. This interpretation preserves these important features of Rousseau's educational philosophy, while making clear their relationship to other elements of his thought. It also explains why manipulation plays the part it does in Rousseau's educational thought. A growth interpretation of *Emile* cannot account for the fact that Emile's tutor is supposed to manipulate and control him, even when he is removed from the corrupting influences of society. Rousseau's manipulative principle, which clearly governs Sophie's education as well as Emile's, constitutes an anomaly for the conception of the educator as gardener.[35] When, however, it is understood that the task of Emile's tutor is to produce an end product along predetermined specifications, the principle that the educator should give the pupil the illusion of freedom—all the while controlling carefully what the pupil learns—is no longer anomalous, but is exactly what one would expect of an educational theory which tells the teacher to be humane but gives that teacher a hidden agenda.

Concluding Remarks

In *The Language of Education*, Israel Scheffler has said that the metaphor of growth "embodies a modest conception of the teacher's role, which is to study and then indirectly to help the development of the child, rather than to shape him into some preconceived form."[36] Given the total control the tutor exercises over Emile's education, it is difficult to understand how standard texts in the history of educational thought could have attributed to Rousseau a growth conception of education. Scheffler criticizes the growth metaphor for masking the fact that the educator must make choices no gardener ever faces.[37] I would add to this the criticism that in drawing attention to the development of the child, the growth metaphor ignores the social and political dimensions of education. The opening pages of *Emile* testify to the fact that Rousseau himself recognized that the educational is the political. He used the language of growth, but he was not fooled by that language. His interpreters have been fooled by it and have done Rousseau the injustice of supposing that the large political concerns with which he wrestled all his life play no role in the education he prescribes for Emile.

A production interpretation of Rousseau's educational thought acknowledges his concern for the political. It enables one to see that even though Emile is to be raised in isolation, from a theoretical standpoint Rousseau, like Plato, envisions education as an enterprise which is linked closely to political purposes and ideals.[38] While Emile is to be educated for the role of citizen, and hence for the political realm, Sophie is not. Although Rousseau grudgingly acknowledges that she could acquire the rationality, objectivity, and independence he demands of those who participate in the General Will, the education Sophie is to receive will ensure that she will develop none of those attributes. Sophie will inhabit the home; she will not be qualified to venture out of it into the political realm. As head of family Emile will also inhabit the home: yet his role of patriarch will not exclude him from being a full-fledged member of the political sphere. Indeed, Rousseau says that it is "the good son, the good husband, and the good father who make the good citizen" (p. 363). The personal autonomy that Sophie must have to be a citizen is precluded by being wife and mother. Emile, however, must be an autonomous agent within the family as in the state; indeed, his role of patriarch can be understood as Rousseau's ideal citizen writ small.

Bloom considers the relationship between Emile and Sophie to be a union of complementary equals.[39] Yet, a union in which one person must always obey the other, as Sophie must obey Emile, is scarcely one of equals. It is true that Rousseau would educate Sophie to wield power over Emile through the judicious use of manipulation and guile. Since he does not grant her the right to make her own decisions, let alone Emile's, one must conclude, against Bloom, that the egalitarian ideal for which Rousseau is famous is to hold in the political—but not the private—domain. Since the political domain is not open to Sophie, the limits to his egalitarianism are clear: equality is a principle intended to govern relations among males, not relations between males and females. That Sophie's place is not the political realm, but the home, is itself, then, a political commitment of Rousseau's.

I have argued that the standard interpretation of Rousseau's educational philosophy cannot explain the education of Sophie because it is based solely on Rousseau's account of Emile. In this respect it is like those psychological theories of development that have difficulty incorporating findings about females because they are derived from male research data.[40] The response of the psychologists to this difficulty is to impose on their female subjects a masculine mold. The response of historians of educational thought to Sophie is either to banish her from their texts or to acknowledge her existence while making no effort to understand or explain her plight.

It is tempting to say that the standard interpretation of *Emile* ignores Book V because historians of educational thought have wanted to protect Rousseau from the scorn of modern readers who would not share his views about the place of women.[41] This is too facile an explanation, however, for historians also ignore Book V of the *Republic*, in which Plato argues that women as well as men can be suited by nature to be rulers of the Just State, and that future female rulers should receive an education identical to that of future male rulers. The sad truth is that historians of educational thought have ignored not only Rousseau's sex bias, but the whole topic of the education of women. They have neglected Sophie because they have implicitly defined their subject matter as the education of male human beings, rather than the education of all human beings.

When the education of females is excluded from the subject matter of the history of educational thought, we are all losers. Women lose because their experience is neither reflected nor interpreted in the works they are made to study and because they are denied the chance to understand and evaluate the range of ideals—from Sophie to Plato's guardians—which the great educational theorists of the past have held for them. Men lose because they are made to believe that the education of women has never been, and hence must not be, a topic worthy of philosophical discussion, and because they are not given an opportunity to ponder the question of whether sex or gender is a relevant category in educational thought. The loss to the history of educational thought itself is perhaps the greatest, for, as I have tried to show through the example of Rousseau, interpretations that neglect the education of women certainly will be incomplete and may even be thoroughly mistaken.

Notes

I wish to thank Ann Diller, Carol Gilligan, Michael Martin, Beatrice Nelson, and Janet Farrell Smith for helpful comments on the original draft.

1. See Robert Ulich, *History of Educational Thought* (New York: American Book, 1945) and *Three Thousand Years of Educational Wisdom* (Cambridge, Mass.: Harvard Univ. Press, 1948); Robert S. Brumbaugh and Nathaniel M. Lawrence, *Philosophers on Education: Six Essays on the Foundations of Western Thought* (Boston: Houghton Mifflin, 1963); Robert R. Rusk, *The Doctrines of the Great Educators,* rev. 3rd ed. (New York: St. Martin's, 1965); Paul Nash, Andreas M. Kazamias, and Henry J. Perkinson, *The Educated Man: Studies in the History of Educational Thought* (New York: Wiley, 1965); Kingsley Price, *Education and Philosophical Thought,* 2nd ed. (Boston: Allyn & Bacon, 1967); Paul Nash, *Models of Man: Explorations in the Western Educational Tradition* (New York: Wiley, 1968); and Steven M. Cahn, *The Philosophical Foundations of Education* (New York: Harper & Row, 1970).

2. Allan Bloom, trans., *Emile* by Jean-Jacques Rousseau (New York: Basic Books, 1979), p. 4. All references to *Emile* will be to this translation and will appear in the text.

3. For example. see Cahn, Price, and Ulich. Insofar as commentators on Rousseau's general philosophy have discussed his views on education, they, too, have tended to slight Book V of *Emile.* See Roger D. Masters, *The Political Philosophy of Rousseau* (Princeton: Princeton Univ. Press, 1968); Merle L. Perkins, *Jean-Jacques Rousseau* (Lexington: Univ. Press of Kentucky, 1974); Kennedy F. Roche, *Rousseau: Stoic & Romantic* (London: Methuen, 1974). One notable exception to this tendency of Rousseau scholars is J. H. Broome, *Rousseau: A Study of His Thought* (London: Edward Arnold, 1963).

4. See Brumbaugh and Lawrence, Nash, Rusk; and also R.L. Archer, ed., *Jean-Jacques Rousseau: His Educational Theories Selected from Emile, Julie and Other Writings* (Woodbury, N.Y.: Barron's Educational Series, 1964). Although Archer contains lengthy selections from Book V of *Emile,* the introduction by S.E. Frost simply says: "*Rousseau's theory of the education of girls.* In this he contradicts all he has advocated for Emile. The girl is educated to please the man and everything she is to learn is relative to men." Excerpts from Book V of *Emile* in *The Emile of Jean-Jacques Rousseau,* ed. William Boyd (New York: Teachers College Press, 1956) appear in a chapter entitled "Marriage" although Rousseau himself calls the relevant section of Book V, "Sophie, or the Woman."

5. Susan Moller Okin, *Women in Western Political Thought* (Princeton: Princeton Univ. Press, 1979), Ch. 6; and Lynda Lange, "Rousseau: Women and the General Will," in *The Sexism of Social and Political Theory,* ed. Lorenne M.G. Clark and Lynda Lange (Toronto: Univ. of Toronto Press, 1979), pp. 41–52. See also Ron Christianson, "The Political Theory of Male Chauvinism: J.J. Rousseau's Paradigm," *Midwest Quarterly 13* (1972), 291–299; Victor G. Wexler," 'Made for Man's Delight': Rousseau as Antifeminist," *American Historical Review 81* (1976), pp. 266–291; and Zillah Eisenstein, *The Radical Future of Liberal Feminism* (New York: Longman, 1981), Ch. 4.

6. Bloom, p. 40.

7. Plato, *Republic*, 396b. References to his work will be to *Plato's Republic*, trans. G.M.A. Grube (Indianapolis: Hackett, 1974).

8. *Republic*, 369c.

9. *Republic*, 370a.

10. *Republic*, 370b.

11. *Republic*, 370b, c.

12. On this point see Lange, "The Function of Equal Education in Plato's *Republic* and *Laws*" in Clark and Lange.

13. Some interpreters of Plato would argue that Socrates assumes a parallelism between human nature and societal needs. However, the account of education contained in the *Republic* makes plausible the interpretation given here.

14. Nicholas P. White abstracts from *Republic* II a principle of the Natural Division of Labor which encompasses what I am calling the Postulate of Specialized Natures and the Postulate of Correspondence. For the present purpose, however, it is important to keep these postulates separate. See White's *A Companion to Plato's Republic* (Indianapolis: Hackett, 1979), pp. 84–85.

15. *Republic*, 537a.

16. *Republic*, 452a.

17. These might well be considered to be two distinct roles, but Rousseau clearly views them as forming a single one.

18. *Republic*, 454b–e.

19. *Republic*, 457d, 458d, 462b–d.

20. *Republic*, 455e.

21. Okin, p. 135

22. Okin, p. 135.

23. *Social Contract* (New York: Hafner, 1947), Book II, Ch. 2 ff.

24. *Social Contract*, p. 19.

25. Bloom, p. 27. See also John Plamenatz, "Ce Qui Ne Signifie Autre Chose Sinon Qu'on Le Forcera D'Être Libre," in *Hobbes and Rousseau*, ed. Maurice Cranston and R.S. Peters (New York: Doubleday, 1972), p. 326; Masters, p. 42; Broome, Ch. 5.

26. On this point see Lange, "Rousseau: Woman and the General Will." She argues, moreover, that the obvious strategy of eliminating the sexism of Rousseau's theory of the General Will by eliminating the patriarchal family is not feasible. See also Okin, p. 134; and Christianson, p. 292.

27. Okin, p. 119.

28. Okin, p. 135.

29. "The first education ought to be purely negative. It consists not at all in teaching virtue

or truth but in securing the heart from vice and the mind from error," (*Emile*, p. 93). Judith N. Shklar argues that this "negative education" is necessary because Emile is to be educated to be his real self. She forgets that since Emile is to be educated apart from society, there is no need for the tutor to protect him to the extent that he does against society. See "Rousseau's Images of Authority," in *Hobbes and Rousseau*, ed. Cranston and Peters, p. 360; see also Shklar, *Men and Citizens* (Cambridge, Eng.: Cambridge Univ. Press, 1969), p. 148.

30. See Lange, "Rousseau: Woman and the General Will."

31. Daniel Pekarsky, "Education and Manipulation," in *Philosophy of Education 1977: Proceedings of the 33rd Annual Meeting of the Philosophy of Education Society*, ed. Ira S. Steinberg (Urbana: Univ. of Illinois, 1977), p. 356.

32. This point is compatible with my claim that Rousseau is committed to the Difference Postulate. That Postulate holds that Sophie and Emile must be given different educational treatment, not that the principles governing their treatment must be different. Compare Broome, p. 99.

33. For an account of open classrooms see Joseph Featherstone, "The British Infant Schools," in *Radical School Reform*, ed. Ronald and Beatrice Gross (New York: Simon & Schuster, 1969), pp. 195–205; Charles H. Rathbone, ed., *Open Education* (New York: Citation Press, 1971); Ewald B. Nyquist and Gene R. Hawes, ed., *Open Education* (New York: Bantam, 1972): and Charles E. Silberman, ed., *The Open Classroom Reader* (New York: Vintage, 1973).

34. Some may wonder if principles of teaching and learning which were advocated by proponents of open classrooms are compatible with the model of education I am attributing to Rousseau. A production model does not entail the harsh methods of teaching and the rigid structures that radical school reformers rejected. Since the Identity and Difference Postulates are purely formal, the methods to be used in equipping people for a given role or function in society can be harsh, but they can also be humane; moreover, they can be employed in a wide range of contexts, the traditional school being only one.

35. I am assuming here the "naive" conception of gardening spelled out by Israel Scheffler in *The Language of Education* (Springfield, Ill.: Thomas, 1960), since it is the one employed in the standard interpretation of *Emile* (see fn. 38). Rousseau's manipulative principle might well be compatible with a different conception of that activity.

36. Scheffler, p. 37.

37. Scheffler, pp. 50 ff.

38. Emile's isolation raises questions, however, about whether he can be educated to fulfill the roles assigned him.

39. P. 22. On this issue see also Wexler, p. 274; Broome, pp. 98–101.

40. See Carol Gilligan, "In a Different Voice: Women's Conceptions of Self and Morality," *Harvard Educational Review 47* (1977), 481–517 and "Woman's Place in Man's Life Cycle," *Harvard Educational Review 49* (1979), 431–446.

41. Not all modern readers find Rousseau's discussion of Sophie objectionable. See Bloom, p. 23; Broome, p. 98 ff.

CHAPTER 3

The Ideal of the Educated Person

My Presidential Address to the 1981 Annual Meeting of the Philosophy of Education Society, "The Ideal of the Educated Person" was written while I was a Fellow at the Mary Ingraham Bunting Institute of Radcliffe College. One of the themes that dominated the research I did before I began my study of the place of women in educational thought was that the prevailing conception of education was too narrow, by far. By bringing women into the picture and thus revealing the genderization of education's governing philosophical ideal, this paper introduced a new dimension into that earlier argument. Representing my very first inquiry into the place of women in contemporary educational thought, it also considerably enlarged the scope of my new research program.

R. S. Peters calls it an ideal.[1] So do Nash, Kazemias and Perkinson who, in their introduction to a collection of studies in the history of educational thought, say that one cannot go about the business of education without it.[2] Is it the good life? the responsible citizen? personal autonomy? No, it is the educated man.

The educated man! In the early 1960s when I was invited to contribute to a book of essays to be entitled *The Educated Man*, I thought nothing of this phrase. By the early 1970s I felt uncomfortable whenever I came across it but I told myself it was the thought not the words that counted. It is now the early 1980s. Peters's use of the phrase "educated man" no longer troubles me for I think it fair to say that he intended it in a gender-neutral way.[3] Despite one serious lapse which indicates that on some occasions he was thinking of his educated man as male, I do not doubt that the ideal he set forth was meant for males and females alike.[4] Today my concern is not Peters's language but his conception of the educated man—or person, as I will henceforth say. I will begin by outlining Peters's ideal for you and will then show that it does serious

This essay was originally published in *Educational Theory*, 31:2 (1981), copyright © The University of Illinois, and in *Philosophy of Education 1981: Proceedings of the 37th Annual Meeting of the Philosophy of Education Society*, copyright © 1982 by the Philosophy of Education Society. Reprinted by permission.

harm to women. From there I will go on to argue that Peters's ideal is inadequate for men as well as women and, furthermore, that its inadequacy for men is intimately connected to the injustice it does women. In conclusion I will explore some of the requirements an adequate ideal must satisfy.

Let me explain at the outset that I have chosen to discuss Peters's ideal of the educated person here because for many years Peters has been perhaps the dominant figure in philosophy of education. Moreover, although Peters's ideal is formulated in philosophically sophisticated terms, it is certainly not idiosyncratic. On the contrary, Peters claims to have captured our concept of the educated person, and he may well have done so. Thus, I think it fair to say that the traits Peters claims one must possess to be a truly educated person and the kind of education he assumes one must have in order to acquire those traits would, with minor variations, be cited by any number of people today if they were to describe their own conception of the ideal. I discuss Peters's ideal, then, because it has significance for the field of philosophy of education as a whole.

I. R.S. Peters's Educated Person

The starting point of Peters's philosophy of education is the concept of the educated person. While granting that we sometimes use the term "education" to refer to any process of rearing, bringing up, instructing, etc., Peters distinguishes this very broad sense of "education" from the narrower one in which he is interested. The concept of the educated person provides the basis for this distinction: whereas "education" in the broad sense refers to any process of rearing, etc., "education" in the narrower, and to him philosophically more important, sense refers to the family of processes which have as their outcome the development of an educated person.[5]

Peters set forth his conception of the educated person in some detail in his book, *Ethics and Education*.[6] Briefly, an educated person is one who does not simply possess knowledge. An educated person has a body of knowledge and some kind of conceptual scheme to raise this knowledge above the level of a collection of disjointed facts which in turn implies some understanding of principles for organizing facts and of the "reason why" of things. Furthermore, the educated person's knowledge is not inert: it characterizes the person's way of looking at things and involves "the kind of commitment that comes from getting on the inside of a form of thought and awareness"; that is to say, the educated person cares about the standards of evidence implicit in science or the canons of proof inherent in mathematics. Finally, the educated person has cognitive perspective. In an essay entitled "Education and the Educated Man," published several years later, Peters added to this portrait that the educated person's pursuits can be practical as well as theoretical so long as the person delights in them for their own sake, and that both sorts of pursuits involve standards to which the person must be sensitive.[7] He also made it clear that knowledge enters into his conception of the educated person in three ways, namely, depth, breadth and knowledge of good.

In their book, *Education and Personal Relationships*, Downie, Loudfoot and Teller presented a conception of the educated person which is a variant on Peters's.[8] I cite it here not because they, too, use the phrase "educated man," but to show that alternate philosophical conceptions of the educated person differ from Peters's only in detail. Downie, Loudfoot and Telfer's educated person has knowledge which is wide ranging in scope, extending from history and geography to the natural and social sciences and to current affairs. This knowledge is important, relevant and grounded. The educated person understands what he or she knows, knows how to do such things as history and science, and has the inclination to apply this knowledge, to be critical, and to have curiosity in the sense of a thirst for knowledge. Their major departure from Peters's conception—and it is not, in the last analysis, very major—is to be found in their concern with knowledge by acquaintance: the educated person must not merely have knowledge *about* works of art—and, if I understand them correctly, about moral and religious theories—but must know these as individual things.

Consider now the knowledge, the conceptual scheme which raises this knowledge above the level of disjointed facts, and the cognitive perspective Peters's educated person must have. It is quite clear that Peters does not intend that these be acquired through the study of cooking and driving. Mathematics, science, history, literature, philosophy—these are the subjects which constitute the curriculum for his educated person. In short, his educated person is one who has had—and profited from—a liberal education of the sort outlined by Paul Hirst in his famous essay, "Liberal Education and the Nature of Knowledge." Hirst describes what is sought in a liberal education as follows:

> first, sufficient immersion in the concepts, logic and criteria of the discipline for a person to come to know the distinctive way in which it 'works' by pursuing these in particular cases; and then sufficient generalisation of these over the whole range of the discipline so that his experience begins to be widely structured in this distinctive manner. It is this coming to look at things in a certain way that is being aimed at, not the ability to work out in minute particulars all the details that can be in fact discerned. It is the ability to recognise empirical assertions or aesthetic judgments for what they are, and to know the kind of consideration on which their validity will depend, that matters.[9]

If Peters's educated person is not in fact Hirst's liberally educated person, he or she is certainly its identical twin.

Liberal education, in Hirst's view, consists in an initiation into what he calls the forms of knowledge. There are, on his count, seven of them. Although he goes to some lengths in his later writings on the topic to deny that these forms are themselves intellectual disciplines, it is safe to conclude that his liberally educated person, and hence Peters's educated person, will acquire the conceptual schemes and cognitive perspectives they are supposed to have through a study of mathematics, physical science, history, the human sciences, literature, fine arts, philosophy. These disciplines will not necessarily be studied separately: an interdisciplinary curriculum is compatible with the Peters-Hirst ideal. But it is nonetheless their subject matter, their conceptual apparatus, their standards of proof and adequate evidence, their way of looking at things that must be acquired if the ideal is to be realized.

II. Initiation into Male Cognitive Perspectives

What is this certain way in which the educated person comes to look at things? What is the distinctive manner in which that person's experience is structured? A body of literature documenting the many respects in which the disciplines of knowledge ignore or misrepresent the experience and lives of women has developed over the last decade. I cannot do justice here to its range of concerns or its sophisticated argumentation. Through the use of examples, however, I will try to give you some sense of the extent to which the intellectual disciplines incorporate a male cognitive perspective, and hence a sense of the extent to which Hirst's liberally educated person and its twin—Peters's educated person—look at things through male eyes.

Let me begin with history. "History is past politics" was the slogan inscribed on the seminar room wall at Johns Hopkins in the days of the first doctoral program.[10] In the late 1960s the historian, Richard Hofstaedter, summarized his field by saying: "Memory is the thread of personal identity, history of public identity." History has defined itself as the record of the public and political aspects of the past; in other words, as the record of the productive processes—man's sphere—of society. Small wonder that women are scarcely mentioned in historical narratives! Small wonder that they have been neither the objects nor the subjects of historical inquiry until very recently! The reproductive processes of society which have traditionally been carried on by women are excluded by *definition* from the purview of the discipline.

If women's lives and experiences have been excluded from the subject matter of history, the works women have produced have for the most part been excluded from literature and the fine arts. It has never been denied that there have been women writers and artists, but their works have not often been deemed important or significant enough to be studied by historians and critics. Thus, for example, Catherine R. Stimpson has documented the treatment accorded Gertrude Stein by two journals which exert a powerful influence in helping to decide what literature is and what books matter.[11] Elaine Showalter, pursuing a somewhat different tack, has documented the double standard which was used in the nineteenth century to judge women writers: all the most desirable aesthetic qualities—for example, power, breadth, knowledge of life, humor—were assigned to men; the qualities assigned to women, such as refinement, tact, precise observation, were not considered sufficient for the creation of an excellent novel.[12]

The disciplines are guilty of different kinds of sex bias. Even as literature and the fine arts exclude women's works from their subject matter, they include works which construct women according to the male image of her. One might expect this tendency to construct the female to be limited to the arts, but it is not. Naomi Weisstein has shown that psychology constructs the female personality to fit the preconceptions of its male practitioners, clinicians either accepting theory without evidence or finding

in their data what they want to find.[13] And Ruth Hubbard has shown that this tendency extends even to biology where the stereotypical picture of the passive female is
projected by the male practitioners of that field onto the animal kingdom.[14]

There are, indeed, two quite different ways in which a discipline can distort the
lives, experiences and personalities of women. Even as psychology constructs the female
personality out of our cultural stereotype, it holds up standards of development for
women to meet which are derived from studies using male subjects.[15] Not surprisingly,
long after the source of the standards is forgotten, women are proclaimed to be under-
developed and inferior to males in relation to these standards. Thus, for example,
Carol Gilligan has pointed out that females are classified as being at Stage 3 of Kohlberg's
six stage sequence of moral development because important differences in moral development between males and females are ignored.[16]

In the last decade scholars have turned to the study of women. Thus, historical narratives and analyses of some aspects of the reproductive processes of society—of birth
control, childbirth, midwifery, for example—have been published.[17] The existence of
such scholarship is no guarantee however, of its integration into the mainstream of
the discipline of history itself, yet this latter is required if initiation into history as a
form of knowledge is not to constitute initiation into a male cognitive perspective.
The title of a 1974 anthology on the history of women, *Clio's Consciousness Raised*, is
unduly optimistic.[18] Certainly, the consciousness of some historians has been raised,
but there is little reason to believe that the discipline of history has redefined itself so
that studies of the reproductive processes of society are not simply tolerated as periph-
erally relevant, but are considered to be as central to it as political, economic and
military narratives are. Just as historians have begun to study women's past, scholars
in literature and the fine arts have begun to bring works by women to our attention
and to reinterpret the ones we have always known.[19] But there is still the gap between
feminist scholarship and the established definitions of literary and artistic significance
to be bridged, and until it is, the initiation into these disciplines provided by a liberal
education will be an initiation into male perspectives.

In sum, the intellectual disciplines into which a person must be initiated to become
an educated person *exclude* women and their works, *construct* the female to the male
image of her and *deny* the truly feminine qualities she does possess. The question remains
of whether the male cognitive perspective of the disciplines is integral to Peters's ideal
of the educated person. The answer to this question is to be found in Hirst's essay, "The
Forms of Knowledge Revisited."[20] There he presents the view that at any given time a
liberal education consists in an initiation into *existing* forms of knowledge. Hirst acknowledges that new forms can develop and that old ones can disappear. Still, the analysis he
gives of the seven distinct forms which he takes to comprise a liberal education today is
based, he says, on our present conceptual scheme. Thus, Peters's educated person is not
one who studies a set of ideal, unbiased forms of knowledge; on the contrary, that person is one who is initiated into whatever forms of knowledge exist in the society at that
time. In our time the existing forms embody a male point of view. The initiation into
them envisioned by Hirst and Peters is, therefore, one in male cognitive perspectives.

Peters's educated person is expected to have grasped the basic structure of science, history and the like rather than the superficial details of content. Is it possible that the feminist critique of the disciplines therefore leaves his ideal untouched? It would be a grave misreading of the literature to suppose that this critique presents simply a sur-face challenge to the disciplines. Although the examples I have cited here may have suggested to you that the challenge is directed at content alone, it is in fact many pronged. Its targets include the questions asked by the various fields of inquiry and the answers given them; the aims of those fields and the ways they define their subject matter; the methods they use, their canons of objectivity, and their ruling metaphors. It is difficult to be clear on precisely which aspects of knowledge and inquiry are at issue when Hirst speaks of initiation into a form of knowledge. A male bias has been found on so many levels of the disciplines, however, that I think we can feel quite con-fident that it is a property also of the education embodied in Peters's ideal.

III. Genderized Traits

The masculinity of Peters's educated person is not solely a function of a curricu-lum in the intellectual disciplines, however. Consider the traits or characteristics Peters attributes to the educated person. Feelings and emotions only enter into the makeup of the educated person to the extent that being committed to the standards of a the-oretical pursuit such as science, or a practical one such as architecture, counts as such. Concern for people and for interpersonal relationships has no role to play: the edu-cated person's sensitivity is to the standards immanent in activities, not to other human beings; an imaginative awareness of emotional atmosphere and interpersonal rela-tionships need be no part of this person's makeup, nor is the educated person thought to be empathetic or supportive or nurturant. Intuition is also neglected. Theoretical knowledge and what Woods and Barrow—two more philosophers who use the phrase "educated man"—call "reasoned understanding" are the educated person's prime characteristics[21]: even this person's practical pursuits are to be informed by some the-oretical perspectives; moreover, this theoretical bent is to be leavened neither by imaginative nor intuitive powers, for these are never to be developed.

The educated person as portrayed by Peters, and also by Downie, Loudfoot and Teller, and by Woods and Barrow, coincides with our cultural stereotype of a male human being. According to that stereotype men are objective, analytic, rational; they are interested in ideas and things; they have no interpersonal orientation; they are nei-ther nurturant nor supportive, empathetic or sensitive. According to the stereotype, nurturance and supportiveness, empathy and sensitivity are female attributes. Intuition is a female attribute, too.[22]

This finding is not really surprising. It has been shown that psychologists define moral development, adult development, and even human development in male terms and that therapists do the same for mental health.[23] Why suppose that philosophers of education have avoided the androcentric fallacy?[24] Do not misunderstand! Females can acquire the traits and dispositions which constitute Peters's conception of the educated person; he espouses an ideal which, if it can be attained at all, can be by both sexes.[25] But our culture associates the traits and dispositions of Peters's educated person with males. To apply it to females is to impose on them a masculine mold. I realize that as a matter of fact some females fit our male stereotype and that some males do not, but this does not affect the point at issue, which is that Peters has set forth an ideal for education which embodies just those traits and dispositions our culture attributes to the male sex and excludes the traits our culture attributes to the female sex.

Now it might seem that if the mold is a good one, it does not matter that it is masculine; that if the traits which Peters's educated person possesses are desirable, then it makes no difference that in our society they are associated with males. Indeed, some would doubtless argue that in extending to women cognitive virtues which have long been associated with men and which education has historically reserved for men, Peters's theory of education strikes a blow for sex equality. It does matter that the traits Peters assigns the educated person are considered in our culture to be masculine, however. It matters because some traits which males and females can both possess are *genderized*; that is, they are appraised differentially according to sex.[26]

Consider aggressiveness. The authors of a book on assertive training for women report that in the first class meetings of their training courses they ask their students to call out the adjectives which come to mind when we say "aggressive woman" and "aggressive man." Here is the list of adjectives the women used to describe an aggressive man: "masculine," "dominating," "successful," "heroic," "capable," "strong," "forceful," "manly." Need I tell you the list of adjectives they used to describe an aggressive woman?: "harsh," "pushy," "bitchy," "domineering," "obnoxious," "emasculating ," "uncaring."[27]

I submit to you that the traits Peters attributes to the educated person are, like the trait of aggressiveness, evaluated differently for males and females. Imagine a woman who is analytical and critical, whose intellectual curiosity is strong, who cares about the canons of science and mathematics. How is she described? "She thinks like a man," it is said. To be sure, this is considered by some to be the highest accolade. Still, a woman who is said to think like a man is being judged to be masculine, and since we take masculinity and femininity to lie at opposite ends of a single continuum, she is thereby being judged to be lacking in femininity.[28] Thus, while it is possible for a woman to possess the traits of Peters's educated person, she will do so at her peril: her possession of them will cause her to be viewed as unfeminine, i.e., as an unnatural or abnormal woman.

IV. A Double Bind

It may have been my concern over Peters's use of the phrase "educated man" which led me to this investigation in the first place, but as you can see, the problem is not one of language. Had Peters consistently used the phrase "educated person" the conclusion that the ideal he holds up for education is masculine would be unaffected.

To be sure, Peters's educated person can be male or female, but he or she will have acquired male cognitive perspectives and will have developed traits which in our society are genderized in favor of males.

I have already suggested that Peters's ideal places a burden on women because the traits constituting it are evaluated negatively when possessed by females. The story of Rosalind Franklin, the scientist who contributed to the discovery of the structure of DNA, demonstrates that when a woman displays the kind of critical, autonomous thought which is an attribute of Peters's educated person, she is derided for what are considered to be negative, unpleasant characteristics.[29] Rosalind Franklin consciously opted out of "woman's sphere" and entered the laboratory. From an abstract point of view the traits she possessed were quite functional there. Nonetheless she was perceived to be an interloper, an alien who simply could not be taken seriously in relation to the production of new, fundamental ideas no matter what her personal qualities might be.[30]

But experiencing hostility and derision is the least of the suffering caused women by Peters's ideal. His educated person is one who will know nothing about the lives women have led throughout history and little if anything about the works of art and literature women have produced. If his educated person is a woman, she will have been presented with few female role models in her studies whereas her male counterpart will be able to identify with the doers and thinkers and makers of history. Above all, the certain way in which his educated man and woman will come to look at the world will be one in which men are perceived as they perceive themselves and women are perceived as men perceive them.

To achieve Peters's ideal one must acquire cognitive perspectives through which one sex is perceived on its own terms and one sex is perceived as the Other.[31] Can it be doubted that when the works of women are excluded from the subject matter of the fields into which they are being initiated, students will come to believe that males are superior and females are inferior human beings? That when in the course of this initiation the lives and experiences of women are scarcely mentioned, students will come to believe that the way in which women have lived and the things women have done throughout history have no value? Can it be doubted that these beliefs do female students serious damage? The woman whose self-confidence is bolstered by an education which transmits the message that females are inferior human beings is rare. Rarer still is the woman who, having been initiated into alien cognitive perspectives, gains confidence in her own powers without paying the price of self-alienation.

Peters's ideal puts women in a double bind. To be educated they must give up their own way of experiencing and looking at the world, thus alienating themselves from themselves. To be unalienated they must remain uneducated. Furthermore, to be an educated person a female must acquire traits which are appraised negatively when she possesses them. At the same time, the traits which are evaluated positively when possessed by her—for example, being nurturant and empathetic—are excluded from the ideal. Thus a female who has acquired the traits of an educated person will not be evaluated positively for having them, while one who has acquired those traits for which she will be positively evaluated will not have achieved the ideal. Women are placed in this double bind because Peters's ideal incorporates traits genderized in favor of males and excludes traits genderized in favor of females. It thus puts females in a no-win situation. Yes, men and women can both achieve Peters's ideal. However, women suffer, as men do not, for doing so.

Peters's masculine ideal of the educated person harms males as well as females, however. In a chapter of the 1981 NSSE Yearbook, I argued at some length that Hirst's account of liberal education is seriously deficient.[32] Since Peters's educated person is to all intents and purposes Hirst's liberally educated person, let me briefly repeat my criticism of Hirst here. The Peters-Hirst educated person will have knowledge about others, but will not have been taught to care about their welfare, let alone to act kindly toward them. That person will have some understanding of society, but will not have been taught to feel its injustices or even to be concerned over its fate. The Peters-Hirst educated person is an ivory tower person: a person who can reason yet has no desire to solve real problems in the real world; a person who understands science but does not worry about the uses to which it is put; a person who can reach flawless moral conclusions but feels no care or concern for others.

Simply put, quite apart from the burden it places on women, Peters's ideal of the educated person is far too narrow to guide the educational enterprise. Because it presupposes a divorce of mind from body, thought from action, and reason from feeling and emotion, it provides at best an ideal of an educated *mind*, not an educated *person*. To the extent that its concerns are strictly cognitive however, even in that guise it leaves much to be desired.

V. Education For Productive Processes

Even if Peters's ideal did not place an unfair burden on women it would need to be rejected for the harm it does men, but its inadequacy as an ideal for men and the injustice it does women are not unconnected. In my Yearbook essay I sketched in the rough outlines of a new paradigm of liberal education, one which would emphasize the development of persons and not simply rational minds; one which would join thought to action, and reason to feeling and emotion. I could just as easily have called it a new conception of the educated person. What I did not realize when I wrote that essay is that the aspects of the Peters-Hirst ideal which I found so objectionable are directly related to the role, traditionally considered to be male, which their educated person is to play in society.

Peters would vehemently deny that he conceives of education as production. Nonetheless, he implicitly attributes to education the task of turning raw material, namely the *un*educated person, into an end product whose specifications he sets forth in his account of the concept of the educated person. Peters would deny even more vehemently that he assigns to education a societal function. Yet an examination of his conception of the educated person reveals that the end product of the education he envisions is designed to fit into a specific place in the social order; that he assigns to education the function of developing the traits and qualities, and to some extent the skills, of one whose role is to use and produce ideas.[33]

Peters would doubtless say that the production and consumption of ideas is everyone's business and that an education for this is certainly not an education which fits people into a particular place in society. Yet think of the two parts into which the social order has traditionally been divided. Theorists have put different labels on them, some referring to the split between work and home, others to the public and private domains and still others to productive and reproductive processes.[34] Since the public/private distinction has associations for educators which are not germane to the present discussion, while the work/home distinction obscures some important issues, I will speak here of productive and reproductive processes. I do not want to make terminology the issue, however. If you prefer other labels, by all means substitute them for mine. My own is only helpful, I should add, if the term "reproduction" is construed broadly. Thus I use it here to include not simply biological reproduction of the species, but the whole process of reproduction, from conception until the individual reaches more or less independence from the family.[35] This process I take to include not simply childcare and rearing, but the related activities of keeping house, running the household, and serving the needs and purposes of all the family members. Similarly, I interpret the term "production" broadly to include political, social and cultural activities and processes as well as economic ones.

Now this traditional division drawn within the social order is accompanied by a separation of the sexes. Although males and females do in fact participate in both the reproductive and productive processes of society, the reproductive processes are considered to constitute "woman's sphere" and the productive processes "man's sphere." Although Peters's educated person is ill-equipped for jobs in trades or work on the assembly line, this person is tailor-made for carrying on certain of the productive processes of society, namely those which require work with heads, not hands. Thus his educated person is designed to fill a role in society which has traditionally been considered to be male. Moreover, he or she is not equipped by education to fill roles associated with the reproductive processes of society, i.e., roles traditionally considered to be female.

Once the functionalism of Peters's conception of the educated person is made explicit, the difficulty of including in the ideal feelings and emotions such as caring and compassion, or skills of cooperation and nurturance, becomes clear. These fall under our culture's female stereotype. They are considered to be appropriate for those who carry on the reproductive processes of society but irrelevant, if not downright dysfunctional, for those who carry on the productive processes of society. It would therefore be irrational to include them in an ideal which is conceived of solely in relation to productive processes.

I realize now, as I did not before, that for the ideal of the educated person to be as broad as it should be, the two kinds of societal processes which Peters divorces from one another must be joined together.[36] An adequate ideal of the educated person must give the reproductive processes of society their due. An ideal which is tied solely to the productive processes of society cannot readily accommodate the important virtues of caring and compassion, sympathy and nurturance, generosity and cooperation which are genderized in favor of females.

To be sure, it would be possible in principle to continue to conceive of the educated person solely in relation to the productive processes of society while rejecting the stereotypes which produce genderized traits. One could include caring and compassion in the ideal of the educated person on the grounds that although they are thought to be female traits whose home is in the reproductive processes of society, they are in fact functional in the production and consumption of ideas. The existence of genderized traits is not the only reason for giving the reproductive processes of society their due in an ideal of the educated person, however. These processes are themselves central to the lives of each of us and to the life of society as a whole. The dispositions, knowledge, skills required to carry them out well are not innate, nor do they simply develop naturally over time. Marriage, childrearing, family life: these involve difficult, complex, learned activities which can be done well or badly. Just as an educated person should be one in whom head, hand and heart are integrated, he or she should be one who is at home carrying on the reproductive processes of society, broadly understood, as well as the productive processes.

Now Peters might grant that the skills, traits, and knowledge necessary for carrying on reproductive processes are learned—in some broad sense of the term, at least—but argue that one does not require an education in them, for they are picked up in the course of daily living. Perhaps at one time they were picked up in this way, and perhaps in some societies they are now. But it is far from obvious that, just by living, most adults in our society today acquire the altruistic feelings and emotions, the skills of childrearing, the understanding of what values are important to transmit and which are not, and the ability to put aside one's own projects and enter into those of others which are just a few of the things required for successful participation in the reproductive processes of society.

That education is needed by those who carry on the reproductive processes is not in itself proof that it should be encompassed by a conception of the educated person, however, for this conception need not be all-inclusive. It need not be all-inclusive but, for Peters, education which is not guided by his ideal of the educated person scarcely deserves attention. Moreover, since a conception of the educated person tends to function as an ideal, one who becomes educated will presumably have achieved something worthwhile. Value is attached to being an educated person: to the things an educated person knows and can do; to the tasks and activities that person is equipped to perform. The exclusion of education for reproductive processes from the ideal of the educated person thus carries with it an unwarranted, negative value judgment about the tasks and activities, the traits and dispositions which are associated with them.

VI. Redefining the Ideal

An adequate ideal of the educated person must give the reproductive processes of society their due, but it must do more than this. After all, these processes were acknowledged by Rousseau in Book V of *Emile*.[37] There he set forth two distinct ideals of the educated person, the one for Emile tied to the productive processes of society and the one for Sophie tied to the reproductive processes. I leave open here the question Peters never asks, of whether we should adopt one or more ideals of the educated person.[38] One thing is clear, however. We need a conception which does not fall into the trap of assigning males and females to the different processes of society, yet does not make the mistake of ignoring one kind of process altogether. We all participate in both kinds of processes and both are important to all of us. Whether we adopt one or many ideals, a conception of the educated person which is tied only to one kind of process will be incomplete.

An adequate ideal of the educated person must also reflect a realistic understanding of the limitations of existing forms or disciplines of knowledge. In my Yearbook chapter I made a case for granting them much less "curriculum space" than Hirst and Peters do. So long as they embody a male cognitive perspective, however, we must take into account not simply the amount of space they occupy in the curriculum of the educated person, but the hidden messages which are received by those who are initiated into them. An ideal of the educated person cannot itself rid the disciplines of knowledge of their sex bias. But it can advocate measures for counteracting the harmful effects on students of coming to see things solely through male eyes.

The effects of an initiation into male cognitive perspectives constitute a hidden curriculum. Alternative courses of action are open to us when we find a hidden curriculum and there is no reason to suppose that only one is appropriate. Let me say a few words here, however, about a course of action that might serve as at least a partial antidote to the hidden curriculum transmitted by an education in male biased disciplines.[39] When we find a hidden curriculum we can show it to its recipients; we can raise their consciousness, if you will, so that they will know what is happening to them. Raising to consciousness the male cognitive perspective of the disciplines of knowledge in the educated person's curriculum is no guarantee, of course, that educated females will not suffer from a lack of self-confidence and from self-alienation. Yet knowledge can be power. A curriculum which, through critical analysis, exposes the biased view of women embodied in the disciplines and which, by granting ample space to the study of women shows how unjust that view is, is certainly preferable to a curriculum which, by its silence on the subject, gives students the impression that the ways in which the disciplines look at the world are impartial and unbiased.

Now it might seem to be a relatively simple matter both to give the reproductive processes of society their due in an ideal of the educated person and to include in that ideal measures for counteracting the hidden curriculum of an education in the existing disciplines of knowledge. Yet given the way philosophy of education conceives of its subject matter today, it is not. The productive-reproductive dualism is built not simply into Peters's ideal but into our discipline.[40] We do not even have a vocabulary for discussing education in relation to the reproductive processes of society, for the distinction between liberal and vocational education which we use to cover the kinds of education we take to be philosophically important applies within productive processes: liberal and vocational education are both intended to fit people to carry on productive processes, the one for work with heads and the other for work with hands. The aims of education we analyze—critical thinking, rationality, individual autonomy, even crea-tivity—are also associated in our culture with the productive, not the reproductive, processes of society. To give the reproductive processes their due in a conception of the educated person we will have to rethink the domain of philosophy of education.

Given the way we define our subject matter it is no more possible for us to take seriously the hidden curriculum I have set before you than the reproductive processes of society. Education, as we conceive of it, is an intentional activity.[41] Teaching is too.[42] Thus, we do not consider the unintended outcomes of education to be our concern. Moreover, following Peters and his colleagues, we draw a sharp line between logical and contingent relationships and treat the latter as if they were none of our business even when they are the expected outcomes of educational processes.[43] In sum, we leave it to the psychologists, sociologists and historians of education to worry about hidden curricula, not because we consider the topic unimportant—although perhaps some of us do—but because we consider it to fall outside our domain.

The redefinition of the subject matter of philosophy of education required by an adequate ideal of the educated person ought not to be feared. On the contrary, there is every reason to believe that it would ultimately enrich our discipline. If the experi-ence and activities which have traditionally been considered to belong to women are included in the educational realm, a host of challenging and important issues and problems will present themselves for study. If the philosophy of education tackles questions about childrearing and the transmission of values, if it develops accounts of gender education to inform its theories of liberal education, if it explores the forms of thinking, feeling and acting associated with childrearing, marriage and the family, if the concepts of coeducation, mothering and nurturance become fair game for philo-sophical analysis, philosophy of education will be invigorated.

It would also be invigorated by taking seriously contingent, as well as logical, rela-tionships. In divorcing educational processes from their empirical consequences and the mental structures which are said to be intrinsically related to knowledge from the empirical consequences of having them, we forget that education is a practical endeavor. It is often said that philosophy of education's concerns are purely conceptual, but the conclusion is inescapable that in analyzing such concepts as the educated person and liberal education we make recommendations for action. For these to be justified, the contingent relationships which obtain between them and both the good life and the good society must be taken into account. A redefinition of our domain would allow us to provide our educational theorizing with the kind of justification it requires. It would also allow us to investigate the particularly acute and very challenging value questions that arise in relation to hidden curricula of all kinds.

VII. Conclusion

In conclusion I would like to draw for you two morals which seem to me to emerge from my study of Peters's ideal of the educated person. The first is that Plato was wrong when, in Book V of the *Republic,* he said that sex is a difference which makes no difference.[44] I do not mean by this that there are inborn differences which suit males and females for separate and unequal roles in society. Rather, I mean that identical educational treatment of males and females may not yield identical results so long as that treatment contains a male bias. There are sex differences in the way people are perceived and evaluated and there may well be sex differences in the way people think and learn and view the world. A conception of the educated person must take these into account. I mean also that the very nature of the ideal will be skewed. When sex or gender is thought to make no difference, women's lives, experiences, activities are overlooked and an ideal is formulated in terms of men and the roles for which they have traditionally been considered to be suited. Such an ideal is necessarily narrow, for it is rooted in stereotypical ways of perceiving males and their place in society.

For some time I assumed that the sole alternative to a sex-biased conception of the educated person such as Peters set forth was a gender-free ideal, that is to say an ideal which did not take sex or gender into account. I now realize that sex or gender has to be taken into account if an ideal of the educated person is not to be biased. To opt at this time for a gender-free ideal is to beg the question. What is needed is a *gender-sensitive* ideal, one which takes sex or gender into account when it makes a difference and ignores it when it does not. Such an ideal would truly be gender-just.

The second moral is that *everyone* suffers when an ideal of the educated person fails to give the reproductive processes of society their due. Ideals which govern education solely in relation to the productive processes of society will necessarily be narrow. In their failure to acknowledge the valuable traits, dispositions, skills, traditionally associated with reproductive processes, they will harm both sexes, although not always in the same ways.[45]

Notes

I wish to thank Ann Diller, Carol Gilligan, Michael Martin and Janet Farrell Smith for helpful comments on earlier versions of this essay.

1. R. S. Peters, "Education and The Educated Man," in R. F. Dearden, P. H. Hirst, and R. S. Peters, eds., *A Critique of Current Educational Aims* (London: Routledge & Kegan Paul, 1972), pp. 7–9.

2. Paul Nash, Andreas M. Kazemias, and Henry J. Perkinson, eds., *The Educated Man: Studies in the History of Educational Thought* (New York: John Wiley & Sons, 1965), p. 25.

3. For a discussion of "man" as a gender-neutral term see Janice Moulton, "The Myth of the Neutral 'Man'," in Mary Vetterling-Braggin, Frederick A. Elliston, and Jane English, eds., *Feminism and Philosophy* (Totowa, NJ: Littlefield, Adams, 1977), pp. 124–137. Moulton rejects the view that "man" has a gender-neutral use.

4. Peters, "Education and The Educated Man," p. 11. Peters says in connection with the

concept of the educated man: "For there are many who are not likely to go far with the-oretical enquiries and who are unlikely to develop much depth or breadth of understanding to underpin and transform their dealings as workers, *husbands* and *fathers*" (emphasis added).

5. Ibid., p. 7.

6. R.S. Peters, *Ethics and Education* (London: George Allen & Unwin, 1966). Page references are to the American edition published by Scott, Foresman and Company, 1967.

7. Peters, "Education and The Educated Man," pp. 9–11.'

8. R.S. Downie, Eileen M. Loudfoot, and Elizabeth Telfer, *Education and Personal Relationships* (London: Methuen & Co., 1974), p. 11ff.

9. In Paul Hirst, *Knowledge and the Curriculum* (London: Routledge & Kegan Paul, 1974), p. 47.

10. Nancy Schrom Dye, "Clio's American Daughters," in Julia A. Sherman and Evelyn Torton Beck, eds., *The Prism of Sex* (Madison: University of Wisconsin Press, 1979), p. 9.

11. Catherine R. Stimpson, "The Power to Name," in Sherman and Beck, eds., *Prism*, pp. 55–77.

12. Elaine Showalter, "Women Writers and the Double Standard," in Vivian Gornick and Barbara Moran, eds., *Women in Sexist Society* (New York: Basic Books, 1971), pp. 323–343.

13. Naomi Weisstein, "Psychology Constructs the Female," in Gornick and Moran, eds., *Women in Sexist Society*, pp. 133–146.

14. Ruth Hubbard, "Have Only Men Evolved?" in Ruth Hubbard, Mary Sue Henifin, and Barbara Fried, eds., *Women Look at Biology Looking at Women* (Cambridge: Schenkman Publishing Co., 1979), pp. 7–35.

15. Carol Gilligan, "Women's Place in Man's Life Cycle," *Harvard Educational Review 49*, 4 (1979): 431–446.

16. Carol Gilligan, "In a Different Voice: Women's Conceptions of Self and of Morality," *Harvard Educational Review 47*, 4 (1979): 481–517.

17. See, for example, Linda Gordon, *Woman's Body, Woman's Right: A Social History of Birth Control in America* (New York: Viking, 1976); Richard W. Wertz and Dorothy C. Wertz, *Lying-In* (New York: Free Press, 1977); Jean Donnison, *Midwives and Medical Men: A History of Interprofessional Rivalries and Women's Rights* (New York: Schocken Books, 1977).

18. Mary Hartman and Lois W. Banner, eds., *Clio's Consciousness Raised* (New York: Harper & Row, 1974).

19. See, for example, Carolyn G. Heilbrun, *Toward a Recognition of Androgyny* (New York: Alfred A. Knopf, 1973); Patricia Meyer Spacks, *The Female Imagination* (New York: Avon, 1975); Ellen Moers, *Literary Women* (New York: Anchor Books, 1977); Elaine Showalter, *A Literature of Their Own: British Women Novelists from Bronte to Lessing* (Princeton: Princeton University Press, 1977); Ann Sutherland Harris and Linda Nochlin, *Women Artists: 1550–1950* (New York: Alfred A. Knopf, 1976); Elsa Honig Fine, *Women and Art: A History of Women Painters and Sculptors from the Renaissance to the Twentieth*

Century (Montclair and London: Allanheld & Schram/Prior, 1978); and Karen Peterson and J.J. Wilson, *Women Artists: Recognition and Reappraisal from the Early Middle Ages to the Twentieth Century* (New York: New York University Press, 1976).

20. In Paul Hirst, *Knowledge and the Curriculum*, p. 92.

21. R.G. Woods and R. St. C. Barrow, *An Introduction to Philosophy of Education* (Methuen & Co., 1975), Ch. 3.

22. For discussions of our male and female stereotypes see, e.g., Alexandra G. Kaplan and Joan P. Bean, eds., *Beyond Sex-role Stereotypes* (Boston: Little, Brown, 1976); and Alexandra G. Kaplan and Mary Anne Sedney, *Psychology and Sex Roles* (Boston: Little, Brown, 1980).

23. Carol Gilligan, "Women's Place"; I. Broverman, D. Broverman, F. Clarkson, P. Rosencrantz and S. Vogel, "Sex-role Stereotypes and Clinical Judgements of Mental Health," *Journal of Consulting and Clinical Psychology 34* (1970): 1–7; Alexandra G. Kaplan, "Androgyny as a Model of Mental Health for Women: From Theory to Therapy," in Kaplan and Bean, eds., *Beyond Sex-role Stereotypes*, pp. 353–362.

24. One commits the androcentric fallacy when one argues from the characteristics associated with male human beings to the characteristics of all human beings. In committing it one often commits the naturalistic fallacy because the traits which are said to be natural to males are held up as ideals for the whole species.

25. I say *if* it can be attained by all, because it is not entirely clear that the ideal can be attained by *anyone* insofar as it requires mastery of Hirst's seven forms of knowledge.

26. See Elizabeth Beardsley. "Traits and Genderization," in Vetterling-Braggin, et al., eds., *Feminism and Philosophy*, pp. 117–123. Beardsley uses the term "genderization" to refer to language, while I use it here to refer to traits themselves.

27. Lynn Z. Bloom, Karen Coburn, Joan Pearlman, *The New Assertive Woman* (New York: Delacorte Press, 1975), p. 12.

28. For discussion of the assumption that masculinity-femininity is a bipolar dimension see Anne Constantinople, "Masculinity-Femininity: An Exception to a Famous Dictum"; and Sandra L. Bern, "Probing the Promise of Androgyny," in Kaplan and Bean, eds., *Beyond Sex-role Stereotypes*.

29. Anne Sayre, *Rosalind Franklin & DNA* (New York: W.W. Norton & Co., 1975). See also James D. Watson, *The Double Helix* (New York: Atheneum, 1968); and Horace Freeland Judson, *The Eighth Day of Creation* (New York: Simon and Schuster, 1979).

30. It is important to note, however, that some colleagues did take her seriously as a scientist; see Sayre, ibid. Adele Simmons cites historical evidence of the negative effects of having acquired such traits on women who did not opt out of "woman's sphere" in "Education and Ideology in Nineteenth-Century America: The Response of Educational Institutions to the Changing Role of Women," in Berenice A. Carroll, ed., *Liberating Women's History* (Urbana, IL: University of Illinois Press, 1976), p. 123. See also Patricia Meyer Spacks, *The Female Imagination* (New York: Avon Books, 1976), p. 25.

31. See Simone de Beauvoir, *The Second Sex* (New York: Bantam Books, 1961) for an extended discussion of woman as the Other.

32. Jane Roland Martin, "Needed: A New Paradigm for Liberal Education," see Chapter 9 in this volume.

33. For an account of education as production see Jane Roland Martin, "Sex Equality and Education: A Case Study," in Mary Vetterling-Braggin, ed., *"Femininity," "Masculinity," and "Androgyny"* (Totowa, N.J.: Littlefield, Adams, 1982). It should be noted that an understanding of the societal role for which Peters's educated person is intended illuminates both the sex bias and the class bias his ideal embodies.

34. For an interesting discussion and criticism of the two-sphere analysis of society, see Joan Kelly, "The Doubled Vision of Feminist Theory: A Postscript to the 'Women and Power' Conference," *Feminist Studies 5*, 1 (1979): 216–227. Kelly argues that a two-sphere analysis distorts reality and that feminist theory should discard it. I use it here as a convenient theoretical device.

35. I am indebted here to Lorenne M.G. Clark, "The Rights of Women: The Theory and Practice of the Ideology of Male Supremacy," in William R. Shea and John King-Farlow, eds., *Contemporary Issues in Political Philosophy* (New York: Science History Publications, 1976), 49–65.

36. In saying that an adequate conception of the educated person must reject a sharp separation of productive and reproductive processes I do not mean that it must be committed to a specific philosophical theory of the relationship of the two. An adequate conception of the educated person should not divorce mind and body, but it does not follow from this that it must be committed to a specific view of the mind-body relationship; indeed, the union of mind and body in a theory of education is quite compatible with a dualistic philosophical account of the relationship between the two. Similarly, a theory of the educated person must not divorce one kind of societal process from the other even if the best account of the relationship of productive to reproductive processes should turn out to be dualistic.

37. Jean-Jacques Rousseau, *Emile* (New York: Basic Books, 1979, Allan Bloom, trans.). See also Lynda Lange, "Rousseau: Women and the General Will," in Lorenne M.G. Clark and Lynda Lange, eds., *The Sexism of Social and Political Theory* (Toronto: University of Toronto Press, 1979), pp. 41–52; Susan Moller Okin, *Women in Western Political Thought* (Princeton: Princeton University Press, 1979); and Jane Roland Martin "Sophie and Emile: A Case Study of Sex Bias in the History of Educational Thought," see Chapter 2 in this volume.

38. I also leave open the question of whether any ideal of the educated person should guide and direct education as a whole.

39. For more on this question see Jane Roland Martin, "What Should We Do with a Hidden Curriculum When We Find One?," Chapter 8 in this volume.

40. On this point see Jane Roland Martin, "Excluding Women from the Educational Realm," Chapter 1 in this volume.

41. See, for example, Peters, *Ethics and Education*.

42. See, for example, Israel Scheffler, *The Language of Education* (Springfield, IL: Charles C. Thomas, 1960), Chs. 4, 5.

43. For a discussion of this point see Jane Roland Martin, "Response to Roemer," in Jerrold

R. Coombs, ed., *Philosophy of Education 1979* (Normal, IL: Proceedings of the 35th Annual Meeting of the Philosophy of Education Society, 1980).

44. This point is elaborated on in Jane Roland Martin, "Sex Equality and Education: A Case Study."

CHAPTER 4

Romanticism Domesticated:
Maria Montessori and the
Casa dei Bambini

"Romanticism Domesticated: Maria Montessori and the Casa dei Bambini" was writ-
ten the year I was a Visiting Scholar at Radcliffe College and a John Simon Guggenheim
Memorial Foundation Fellow. The immediate occasion was an invitation to contribute
an essay to a book celebrating the Educational Legacy of Romanticism. That volume and
the seminar in October 1988 that brought together the contributors to it was sponsored
by the Calgary Institute for the Humanities. I am grateful to those participants in that
quite unusual meeting who gave me constructive criticism and especially to John Willinsky,
the book's editor and the conference convenor, for allowing me first to refuse the topic that
he assigned me and then to reject the one that I myself named. In so doing he gave me my
first chance to present publicly one of the several strands of research that came together a
few years later in The Schoolhome.

In tracing Maria Montessori's intellectual lineage to "the Rousseau-Pestalozzi-
Froebel group" critics and admirers alike place her squarely in the Romantic tradition
of educational thought (Kilpatrick; cf. Rusk). This characterization seems apt given
Montessori's emphasis on the child, her faith in its inherent capacities, her belief that
the educational process should follow the child's natural development, her commitment to the child's freedom and self-expression, and her insistence on the
importance in a child's education of direct sense experience. When one notices the
allusions to Wordsworth in her writings, it appears to be all the more fitting. Yet
when the Casa dei Bambini is added to the equation, Montessori's standing as a
Romantic becomes problematic.

This essay has been previously published in *The Educational Legacy of Romanticism*, edited
by John Willinsky (Waterloo: Wilfrid Laurier University Press, 1990) pp. 159–174.

Speaking in 1907 at the opening of a Casa dei Bambini in Rome, Montessori said: "We Italians have elevated our word 'casa' to the almost sacred significance of the English word 'home,' the enclosed temple of domestic affection, accessible only to dear ones" (*Method* 53). Notwithstanding this emphasis on "home," from the beginning her term for school has been rendered in English as "The House of Childhood" or "The Children's House." Indeed, in 1912 the speech containing her cautionary note was published as chapter 3 of the first English language edition of *The Montessori Method* under the title "Inaugural Address Delivered on the Occasion of the Opening of One of the 'Children's Houses.'"

Read "casa" as house and one's attention is drawn to the child-size furniture, the exercises in dressing and washing, and perhaps the extended day. Read "casa" as home and one discovers a moral and social dimension to her theory that belies the Romantic label. Moreover, just as the designation of Montessori as a Romantic theorist of education is cast in question by a rereading of her accounts of the Casa dei Bambini, the interpretations that have been placed on her theory lose their initial plausibility. When it is understood that Montessori thought of school on the model of home, the elements of her system take on a different configuration. Where once small individuals were seen busily manipulating materials designed especially for learning, a domestic scene now emerges with its own special form of social life and education. In addition, her theory acquires an uncanny relevance to our own time and place.

The Casa dei Bambini

The Casa dei Bambini was designed for poor children whose mothers worked each day outside their own homes. In *A Montessori Mother*, written in 1912 for mothers, Dorothy Canfield Fisher noted that enterprises like laundry and baking, which had once been undertaken by women in the home, were now being carried on outside. Prophesying that the education of children under six would soon follow suit, she wrote: "At some time in the future, society will certainly recognize this close harmony of the successful Casa dei Bambini with the rest of the tendencies of our times" (236–237). If anything, Fisher's metaphor of harmony underestimates the significance for today of Montessori's idea of school.

I cannot help thinking that Canfield's prescience stemmed at least in part from the fact that she read "Casa dei Bambini" as Montessori meant it. "The phrase Casa dei Bambini is being translated everywhere nowadays by English-speaking people as 'The House of Childhood,'" Fisher wrote, "whereas its real meaning, both linguistic and spiritual, is, 'The Children's Home'" (31). "I feel like insisting upon this rendering, which gives us so much more idea of the character of the institution," she added (33).

Subtract the Children's Home from Montessori's system and her method sounds like a recipe for those British and North American open classrooms of the 1960s and 1970s to which the Romantic label is so often attached.[1] Her emphasis on children learning rather than teachers teaching, on the child's manipulation of concrete materials, on freedom and the absence of compulsion in the schoolroom were commonplaces of open classrooms. To be sure, advocates of open education undoubtedly considered the apparatus Montessori prescribed for learning too confining and, had they known of it, they would have thought that her conceptualization of the child's activities in school as *exercises* reflected an unfortunate rigidity as to the way skills are both acquired and put into practice. She, in turn, would probably have frowned upon the use of one and the same object for different purposes and would certainly have disapproved of what would have seemed to her the haphazard way in which concepts were learned and skills acquired in open classrooms. Still, the open-classroom teacher like the Montessori Directress was not supposed to take center stage. Nor was that teacher supposed to tell children the answer as opposed to helping them figure things out. Moreover, the distinction between work and play was as blurred in open classrooms as it is in Montessori's theory and the location of both in time and place was as fluid.

The open-classroom movement did not share Montessori's conception of school, however. Rejecting the features of traditional schools that had led critics to characterize them as prisons, open classroom advocates were determined to remove the barriers between school and world. Allowing children to cross the threshold into the out-of-doors, bringing materials from the "outside" world into the classroom, inviting members of the community into school to demonstrate their skills, they saw school more as a replica in miniature of the world than as a home. Indeed, the very presence in many open classrooms of a "family *corner*" indicated that whatever the rest of school was seen as, it was not seen as home. One homelike area does not transform a school or even a classroom into a home.

In any event, it is not the furniture that makes the Casa dei Bambini a child's surrogate home. In *Education for Peace*, a collection of lectures Montessori delivered in the 1930s, she distinguished a negative concept of peace, as merely the cessation of war, from a positive one. Introducing an analogy to good health which, she said, is not simply a matter of the absence of disease but is based on a strong well-developed body relatively resistant to infection, she argued that positive or genuine peace requires a transformation of moral life. Peace, wrote Montessori, is not "a partial truce between separate nations, but a permanent way of life for all mankind" (*Peace* 70). How is this to be achieved? The child must be the starting point for the transformation since "the hope of altering adults is vain" (*Mind* 73).

Calling the child a "spiritual embryo," Montessori drew upon Wordsworth in her later writings as she had in her earliest. In the last paragraph of *The Montessori Method* she had said:

> I understand how the great English poet Wordsworth, enamored as he was of nature, demanded the secret of all her peace and beauty. It was at last revealed to him—the secret of all nature lies in the soul of a little child. He holds there the true meaning of that life which exists throughout humanity. But this beauty which "lies about us in our infancy" becomes obscured; "shades of the prison house, begin to close about the growing boy . . . at last the man perceives it die away, and fade into the light of common day." (*Method* 376)

More than two decades later Montessori told European audiences that the child "must no longer be considered as the son of man, but rather as the creator and the father of man" (*Peace* 104).

The spiritual embryo's promise will only be fulfilled if the child is allowed to develop normally, Montessori insisted. Since its psychic life begins at birth, the problem of peace becomes, then, one of educating young children. Just as the physical embryo derives its nutriments from the womb, the spiritual embryo absorbs them from its surroundings. Put children in the wrong environment, their development will be abnormal and they will become the deviated adults we now know. Create the right environment for them and their characters will develop normally. The "second womb" is what she called the young child's proper environment. From perhaps the age of two the Casa dei Bambini is that second womb.

If Montessori's own words in her Inaugural Lecture that "casa" means "home" are not convincing, these references to a child's very first home should be decisive. What is the character of the institution called home? One dwells in a house. One feels secure, loved, at ease—that is, "at home"—in a home, at least in the kind of home envisioned by Montessori.

Let there be no misunderstanding. Montessori did not model her school on just any home. Maintaining in her Inaugural Address that the Casa dei Bambini "is not simply a place where the children are kept, not just an *asylum*, but a true school for their education" (*Method* 62), she indicated that even its home-likeness was to be educative. Montessori reminded her audience that the Casa dei Bambini then opening was located in buildings in which, until they had been renovated, the poor had been living in unspeakable conditions. Upon completion of the project, the authorities had found themselves faced with an unexpected problem: the children under school age living in the new apartments were running wild while their parents were at work. In her words, they were becoming "ignorant little vandals, defacing the walls and stairs" (60). Convinced that these children were neither being cared for properly nor learning what they should at home, Montessori designed the school she had been asked to establish *in* the housing project *for* the housing project children as the kind of home to which the resident poor should aspire. Making it their school by giving them collective ownership (63), she nevertheless modeled it on a version of home many of them did not know.

Montessori's description of what the literal home in the project might one day become captures the spirit of that metaphorical home named school: "It may be said to embrace its inmates with the tender, consoling arms of a woman. It is the giver of moral life, of blessings; it cares for, it educates and feeds the little ones" (*Method* 68–69). Her idealized version of home was based in part, but only in part, on her image of a womb. Like a womb the Casa dei Bambini would provide a safe and secure, supportive and nurturant environment for children. Over and beyond this, the children in the Casa dei Bambini would have a double sense of belonging: they would feel that they belonged to this home *and also* that it belonged to them. Deriving not from possessiveness but attachment—to the school itself, to its physical embodiment, to the people in it—this latter feeling explains the children's zeal in keeping the schoolrooms neat and clean, their pride in showing the school to visitors, their joy in serving each other hot lunches.[2]

One clear implication of Montessori's image of school as home is that the inhabitants of school are to see themselves as a family. When this element of her system is overlooked, Montessori's belief in self-education makes Robert R. Rusk's claim that "the most significant feature of the system is the individualisation of instruction" (306) seem warranted. The conclusions reached in 1914 by William Heard Kilpatrick that Montessori "does not provide situations for more adequate social cooperation" (20) and in 1964 by J. McV. Hunt, a more sympathetic interpreter than Kilpatrick, that her pedagogy underemphasizes "the role and importance of interpersonal relationships" (in Montessori, *Method* xxxiii) also appear so credible that one must either discount the reports of the unselfish behavior of the children in her schools and their genuine concern for each other's welfare or else consider these phenomena to be miraculous. A description like Fisher's of the smiling faces of several children who witnessed one boy's long and ultimately successful struggle to tuck his napkin under his chin and of the way one then patted the napkin "as its proud wearer passed" (25) makes perfect sense, however, if one remembers that they and he are bound together by "domestic affection."

School, Home, and World

Sharing Montessori's belief in the value of domestic life, Fisher understood that the Casa dei Bambini was intended as a surrogate home for children. A home away from home, one is tempted to say, except for the fact that it was situated in the very building in which the children lived and the parents—or at any rate the mothers—were expected to make frequent visits. Foreseeing that one day in the United States women of all classes would be working outside their own homes and that most children would therefore be in need of surrogate homes, Fisher glimpsed the significance for her own country of Montessori's idea. But women at work outside the home is only part of the latter day domestic situation to which the Casa dei Bambini speaks.

Perhaps two million, possibly even three or four million people in the United States today, the great majority of whom live in families with children, are homeless (Kozol). Living on the streets or in rat-ridden, roach-infested shelters, these people can scarcely be said to dwell in a house let alone a home. Telling her audience about the district of Rome in which the Casa dei Bambini was located, Montessori said that children born in this Quarter "do not 'first see the light of day'; they come into a world of gloom . . . Here, there can be no privacy, no modesty, no gentleness; here, there is often not even light, nor air, nor water!" (*Method* 52). Describing the Martinique, a once elegant hotel in New York City now littered with garbage and smelling of urine that in 1987 housed 438 homeless families, Jonathan Kozol gives a graphic sense of this world of gloom:

It is difficult to do full justice to the sense of hopelessness one feels on entering the building. It is a haunting experience and leaves an imprint on one's memory that is not easily erased by time or cheerful company. Even the light seems dimmer here, the details harder to make out, the mere geography of twisting corridors and winding stairs and circular passageways a maze that I found indecipherable at first and still find difficult to figure out. After fifty or sixty nights within this building, I have tried but cannot make a floor plan of the place.

Something of Dickens' halls of chancery comes to my mind whenever I am wandering those floors. It is the knowledge of sorrow, I suppose, and of unbroken dreariness that dulls the vision and impairs one's faculties of self-location and discernment. If it does this to a visitor, what does it do to those for whom this chancery is home? (28)

In the Martinique, where a family of four or even five lives in an unheated room with no chairs, no space to move around in, no stove—indeed, often no food to eat and no clean clothes to wear, there is no Casa dei Bambini. Of the more than 1,400 school-age children living there in 1985, Kozol estimated that over one-third did not usually get to school. Of those who did, many had to travel by bus or subway to outlying districts and even those attending schools nearby fell asleep at their desks and fell behind in their work.

It is not just the homeless who stand to benefit from a Montessorian conception of school, however. In the United States as recently as 1960, 70 percent of all families consisted of children and two parents, only one of whom—the father—worked outside the home (Mintz and Kellogg). By 1987, however, less than 10 percent of families consisted of a male breadwinner, a female housewife, and dependent children (Stacey). One in four children in that year lived in single-parent households and in the majority of two-parent families, both adults went out to work (Schmid). If the concept of school as surrogate home met a need of the poor in the San Lorenzo Quarter of Rome at the beginning of this century, in the United States at century's end it meets a need of almost all.

Fisher's insight into the significance of the Casa dei Bambini deserves closer study than I can possibly give it here. So that history does not repeat itself, however, let us at least ask how it is that she heard Montessori's message when others did not and why those others were unable to hear either the original message or Fisher's reiteration of it.

An adequate answer to this second question turns on the fact that Montessori's domestic imagery violates this culture's basic expectations about the role of school in society. Implicitly dividing social reality into two parts—private home and public world—we take the function of education to be that of transforming children who have heretofore lived their lives in one part into members of the other part. Assuming that membership in the private home is natural, we see no reason to prepare people to carry out the tasks and activities associated with it. Perceiving membership in the public world as something to be achieved and therefore as problematic, we make the business of education preparation for carrying out the tasks and activities associated with it. Our culture's very conception of education, then, rests on the assumption that domestic life is that which we must learn to go beyond.

Of course almost all of us continue to live in homes and be members of families even as we take our place in the world at large. Yet although to go beyond is not necessarily to leave behind, becoming educated is nevertheless thought of not simply as a process of acquiring new ways of thinking, feeling, and acting. It is also assumed to be a matter of casting off the attitudes and values, the patterns of thought and action associated with domesticity. Considering these latter to be impediments to the successful performance of society's productive processes, we demand that education move us away from home and all it represents even as it equips us for life in the world.

Montessori's intention of bringing home and school into close connection thus conflicts with what appears to us to be the *raison d'être* for a society to educate its young. Writing *as* educators *for* educators, her translators and commentators would not, or perhaps could not, break out of the established framework of thought. When, as Hunt did in his introduction to a 1964 edition of *The Montessori Method*, they acknowledged the existence of Fisher's translation, they reverted quickly to the standard one. Even when their own appreciative readings of Montessori stood to be enriched by an acknowledgment of the homelike qualities of the Casa dei Bambini, these were ignored.

Henry Holmes noted in his introduction to the 1912 edition of the same work that "Montessori children often are in a real social enterprise, such as that of serving dinner, cleaning the room, caring for animals, building a toy house, or making a garden" (xxiii). He did not say, because he did not see, that as domestic activities each of these social enterprises takes on a special shape or that when they are considered together they constitute a special form of life. Martin Mayer, in turn, said in the introduction to a 1964 edition of *The Montessori Method* that whatever we do in response to "the scandal of modern education for slum children" (xxxviii), much of it will have to be "informed by the Montessori spirit, and some of it must employ the Montessori method" (xli). Emphasizing the seldom remembered fact that Montessori placed the Casa dei Bambini in "the model tenement where the children lived" (xxxix), and also made that tenement the Directress's home, he wanted it known that the Montessori system is not reducible to a set of techniques, however valuable they may be. Because he overlooked the ways in which the Montessori spirit is informed by domestic imagery, he conveyed to his readers at best a partial understanding of it.

Envisioning school as an extension of home and a means of strengthening that "temple of domestic affection," Montessori assigns it a societal function as different as can be from the one that almost all her interpreters and critics have taken for granted. The system of education that Kilpatrick said had nothing new in it of importance is, thus, nothing short of revolutionary. To be sure, Montessori was not the first person in the history of Western educational thought to deny a radical separation between school and home.[3] She is the one, however, to insist that the atmosphere and affections associated with home be preserved in school.

In the preface to *A Montessori Mother*, Fisher felt it necessary to make explicit the difference between her own standpoint and that of other commentators:

> This volume of impressions is not written by a biologist for other biologists, by a philosopher for an audience of college professors, or by a professional pedagogue to enlighten school superintendents. An ordinary American parent, desiring above all else the best possible chance for her children, addresses this message to the innumerable legion of her companions in that desire. (x)

Writing as a mother who did not want to send her own preschool-age children to school in the outside world, and writing for mothers like herself Fisher was, on the one hand, attuned to Montessori's domestic imagery and, on the other, better situated than her peers to step outside the educational paradigm that controlled their thinking. Had Montessori's more theoretically inclined discussants acknowledged her domestic metaphor and its implications, they would not only have had to rethink the relationship of school and home; they would also have had to reassess the relationship between school and world. Fisher's position made it unnecessary for her to face up to these difficult issues.

Montessori herself did not, to my knowledge, confront them directly. There is ample evidence in *Education for Peace*, however, that she was well aware that school forms people for life in the public world. She might have been reluctant to admit that from the standpoint of maintaining that world a conception of school as home will be considered dysfunctional. Yet she knew full well that a public world hospitable to peace in the positive sense would have to be very different from the one of her acquaintance and that those living in it would have to have been formed by a very different kind of school. Thus, although she did not explicitly formulate a new theory of the relationships obtaining among home, school, and public world, there is every reason to suppose that in her system there is no room for the radical dichotomies so often drawn in both her day and our own between school and home, home and world, world and school.

Romanticism and the Montessori Spirit

"The history of Romanticism is—to a far greater extent than the history of any other artistic or philosophical movement—a history of redefinitions," say Charles Rosen and Henri Zerner (16). Barriers between genres are broken down, they add, as is "the barrier between art and life" (17). Fusing and confusing genres, as according to Friedrich Schlegel's definition of Romanticism the novel does, Montessori proved herself in this respect a true Romantic and an artist among educators. School was to be a home for children. The homes of the poor were to move closer to the ideal home embodied by school. And if positive peace was ever to prevail, the world itself would become "a temple of domestic affection."

Yet if in one way an accurate rendering of Casa dei Bambini strengthens the case that Montessori is a Romantic thinker, in another it weakens it. In a book that attempts to reconcile Romanticism and liberal thought, Nancy Rosenblum distinguishes within "the romantic sensibility" the "militarist opposition to prosaic peace and the law of the heart's opposition to legalism" (6). The content Montessori builds into the term "home"—the domestic form of life the Casa dei Bambini embodies—is fundamentally at odds with both aspects of Romanticism.

"Romantic militarism," says Rosenblum referring to Wordsworth's "Convention of Cintra," "is the invention of sensibilities who usually were not inclined to real aggression, but who imagined war as the prime occasion for perfect freedom and self-expression" (9). Montessori imagined nothing of the sort. Serenity and love, not aggression and war, were to her mind the conditions in which the freedom and self-expression she prized so highly for children would flourish. Whereas in liberal thought liberty is inseparable from legal security and peace, Romantic militarism opposes "the prosaic promises of civil society" (19), Rosenblum continues. Montessori did not make civil society, which in liberal thought stands in opposition to home, the model for school. From the standpoint of Romantic militarism, however, the promises of the model she did adopt are even more prosaic than those of the liberal's public world. Starting as do Romantics from an assumption of individualism,[4] Montessori did not simply purge this position "of its moderating elements" (Rosenblum 10). She endowed it with a domestic dimension that at once nullifies the violence, the unrestrained self-assertion, the heroism that this strand of Romanticism idealizes and nurtures the peaceable qualities and prosaic activities it despises.

Washing and dressing, dusting and sweeping, setting tables and serving meals: these everyday chores are the stuff out of which the practical exercises for children in the Casa dei Bambini were constructed. Equating domesticity with banality and the banal with the boring, Romantic militarism would oppose any system of education that made such activities central. A love shorn of selfishness and possessiveness and purged of passion and transitoriness: this is the relation in which a Casa dei Bambini Directress was to stand to the children and in which they were to learn to stand to each other and to all living things. Glorifying unconstrained expression and extraordinary action, Romantic militarism would consider intolerable the serenity and calm affection embracing the children in Montessori's school.

Rosenblum distinguishes several versions of Romantic militarism, for it is by no means a unified position. While, for example, Wilhelm von Humboldt's emphasis on individuality and spontaneity seems to accord with Montessori's domestic vision, what does not accord is his claim that "the essence of man's value is that he can risk himself, and, when necessary, play freely with his own life" (Rosenblum 14). The attraction of death, or at least of risk to life and limb, is a unifying theme in Romantic militarism, one that contrasts sharply with the Montessori spirit. As the metaphor of a second womb implies, Montessori's hope was to institute an education for our young in which life could flourish. As her lectures to European audiences at a time when war was imminent demonstrate, her object was to prevent adults from waging war by instilling in them as children "a love and a respect for all living beings and all the things that human beings have built through the centuries" (*Peace* 33):

> If man were to grow up fully and with a sound psyche, developing a strong character and a clear mind, he would be unable to tolerate the existence of diametrically opposed moral principles within himself or to advocate simultaneously two sorts of justice—one that fosters life and one that destroys it. He would not simultaneously cultivate two moral powers in his heart, love and hatred. Nor would he erect two disciplines, one that marshals human energies to build, another that marshals them to destroy what has been built. (22)

The psychic transformation Montessori sought would deny the romantic militarist's identification of peace with ennui even as it made extinct his flirtation with death (Martin, *Virtues* 37ff).

The domestic spirit that animates the Montessori system precludes application not just of the Romantic militarist label. Romantic anarchism may not glorify death and danger but it too rejects social conventions (Rosenblum 34). In the works of Friedrich Schiller, for instance, "the law of the heart" stands in opposition to legalism. Yet what are Montessori's practical exercises if not training in those societal conventions that children are expected to learn at home? Striving for boundlessness not order, Romantic anarchism also values spontaneity and impulsiveness not predictability (Rosenblum 45). Yet as designed by Montessori those exercises in domesticity impose an external order on the process of learning even as they make predictable how children will act in society at large. Making "faithfulness to feelings the measure of all things" (Rosenblum 45), this brand of Romanticism in addition emphasizes sincerity and authenticity of the self over that self's ties with others. Yet the family model of human relationships the Casa dei Bambini incorporates constitutes a clear rejection of such "narcissistic self-absorption" (Rosenblum 45).

There is more to Romanticism, of course, than the militarist and anarchist aspects Rosenblum discusses. However, even that most central Romantic component—that authentic experience, self-discovery and wholeness derive from the individual's proximity to nature—is contradicted by the Casa dei Bambini. In Romanticism nature is represented by the open countryside: by mountains, rocks, clouds, flowers, trees, waterfalls. Montessori's school, however, is a creature of the city that in Romantic thought stands in opposition to nature. Geographical considerations aside, from the standpoint of Romanticism Montessori makes the grievous error of interposing home and family between child and nature. Granted, for Romantics like Rousseau home and family are natural institutions.[5] Nevertheless, they necessarily mediate one's relationship with nature. View school as home and instead of the direct unmediated fusion of human being and the natural world desired by the Romantic, the primary relationship in education is of one human being to another.

A rereading of the Casa dei Bambini casts doubt, then, on Montessori's credentials as a Romantic theorist of education.[6] Yet she valued the child's freedom and spontaneity as few educational thinkers have. She rejected arbitrary distinctions and boundaries as a good Romantic must. And she saw in the child intimations of the man. As if this were not enough to make one uneasy about withholding the label, there is also the matter of joy, something Romanticism values highly and most educational theorizing ignores. Consider Fisher's description of a Casa dei Bambini child working with buttons on a frame who then succeeds in fastening a button on his own shirt: "When the bone disk finally shone out, round and whole, on the far side of the buttonhole, the child drew a long breath and looked up at me with so ecstatic a face of triumph that I could have shouted, 'Hurrah!'" (14). In the context of the Casa dei Bambini this experience of joy is not at all extraordinary: Fisher cites several more examples of it and Montessori presents it as an integral part of children's learning (*Method*; White).

Needless to say, in a Casa dei Bambini joy tends to be a byproduct of quiet concentration rather than the explicit goal of exuberant exertion. The Montessori system whose domestic spirit has eluded her interpreters' grasp thus demonstrates that peace is not intrinsically joyless and that domesticity need not be boring. Revealing that independence can flourish in an atmosphere of family affection, that a homelike environment does not entail passivity, and that the home's initiation into society's conventions is compatible with individuality and self-expression, this system allows us to recognize the false dichotomies upon which Romanticism rests.

The domesticity of the Montessori spirit makes the characterization of her educational thought as Romantic a contradiction in terms.[7] If, however, one rejects the terms according to which Romanticism defines domesticity, it is possible to see Montessori as a special kind of Romantic thinker. Call Montessori a Romantic pure and simple and the spirit of her system—the domesticity embodied in the Casa dei Bambini—is lost to view. Call her a theorist of domesticity and the Romantic cast of that spirit is suppressed. Call her a Domestic Romantic, however, and her celebration of child and home, freedom and cooperation, personal autonomy and social interdependence, individuality and connection to others, work and play, prosaicness and spontaneity, concentration and joy is illuminated; her refusal to accept arbitrary boundaries is respected; and the significance for our own day of her attempt to redefine not just the terminology of education but the terms according to which our young are educated is brought into focus.

Is Montessori the only Domestic Romantic in the history of educational thought or have there been others? The answer awaits detailed discussion of the roles played by home and family in the philosophies of the likely candidates. Supposing she is until now the sole member of the class however, the category is still worth establishing. That early twentieth-century Italian creation of hers, the Casa dei Bambini, holds so much promise for late twentieth-century America, who can say how many Domestic Romantics the future of educational thought will contain.[8]

Notes

I wish to thank Ann Diller, Barbara Houston, Michael Martin, Beatrice Nelson, Jennifer Radden, and Janet Farrell Smith for their helpful comments on an earlier draft.

1. For accounts of open education see, for example, Featherstone, Nyquist and Hawes, Rathbone, Silberman.

2. Montessori made it clear that in her idealized version of home women were the equals of men. Thus, in the Casa dei Bambini both boys and girls were to carry out these domestic activities.

3. See, for example, Pestalozzi's pedagogical novel *Leonard and Gertrude* and Dewey's *The School and Society*.

4. For a discussion of individualism in Montessori, see Martin (*Virtues*).

5. For critical discussion of this position see Martin (*Conversation*).

6. There are other reasons for doubt too, most notably her scientific approach to education. The question of the adequacy of the Romantic label in the case of Rousseau, Pestalozzi, and Froebel also arises but that discussion must be reserved for another occasion.

7. This is not to say that the lives of those we classify as Romantics did not include domesticity or that domesticity cannot be discerned as a *suppressed* or *repressed* theme in their works.

8. Montessori's invention must of course be adapted to local conditions. It is important, however, that in all contexts a domestic atmosphere be provided in which individuality can flourish lest the practical domestic exercises in which children engage become occasions simply for the imposition of a veneer of middle-class manners and tastes. It is also essential that measures be instituted to allow parents to cooperate with school people in this endeavor. It should be noted that Montessori herself advocated collective ownership of the Casa dei Bambini by parents.

CHAPTER 5

The Contradiction and the Challenge of the Educated Woman

Written with the support of a grant from the Fund for the Improvement of Post-Secondary Education as the Inaugural Lecture of the Project on the Study of Gender and Education, and first presented at Kent State University, November 18, 1988, "The Contradiction and the Challenge of the Educated Woman" led an active pre-publication life. It served as the basis for "Women's Education for the 21st Century," a brief talk I gave in March 1989 at the conference, Restructuring Reality, sponsored by Radcliffe College. I then made it my contribution—in absentia, as it turned out—to the Research Workshop on Knowledge, Gender, Education and Work held at the University of Calgary. This paper was next given in March 1990 as part of a Harvard Graduate School of Education lecture series on Women, Girls, and Education. Then in October of that year I presented it at the International Symposium, "The Construction of Sex/Gender—What is a Feminist Perspective?," sponsored by the Swedish Research Council. Focusing on six themes, that Stockholm meeting brought together women with a wide range of interests from an even wider range of disciplines. As it happened, one of those was the Norwegian sociologist Hildur Ve whose work is referred to, albeit indirectly, in this paper. At the Stockholm conference's conclusion, she and I and the other members of its Education Workshop had the good fortune to travel with our enterprising convenor Inga Elgqvist-Saltzman, herself a leading Swedish scholar, to the University of Umeå for a day long conference on Gender and Education, sponsored by the Departments of Education and History at the University of Umeå. There I read "The Contradiction and the Challenge of the Educated Woman" to an audience of educational researchers and practitioners and later met with a group of Inga Elgqvist-Saltzman's students who shared with me their ongoing research on women and education.

Reprinted from *Revolutions in Knowledge*, edited by Sue Rosenberg Zalk, 1991, by permission of Westview Press, Boulder, Colorado. It has also appeared in *Women's Studies Quarterly*, Vol. XIX, Nos. 1 & 2, Spring/Summer 1991, pp. 6–27.

"Women who read, much more women who write, are, in the existing constitution of things, a contradiction and a disturbing element," wrote John Stuart Mill in 1861.[1] Mill was not the first great Western thinker to perceive that an educated woman is a perplexity. He differed from most of his philosophical colleagues, however, in his diagnosis of the cause of the problem. An ardent supporter of women's equality and a firm believer that women were as deserving of a good education as men, he located the source of the trouble not in nature but in culture. Change the existing constitution of things and educated women will no longer be contradictions and disturbances: that was the thesis of *The Subjection of Women*, the thin eloquent volume, widely read and hotly debated when it was published in 1869, that Bertrand Russell credited with turning him into a "passionate advocate of equality for women" and Freud criticized on the grounds that "Nature has determined women's destiny."[2]

In the century and a quarter or so since Mill penned those words, conditions have changed. The marriage laws he described as despotic have been repealed. The female suffrage he supported has been won. The male monopoly over occupations, arts, and professions has been ended. Furthermore, women now comprise at least 40 percent of all students enrolled in higher education in his country, 50 percent in ours.[3] Has Mill's analysis of an educated woman become irrelevant? Are we contradictions no longer? As for being disturbing elements, are we not these any longer either?

Virginia Woolf eschewed the logical language of contradiction in *Three Guineas*, published in 1938 but begun in 1931, exactly seventy years after Mill wrote *The Subjection of Women*. Yet she too portrayed educated women as disturbing elements—or, rather, as having the capacity to be such. In contrast to Mill, who wanted to overcome women's status as disturbance, however, Woolf considered our power to disturb a virtue. Look at people in the professions, she urged:

> they lose their senses. Sight goes. They have no time to look at pictures. Sound goes. They have no time to listen to music. Speech goes. They have no time for conversation. They lose their sense of proportion—the relations between one thing and another. Humanity goes. Money making becomes so important that they must work by night as well as by day. Health goes. And so competitive do they become that they will not share their work with others though they have more than they can do themselves. What then remains of a human being who has lost sight, sound, and sense of proportion? Only a cripple in a cave.[4]

The cripples she described—"sans teeth, sans eyes, sans taste, sans everything"—are not in that age of man that Shakespeare called "second childishness and mere oblivion." They are educated men. The question Woolf posed in *Three Guineas* is: How can women be educated and enter the professions and yet remain, "civilized human beings; human beings, that is, who wish to prevent war"? (75). Her answer: only by disturbing the existing constitution of things.

Here I want first to explain why Mill was justified in using the language of contradiction and why his analysis is still relevant. I will then turn to Woolf's thesis to see how well it survives the development of twentieth-century feminism.

The Contradiction of the Educated Woman

What makes an educated woman a contradiction? There are so many versions of the argument one scarcely knows which to cite.

"A woman who has a head full of Greek . . . or carries on fundamental controversies about mechanics . . . might as well even have a beard," wrote Immanuel Kant. He added:

> A woman therefore will learn no geometry; of the principle of sufficient reason or the monads she will know only so much as is needed to perceive the salt in a satire . . . . The fair can leave Descartes his vortices to whirl forever without troubling themselves about them. . . . In history they will not fill their heads with battles, nor in geography with fortresses, for it becomes them just as little to reek of gunpowder as it does the males to reek of musk.[5]

The reek of gunpowder is precisely what worries Woolf. But if Kant seems to be confirming Woolf's worst fear, namely that an interest in war is natural to men, it is nevertheless clear from his remarks that he knew that females *could* learn geometry and Greek and *could* understand Leibnitz's and Descartes's philosophies. Kant's point was that, insofar as women did "master" these subjects, we would not be women; we would be men.

Ultimately, the various versions of the claim that an educated woman is a contradiction reduce to this. Beginning with the twin assumptions that to be a female of the human species is to be a woman and to be an educated human being is to be a man, and adding to these the truism that a man is not a woman, the argument leads inexorably to the conclusion that to be an educated female human being is to be and not to be a woman—a contradiction if there ever were one.

At least Kant acknowledged the existence of the living contradictions called educated women. Arthur Schopenhauer seems to have viewed us as physical impossibilities. Women, he said, "are big children all their life long—a kind of intermediate stage between the child and the full-grown man, who is man in the strict sense of the word."[6] Having no sense of justice, a weak reasoning faculty, and an innate tendency to dissimulate as well as being intellectually shortsighted, women in his view could not possibly acquire the rationality, theoretical knowledge and understanding that are the marks of an educated person. If we could, however, we would surely have the status of contradictions: not fully human because of being female, we would be fully human by dint of being educated; or, to put it another way, being women by dint of being female, we would be men, hence not women, because of being educated.

Although Jean-Jacques Rousseau suggested that behind every woman of great talent a man was holding the pen or brush, this thinker who so influenced Kant did not doubt that women could learn philosophy, mathematics, and military history. He warned, however, that if we did we would suffer for it. "A brilliant wife," said Rousseau, "is a plague to her husband, her children, her friends, her valets, everyone. . . . Outside her home she is always ridiculous and very justly criticized." Yet the hardships an educated woman is bound to experience were not his real concern. Like Kant, Rousseau represented her as a violation of nature: "Believe me, judicious mother, do not make a decent man of your daughter, as though you would give nature the lie."[7]

Mill did not for a moment think that a woman who could read and write, let alone do philosophy and mathematics, violated nature. On the contrary, he rejected this idea, saying: "I deny that anyone knows, or can know, the nature of the two sexes, as long as they have only been seen in their present relation to one another" (22). Yet he did not call educated women contradictions simply to remind his readers how others saw them. Mill understood that man and woman are social, psychological, and cultural as well as biological categories and that different cultural and social norms govern the two sexes. Thus, while others were maintaining that Nature with a capital *N* circumscribes women's abilities and prescribes her place in society, Mill insisted that these limits were set by culture. "What is now called the nature of women is an eminently artificial thing—the result of forced repression in some directions, unnatural stimulation in others," he wrote (22). Artificial or natural, so long as education fosters "manly" qualities and these are taken to be the polar opposites of "womanly" ones, educated women will constitute contradictions.

To accommodate educated women—to resolve our contradictory status—Mill wanted to reform society. Rousseau, Kant, and Schopenhauer, on the other hand, would have no accommodations made; cultivate woman's and only woman's qualities in society's daughters, Rousseau in effect told readers of book 5 of *Emile*, and they will be neither disturbances nor living contradictions. We must not think, however, that because Mill's analysis is acute and his heart is in the right place, we should accept unquestioningly his solution to educated women's contradictory status, which was to provide freer access to an education originally designed for boys and men and change cultural attitudes toward our knowing geometry and thinking abstractly. Demanding and fighting for the extension to girls and women of the curriculum studied by the educated men in their midst, over the years most women and men who have believed in women's rights and the equality of the sexes have adopted the first part of Mill's program. Too few, however, have perceived the dilemma for women inherent in the achievement of this goal. Thus, until the advent of women's studies programs in our schools, colleges, and universities, the "degenderization" of the qualities built into our cultural concept of an educated person, by which I mean the detaching of them from our cultural construct of masculinity, has seldom been a designated aim of education, and even now it is rarely acknowledged as such.

Make no mistake. Although there are many more qualities our society considers to be a man's than belong to our conception of an educated person, and although many men by virtue of their race or class have been thought to be lacking in just these dimensions, the traits we take to be the marks of an educated individual are the very ones that Rousseau, Kant, and Schopenhauer assigned to men by nature and that Mill knew were denied us by culture. Rationality, a highly developed capacity for abstract analytic thought, self-government, and independence: these were considered in Mill's England to be "man's qualities"—at least a white, middle- or upper-class man's—hence not "a woman's," and they are still perceived in this way by many in our United States.

I do not for a moment mean to suggest that it was wrong for Mill to want to appropriate for England's daughters the education of its sons. This effort was seen by him, as by its adherents in this country to be a necessary step in ending the subordination of women.[8] We need, however, to understand the framework of assumptions about gender within which this program of appropriation operates, for the conjunction of the two creates people who, as living contradictions, may even today have special educational problems and needs.[9]

Needed: A Gender-Sensitive Ideal of the Educated Person

According to a recent report of the Organization for Economic Cooperation and Development (OECD), in Canada, Finland, France, and the United States women make up at least half of all students enrolled in higher education.[10] In most other industrialized Western countries we make up at least 40 percent. Yet the report cautions against complacency over the status of women in higher education. Recognizing that educational equality is not simply a matter of equal admissions, it notes that more males than females attain top scholarships and postgraduate degrees. It notes too that fields of study are sharply divided by sex. On the face of it, this might seem unobjectionable. Surely the ideal of equality does not require that every subject be taken by equal numbers of males and females. The report makes it clear, however, that the subjects in which females predominate are the very ones in which job opportunities have been severely curtailed in recent years and, moreover, that these fields are presently at risk of being downgraded in academic standing and resources.

Given the fact of equal access to higher education, why does there seem to be marked difference in male and female achievement? Why does the same education for the two sexes not yield the same results? Mill's insight into the genderization of the traits associated with "true" education and the consequent contradictory status of an educated woman is relevant here.

Research in coeducational classrooms and their surrounding environments shows that when what was originally a boy's or young man's education is extended to girls and women and the two sexes are educated together, the educational treatment of the sexes will not necessarily be the same.[11] Furthermore, even when the treatment itself is the same, it is frequently experienced differently. Now I want to stress that different educational treatment of males and females is not in itself suspect. Studies of the coeducational classroom climate are important, not because they have uncovered differences where none were thought to exist, but because the differences uncovered are so damaging to women. When you feel peripheral in class, when your participation is not expected and your contributions are not thought to be important, it will scarcely be surprising if you begin to doubt your own intellectual capacity. Nor will it be surprising if, when your academic achievements are minimized and your career goals are not taken seriously, you lose your self-confidence.

With even the best will in the world it is not easy to achieve identical treatment of males and females in coeducational classrooms.[12] But supposing we could readily achieve it, we must ask ourselves if this should be our goal. The hypothesis that the same education for both sexes will yield the same results rests on the assumption that sex or gender is a difference that makes no difference.[13] By all means let us side with Mill against philosophers such as Rousseau, Kant, and Schopenhauer in extending the duties, tasks, and privileges of citizenship to women. But let us not, therefore, suppose that gender is irrelevant to education. In the first place, people with similar talents who might be expected to perform the same tasks with equal proficiency often learn in different ways, thereby benefiting from different modes of instruction. Furthermore, some start with handicaps having nothing to do with natural aptitude that must be overcome if a given end is to be achieved. In either case it is a mistake to assume that an identical education will yield identical results in all instances.

The question, of course, is whether differences in learning styles and learning readiness are systematically related to gender. To ask this question is not to raise the specter of biological determinism. We who are committed to the ideal of sex equality must remember that whether or not identical results require identical educational treatment is an *empirical* question and that, until the necessary research on gender and learning is done, a healthy skepticism must be maintained toward the postulate that the same societal role requires the same education.

Such skepticism is particularly warranted in light of the literature on the socialization of boys and girls.[14] Treated differently almost from birth and with different expectations held up to them within the family and in the early years of schooling, children become aware at an early age of their culture's distinctions between masculine and feminine roles and of their culture's higher valuation of men and masculine roles. This process of socialization, begun in infancy, continues through childhood and adolescence into adulthood. Would it not be astonishing if it had no consequences for learning?

Given that any acknowledgment of the workings of gender in education is likely to be construed as an acceptance of fixed male and female natures, it is tempting to adopt the strategy of ignoring gender entirely. Yet the phenomenon of *trait genderization* invalidates this tactic. As Mill realized, many qualities are genderized—that is, they are appraised differently by a given culture or society when possessed by males and females.[15] Aggressiveness, for example, is judged in North America, at least, to be a desirable trait for males to possess, but not females. So too, a highly developed capacity for abstract reasoning, a self-control in which feeling and emotion are subordinated to the rule of reason, and an independent spirit are qualities for which men—white, middle-class men, to be precise—are praised and women regarded with suspicion, if not downright disdain.[16] Yet these latter are the very qualities an educated woman is supposed to possess.

In the face of the trait genderization embedded in our culture, the dictum that gender is a difference of no consequence to education loses credibility. If, in order to become truly educated people, those born female must acquire the very "man's qualities" for which they are denigrated, will not this negative evaluation reverberate in the way and the extent to which the trails are acquired? No one who has been moved by Mill's arguments in favor of the education of female reason and self-government could possibly want to seal off women's education from every quality now genderized in favor of males. Yet, in rejecting a gender-bound educational philosophy like Rousseau's, let us not forget what Mill knew, namely that traits and gender are related. And let us not ignore the growing literature that shows gender to be a significant dimension of life in classrooms.

"Educational equality between the sexes is still far from having been realized," the OECD report says. I fear that as long as women's education is designed on the one hand to develop traits genderized in favor of males and on the other to ignore gender differences related to learning, this finding will continue to hold true. In the name of identical educational treatment, girls and women will experience difficulties and suffer hardships our male counterparts will never know. But if identical treatment is untenable—if, indeed, it gives us the illusion of gender-neutrality when in fact it intensifies the problems of becoming an educated woman—what is to be done?

There is an alternative to the dictum that sex is a difference that makes no difference that does not commit us to a regressive two-track educational system based on sex. Joining Mill's insights that traits and gender are connected and that roles and gender are not fixed by nature,[17] we can adopt a gender-sensitive ideal as opposed to either an illusory gender-free one or a vicious gender-bound one. Taking gender into account when it makes a difference and ignoring it when it does not, a gender-sensitive ideal allows educators to build into curricula, instructional methods, and learning environments ways of dealing with trait genderization and the many and various other gender-related phenomena—for example, the portrayal of women in the subject matter of the curriculum—that enter into education today.

In acknowledging gender without making us its prisoners, a gender-sensitive ideal allows us to continue Mill's project of building traits genderized in favor of males into the education of females without victimizing women. It also makes possible Virginia Woolf's more revolutionary and absolutely essential project.

The View from the Bridge

If any single image dominates Woolf's *Three Guineas*, it is a bridge connecting two worlds: private and public, home and professions, women's and men's. Woolf invites us in imagination to see "the educated man's daughter"—this is the woman she was writing about—"as she issues from the shadow of the private house, and starts on the bridge which lies between the old world and the new" (16). She then lays before her male readers "a photograph . . . of your world as it appears to us who see it from the threshold of the private house; . . . from the bridge which connects the private house with the world of public life" (18). Asking how to educate the young to hate war, she has us "turn from our station on the bridge across the Thames to another bridge over another river, this time in one of the great universities. Once more, how strange it looks, this world of domes and spires, of lecture rooms and laboratories, from our vantage point! How different it must look to you!" (23). Finally, calling us back to the bridge over the Thames, she tells us to "fix our eyes upon the procession—the procession of sons of educated men" (60). "There they go," Woolf says,

> our brothers who have been educated in public schools and universities, mounting those steps, passing in and out of those doors, ascending those pulpits, preaching, teaching, administering justice, practising medicine, transacting business, making money. It is a solemn sight always. . . . But now, for the past twenty years or so, it is no longer a sight merely, a photograph, or fresco scrawled upon the walls of time, at which we can look with merely an esthetic appreciation. For there, traipsing along at the tail end of the procession, we go ourselves. (60–61)

Watching this procession march into the city and speaking this time to her female readers, she says: "We have to ask ourselves, here and now, do we wish to join the procession, or don't we? On what terms shall we join the procession? Above all, where is it leading us, the procession of educated men?" (62). Her answer takes the form of more questions. Insisting that the professions make those who practice them "possessive, jealous of any infringement of their rights, and highly combative if anyone dares dispute them," Woolf asks:

> Are we not right then in thinking that if we enter the same professions we shall acquire the same qualities? And do not such qualities lead to war? In another century or so if we practise the professions in the same way, shall we not be just as possessive, just as jealous, just as pugnacious, just as positive as to the verdict of God, Nature, Law and Property as these gentlemen are now? (66)

Woolf's eye for the vanities of dress and distinctions of rank in the then male bastions of the bar, the church, the stock exchange, the civil service, medicine, and publishing was merciless. Her perceptions of the connection between these professions and war chill the blood. Yet despite the fact that she has been called a "separatist,"[18] she does not answer her own question by telling women to keep out for she perceives that the daughters of educated men "are between the devil and the deep sea": "Behind us lies the patriarchal system; the private house, with its nullity, its immorality, its hypocrisy, its servility. Before us lies the public world, the professional system, with its possessiveness, its jealousy, its pugnacity, its greed" (74). "Had we not better plunge off the bridge in to the river; give up the game; declare that the whole of human life is a mistake and so end it?" asks Woolf, who three years after the publication of *Three Guineas* took her own life by walking into the water. No, she says, there is another course open.

From reading biographies of educated women who had entered the public world and managed to remain civilized, Woolf had discovered that what Florence Nightingale and the others all shared was instruction from teachers their brothers never knew. Poverty, chastity, derision, and freedom from unreal loyalties, she calls them—not pretty names, but she tempers their impact by redefining their scope. Rather than being destitution, *poverty* is "enough money to live upon. . . . But no more. Not a penny more." *Chastity* does not refer to sexual abstinence but means "when you have made enough to live on by your profession you must refuse to sell your brain for the sake of money." *Derision*—she admits it is a bad word for what she has in mind—means that "you must refuse all methods of advertising merit, and hold that ridicule, obscurity and censure are preferable, for psychological reasons, to fame and praise." And freedom from unreal loyalties means that "you must rid yourself of pride of nationality in the first place; also of religious pride, college pride, school pride, family pride, sex pride and the unreal loyalties that spring from them." Agree to live by these terms and one other, namely "that you help all properly qualified people, of whatever sex, class or colour, to enter your profession" (80), Woolf says to women, and "you can join the professions and yet remain uncontaminated by them; you can rid them of their possessiveness, their jealousy, their pugnacity, their greed. You can use them to have a mind of your own and a will of your own. And you can use that mind and will to abolish the inhumanity, the beastliness, the horror, the folly of war" (83).

Mill was the one who said that women who read and write are a disturbing element as well as a contradiction, but he did not think women disrupted the social order. Rousseau did. He feared that if a woman were a scholar or accountant, a soldier or diplomat, she would perform her "woman's duties" badly or, worse still, neglect them altogether. G.W.F. Hegel, one of Rousseau's direct descendants, went so far as to say that "when women hold the helm of government, the State is at once in jeopardy."[19] Schopenhauer, in turn, wondered if the influence of women on the French court and government did not hasten the Revolution. Like these traditionalists, Woolf sees educated women—at least those of us trained by her four teachers—as bearers of disorder. But she invests our power to disarrange the existing constitution of things with positive value.

In the last scene of the play *Wild Honey*, Anton Chekhov has Anna Petrovna say: "It's terrible to be an educated woman. An educated woman with nothing to do. What am I here for? Why am I alive? . . . They should make me a professor somewhere, or a director of something . . . If I were a diplomat I'd turn the whole world upside down . . . An educated woman. . . . And nothing to do. So I'm no use. Horses, cows, dogs— they all have their uses. Not me, though. I'm irrelevant."[20] Her self-revelation is painful, not the least because through the play's action the audience has come to know Anna Petrovna as the linchpin of the small society gathered on her decaying estate. Occupied not only in trying to save the family home from its creditors but in soothing tempers and mending fractured relationships, she is surely the least idle, least irrelevant of the play's many characters. What matters, however, is Anna Petrovna's view of herself: her feelings of failure, her sense of despair, her perception of the mismatch between the life for which her education prepared her and the one she had actually to live— and also her momentary vision of what she might have accomplished.

Anna Petrovna's dream of herself as a diplomat who would turn the whole world upside down is Virginia Woolf's for educated women as a group. With respect to war the Woolf of *Three Guineas* is indeed a separatist: have nothing at all to do with it, she tells women. But with respect to the professions she is not. She would have us join the procession across the bridge and enter the city of professions *on condition that in so doing we remake man's culture.*

The City on the Hillside

Just over fifty years have elapsed since Woolf bid women stand on the bridge. Does man's culture still need to be remade? In the United States violence at home and in our public spaces is rife. In the world at large war has become even more deadly than Woolf knew it to be. And besides the promise of quick destruction to all living creatures of the nuclear peril born of that war whose end Woolf did not wait to see, we now face the equally grave—possibly far graver—danger of a slow, lingering, planetary death brought on by the human species' arrogant disregard for its earthly surroundings.

Have educated women become "Just as possessive, just as jealous, just as pugnacious, just as positive as to the verdict of God, Nature, Law and Property" as Woolf said professional men were in half the predicted time? Or, remaining civilized human beings, are we the disturbing elements that Woolf wanted us to be and our own upside down world so sorely needs? Come stand on the bridge with me and watch the procession circa 1990.

Look at all those women! They are not just traipsing along at the end as they were in the 1930s. See the ones marching at the head. They are as solemn as the men and seem almost as confident. True, they do not walk as freely. Is that because their gray suits have skirts, not trousers, and their heels are high? And what do you suppose is wrong with the woman over there? She appears to be distraught. You say her child is sick? that she is wondering how to sandwich in a trip to the doctor between clients? But Woolf led us to understand that the daughters and sisters of educated men had the choice of staying in the private, patriarchal home to practice the unpaid professions of marriage and mothering or entering the uncivilized, patriarchal public world to practice the paid professions of the bar and the stock exchange. This woman seems to be practicing both kinds of professions at once. What has happened in these fifty years to nullify Woolf's either-or analysis? And what is happening to the woman with the sick child? She seems to be having trouble keeping up with the men now that the procession has crossed the bridge.

Woolf did not tell us that the city of professions is built on a hillside. She did not say that the doors opening into law, medicine, politics, engineering, banking, and investment are situated on the heights and that the climb is steep. As the procession turns up the high road, you can see some women still walking briskly, but others are stumbling—nay, faltering. Surely their skirts are too narrow, their shoes too tight, and their minds too occupied by home.

Woolf knew that for every person in the procession she watched, except perhaps those few women traipsing behind, there was someone at home practicing the unpaid professions. Today those "someones" have joined the procession. The daughters, sisters, wives, and mothers of well-educated men, somewhat-educated men, poorly educated men, and uneducated men all walk across the bridge each morning into the paid professions or paid work of some kind. Whether by choice, circumstance, necessity, or some combination of the three, most walk back again into the unpaid ones.

But look now at those stragglers on the high road. Not the breathless women but the smiling, incongruously dressed ones who stop along the way to admire the view. They are actually passing the stumblers and, together with their no-nonsense gray-suited sisters, are approaching the entrances to the professions. Not one of those doors is opening automatically when a woman nears! Still, give a strong push and the doors do open; indeed, women are going in and out as if they belong.

Does this mean that men's culture is being turned upside down, which is to say rightside up? Is politics becoming less competitive, the law less pugnacious, banking less acquisitive? Not to my knowledge. Yet some small changes are occurring. That woman in the flowing dress now entering the door marked Medicine has just created a center for victims of violence at the city hospital. The research of the one in the full skirt who is just now opening the academy's portals is shaking the foundations of psychology. That prize-winning novelist is changing the face of African-American studies. The biologist wearing overalls whose corn grows in the field over there is making her colleagues rethink both their theories and their methodologies. The actress walking through the stage door donates her earnings to a black women's college. That law professor is actively trying to change the legal system's understanding of pornography. That scientist is running her laboratory in an egalitarian manner. If Florence Nightingale "left the world better than she found it,"[21] if on our side of the deep sea Alice Hamilton, Jane Addams, Crystal Eastman, and Helen Thompson Woolley did likewise, today professional women of all races and ethnicities are also acting out Anna Petrovna's dream of turning at least their own small portions of the world upside down. Not all, probably not even a majority—possibly only a determined few. But at least that many.

Woolf might not call those women in the gray suits who are entering the doors of the professions contradictions, but, by her own analysis, those of us who would rather adapt than disturb are just that. Given still existing conceptions of masculinity and femininity, in acquiring the "manly" qualities of competitiveness, jealousy, pugnacity, and possessiveness, yet being female human beings, these professionals are both women and not women. The contradictory nature of their position explains many of the problems they confront on the job and at home and is also reflected in such mundane matters as their decisions about dress; their uncertainty about whom to model their speech and behavior on in the university classroom, the courtroom, the boardroom, and the operating room; and, of course, pronouncements such as the one by a *Boston Globe* music critic, who said of the director of a renowned British ensemble touring American concert halls: "Brown is a first-rate violinist. And just like Olympic gold medalist Florence Griffith-Joyner, the strikingly lovely Brown is a woman who knows one can be both a champion in your field and triumphantly feminine. In the first half of the concert, she wore an elegant dark formal gown. In the second half for the concerto, she wore a springtime dress of dazzling white."[22]

Is it easier nonetheless to adjust within the professions than to be disturbing elements? Possibly, but the course Woolf would have us reject takes it toll. It is hard, very hard, to be a living contradiction every minute and hour of every working day and night: the psychic costs are enormous, and the threat of ridicule is ever present. Of course, for the women who refuse to or do not know how to fit in—the ones who remain relatively uncompetitive, unjealous, unpugnacious, and unacquisitive women—derision is not a threat but a fact of life. "Just an old bag who'd been hanging around Cold Spring Harbor for years" is what a famous biologist called Nobel scientist Barbara McClintock.[23] Most disturbing elements are schooled also in poverty and chastity.

But lest we take the burdens of being disturbances too much to heart, let us look again at the procession. What are those stumblers doing as our precious few try to disturb the existing constitution of things and their sisters attempt to adapt to it? Can they be walking back down the hill? Are they giving up and going home? No, few of them can afford to. They are joining that second, much bigger wave of women now spilling off the bridge and onto the low road, the one less traveled by men.

Woolf did not tell us that across the bridge two roads diverge. She did not say that fifty years later the choice for educated women, if *choice* is the right word for what so often is far from being voluntary, would be between walking up to the "male" professions on the heights or down to the "female" ones. See those doors marked Teaching, Nursing, Social Work? She did not say that women's options would consist of two kinds of paid professions, one high and the other low. Nor did she perhaps anticipate that the great majority would pick the "female" ones.

How astonishing that, when women cross the bridge, relatively few follow the men up the hill! Are the doors on the heights too heavy for the rest to open, or have those women taking the road less traveled by men never even wanted to be professors, directors, or diplomats? Has the fear of being judged unnatural prevented them from ever imagining themselves heading a bank or embassy, or did their self-confidence wane during their school and college years until they no longer trusted their own abilities to survive as living contradictions? Perhaps the reason is simply that they see no way of combining the professions on the heights with the unpaid ones they want to practice. Maybe these women truly want to help others.

Whatever the explanation of the unequal distribution of women in the two kinds of paid professions, Woolf would be interested to know that those entering the doors of the "female" professions, otherwise known as the "caring" professions, need take no special vows of poverty, chastity, and derision. These stern task mistresses rule the lowlands. Wages here are perhaps enough to live on by oneself, but they are not a penny more, not even for single mothers. You need not refuse to sell your brain for the sake of money for no money is ever offered you; as for fame and praise, they reside on the heights.

Will these educated women fulfill Anna Petrovna's dream of turning the world upside down? Working on both sides of the bridge in what amounts to a double shift, engaged in the unpaid and low-paid professions that they and their culture devalue, they are perhaps more likely to replicate her feelings of irrelevance and her sense of

being a failure. Sharing her culture's valuation of the domestic activities she performed on her estate, Anna Petrovna did not count them as real work. Hence her
frustration and unhappiness. Today, the professions that impose poverty, chastity,
and derision on their practitioners comprise activities and processes analogous to the
ones performed at home by Chekhov's heroine. It is no accident that they are alternately called "the caring professions" and "women's professions." They involve the
selfsame activities and processes that our culture used to place in the private home
and assign to women. Although they have been transported into the public world,
they stand to the "male" occupations that Woolf was discussing in much the same
relation as the domestic occupations Anna Petrovna performed on her estate stood
to the ones of professor, director, and diplomat that she wished she had been allowed
to undertake in the public world.

The Challenges for Educated Women

Standing on the bridge, it is just possible to see a few women and men in the lowlands packing up their belongings. The cries of the people on the heights leave no
doubt as to what is happening. "Join us up here you teachers, nurses, and social workers," they shout. "Not just for a visit. Come to stay. Forswear poverty, chastity, and
derision forever. Come right now. We have ropes you can use to scale the rocks. Let
us throw them down to you."

In response, more and more people are trying to drag their possessions lock, stock,
and barrel up the face of the cliff. In view of our culture's devaluation of the caring
professions, in view of the denigration that teachers, nurses, and social workers experience, who can blame them for trying to reach higher ground, even if by such an
improbable route? Yet where prestige, fame, and money dwell can competition, jealousy, pugnacity, and possessiveness be far behind? I ask because, as long as they are
under the sway of three of Woolf's teachers, those who take the low road into the city
of professions tend by default, if not by choice, to hold on to their senses. True, from
the points of view of their professions, these civilized teachers, nurses, social workers
are not disturbing elements in Woolf's sense. How can they be when the "female" professions have not for the most part partaken of the war-related qualities possessed by
the "male" professions Woolf had in mind? Nor do these women fulfill Anna Petrovna's
ambition of turning the world upside down. Given the cultural devaluation of their
occupations, they cannot. Many, many, however, succeed in the more modest ambition of making the world a better place by helping the young, the poor, the sick, the
feeble, and the elderly.

Listen now and you can hear some of these women warn the ones headed for the
heights that upon reaching their destination this modest ambition may have to be for-
sworn. You can hear them protest that care cannot be nourished in a competitive
environment; that the young, the poor, the sick, the feeble, and the elderly cannot
obtain the help they need where acquisitiveness and pugnaciousness prevail. If I am

not mistaken, these women are giving voice to Woolf's fear that with professionalization comes decivilization. In the past her anxiety may not have seemed to apply to the "caring" professions. Now, with the pressure mounting for their practitioners to become "genuine" professionals, the risk of losing one's senses also rises. But, whereas Woolf's advice to the women walking off the bridge onto the high road matched Anna Petrovna's dream of turning the world upside down, it translates differently for women in the "caring" professions. Were she still alive, Woolf might well say: "You too must be disturbances for, although your professions are not yet standing on their heads, they are listing dangerously. In your case, therefore, to disturb means both preventing your occupations from being turned upside down and pushing them back into the upright positions that they have long since abandoned."

But Woolf is not alive. She cannot see today's procession move across the bridge and into the city on the hillside, and we cannot ask her if the poverty, chastity, and derision she prescribed are dangerous to women. We must ask ourselves, however, if those who have traditionally been cast in the role of self-sacrificer should really be expected to forgo the personal rewards that "genuine" professions offer when, after long and arduous struggles, they finally manage to cross the bridge.

Woolf was keenly aware and sharply critical of the different wages paid to men and women. She also knew full well the costs to women of the sacrifice of self that was so often the price of helping others. She did not say, but she might have—nay, she should have—that one challenge facing educated women who enter the "caring" professions is how to hold on to their senses, how to keep their fields and themselves civilized without being trapped in the stereotypical female role of self-sacrificer or even victim. She might have also said that another challenge is how to temper the three Cs of care, concern, and connection that are absolutely essential to the sound practice of their professions with reason and critical analysis so that they do not lapse into a well-meaning but ineffectual sentimentality.

Woolf certainly knew that educated women at the heights face opposite problems. As she perceived so clearly, their first challenge is how to live in the realm of fame, money, prestige, and power without being corrupted. But an equally compelling one is how to temper the rationality, critical thinking, and self-governance that are the marks of a "genuine" professional with the care, concern, and connection that are absolutely essential to turning both the professions and the world around. Focusing on the "manliness" of the war-related qualities that govern "men's" professions, Woolf ignored what she knew to be the manliness of the reason, critical thinking, self-sufficiency, and self-governance that are supposed to characterize educated people from whose ranks "genuine" professionals are drawn. Dwelling on what she took to be the evils for society of women becoming competitive, jealous, pugnacious, and possessive as soon as they crossed the bridge, she neglected the perils inhering in the separation of mind from body, thought from action, reason from feeling and emotion, and self from other that are built into our genderized definition of an educated person.[24]

Remarkably, those disturbing elements, those unsolemn women on the high road, those women who refuse to adapt, somehow divest themselves of the "manly" forms of rationality and personal autonomy they learned in school—or did they manage never to "master" these in the first place? Holding on to their senses and their humanity as they practice their professions, they defy established codes by joining reason to passion and harnessing knowledge to the three Cs. If they are disturbances, they are also pioneers who, on a daily basis, are developing new ways to think and work in their chosen fields. Some women in the lowlands are pioneers too. Remaining free from an unreal loyalty to professionalization, they refuse to distance themselves from the interests and needs of their students, patients, and clients. Making these interests and needs their own, they seek ways of linking impersonal knowledge to action and abstract theory to concrete practice.

But those few intrepid women at the heights and in the lowlands should not have to figure out, each for herself and every generation anew, how to bring together the qualities education and the professions tear asunder. It is too much for us to ask, too great a burden for them to bear, too difficult a task to undertake alone.

A short time ago I invited you to stand on the bridge with me to watch the procession. I see now that as educators—as school teachers, teachers of teachers, and educational researchers—we must not linger here. There is too much work to be done in the city on the hillside.

The Challenges for Educators

Even as educated women face challenges themselves, they pose new ones for educators. First and foremost is how to make the knowledge that allows a woman to engage in a profession and remain civilized part and parcel of the education of all so that succeeding generations of educated women will find it easier than ours has to fulfill Anna Petrovna's dream. Another is how to counteract the hidden curriculum of school and society that teaches all of us that the "caring" professions, including school teaching, belong in the lowlands.

Far-reaching changes are required if the former challenge is to be met, for those pioneer women who meet it accomplish the impossible. Transforming themselves from living contradictions—females possessing the "manly" qualities—into people who transcend male as well as female stereotypes, they fuse qualities that some of our greatest philosophers have assured us are incompatible and, as they are presently defined, certainly do resist combination. Following Rousseau and Kant, we build disconnection from others and from our own feelings and emotions into our very concepts of rationality and autonomy and the suspension of critical thought into our ideas of care, concern, and connection, thus making it impossible for a person to exhibit both sorts of qualities simultaneously. Human chameleons and split personalities can prosper under this scheme, for it is possible to be rational at one moment and caring the next. The pioneers in the city on the hillside, however, do not turn their caring and their reason on and off. They exhibit both continuously.

With all the talk today about thinking about thinking, educators need to begin to think about these women. They need to make them their data, not in order to objectify them but to learn from their example how and what to teach our young. Teachers and the teachers of teachers cannot afford, however, to sit back placidly to await the results of that research. While the philosophers in our midst study these pioneers in order to redefine and in the process degenderize rationality and autonomous judgment and also the three Cs of care, concern, and connection; while the educational theorists determine how, in light of these women's lives and work, to do what Mill never dreamed of, namely reconstruct our culture's conception of an educated person so as to include the three Cs; while experts in the various teaching areas figure out how to map onto their respective subject matters the "ansvars retionalitet"—the "caring rationality," or perhaps one should call it the "responsive rationality"[25]—our pioneer women exhibit; while the curriculum specialists redesign the many programs focusing on decision making that now assume a sharp separation of the so-called manly and womanly qualities and honor only the former,[26] let us begin to make those women who have been or now are disturbing elements in Woolf's positive sense vivid presences in the schools, colleges, and university curricula.

Quite apart from the fact that we do not yet fully understand how they did it a century ago, or do it now, it is a significant challenge because the facts contradict the stereotypes that still prevail. As a case in point, Florence Nightingale was not so much a Lady with a Lamp as a woman who, reorganizing hospitals from top to bottom in the Crimean War, performed the function of "an administrative chief."[27] Once back in England she set out in an eight hundred-page document "vast principles of far reaching reform," which provided the basis for a Royal Commission report that for decades remained "the leading authority on the medical administration of armies."[28] Let us fill our classrooms with Nightingale and her sisters, both historical and contemporary, not in the capacity of role models or exemplars but as examples of women who in their lives and work have brought together and in the process transmuted the "manly" qualities of rationality, critical thinking, and autonomous action and the "womanly" ones of care, concern, connection, nurturance, and love.

Scholars who seek to transform the curriculum by integrating women into it have called the introduction of exceptional women a first stage in a complex process and an elitist stage at that.[29] But the challenge is not to show the world that women have made their marks on history. It is to provide students with alternative modes of thinking, perceiving, acting, feeling, and existing in relation to others so that educated women can carry out Anna Petrovna's dream without having to reinvent for themselves the minutest details of daily life. When the examples are drawn from the entire population rather than a privileged segment of it—when they include black, Hispanic, and Asian as well as white women; poor as well as rich women; lesbian as well as heterosexual women; old and young women; married and single women; mothers without partners and women without children—the project of giving Woolf's disturbing elements a central place in the curriculum takes on a new validity.

Of course, examples are not enough. Practice is also required. And, of course, to meet the first challenge to educators our ideal of the educated person will have to be restructured. Since that ideal is linked tightly to the function our culture attributes to education of carrying out society's "productive" processes—by which I mean not just its economic but its political, social, and cultural ones as well—rather than its "reproductive" ones, and I define these broadly to include the rearing of children, caring for the sick, and tending to the needs of family members: the fundamental premise upon which our whole educational system rests will also have to be rethought.[30] "Far-reaching changes" did I say? That is an understatement.

I spoke earlier of the importance of being sensitive to gender. Unless we take to heart the genderization of the attributes both included in and excluded from our present ideal, I do not think we can make the changes we must. Nor can we expect cultural attitudes toward the "caring" professions to change if we ignore the fact that they are also called "female."

In failing to acknowledge that the services provided by teaching, nursing, and social work constitute some of the central reproductive processes of society and that in our culture these have traditionally been considered women's responsibilities, one remains blind to the value hierarchy that situates the "caring" professions in the lowlands and keeps them there. How many today would try to turn them into "genuine" professions without admitting that *genuine* means "male" and without ever quite saying that in the process the three Cs of care, concern, and connection will be replaced by the so-called virtues of distance, objectivity, and efficiency! Be gender-*in*sensitive, and, given the cultural value hierarchy that places male above female and society's productive processes above its reproductive ones, one should not be surprised if, in the course of that move to the top of the hill, the nurturant activity at the heart of each "caring" profession is sacrificed.

The second educational challenge—how to keep the "caring" professions *caring* without their practitioners having to sacrifice themselves in the manner of Anna Petrovna on her estate—is not education's alone. Yet educators can raise the offending value hierarchy to consciousness. They can try to counteract schooling's contribution to the devaluation and denigration of women and of the positive functions and traits that have been assigned to us historically. They can think anew with their students about the significance of society's reproductive processes. As Woolf would remind us, however, the goal is not to turn the value hierarchy upside down. Our challenge is not how to move the "female" professions up to the heights while banishing the "male" ones to the lowlands. It is to find a middle ground where hierarchy vanishes: a large, open, inviting area midway up the hillside where the importance of society's reproductive processes is recognized; where women, and men too, can practice the "caring" professions without having to become uncivilized; and where the professions now called genuine can be as "caring" as those whose legitimacy is now denied.

Conclusion

Mill's program for educating women had two parts: that women be given access to men's education and that society's practices and attitudes be changed so that women who read and write and do history, philosophy, and mathematics will not be viewed as contradictions. In *Three Guineas* Woolf, for whom *The Subjection of Women* was required reading,[31] warns against the first of these. Beware of men's education and the professions for which it prepares them, she says. They lead to war. I am oversimplifying what is perhaps an oversimplified analysis of the roots of war. Yet Woolf is one of the few outspoken figures in our past who believed in women's equality and also, for good reason, had qualms about men's education. If she does not quite do justice to Mill's insight that women who cross the bridge are already living contradictions, she more than compensates for this by the attention she pays us as disturbing elements in the existing constitution of things. Prescribing a regimen of resistance and reform, she casts us as agents of change in a culture attached to war. Making our capacity to be disturbances a virtue possessing moral, political, and social significance, and demanding that we act it out on a public stage, she implicitly suggests that the way for us to overcome our contradictory status is for each in her own way to turn Anna Petrovna's dream into a reality.

Notes

1. John Stuart Mill, *The Subjection of Women*, ed. Wendell Robert Carr (1869; reprint, Cambridge, Mass.: MIT Press, 1970), p. 29. In his introduction to the 1990 edition, Carr gives 1861 as the date (p. vi); the book was published in 1869. References to this edition will henceforth appear in parentheses in the text.

2. Carr, introduction to Mill, *Subjection of Women*, p. xxi.

3. "Women Account for Half of College Enrollment in U.S., Three Other Nations," *Chronicle of Higher Education* (September 17, 1986).

4. Virginia Woolf, *Three Guineas* (New York: Harcourt Brace Jovanovich, 1938), p. 72. References to this work will henceforth appear in parentheses in the text.

5. Immanual Kant, "Of the Distinction of the Beautiful and Sublime in the Interrelations of the Two Sexes," in *Philosophy of Woman*, ed. Mary Briody Mahowald, 2d ed. (Indianapolis: Hackett Publishing, 1983), pp. 194–95.

6. Arnold Schopenhauer, "On Women," in *Philosophy of Woman*, ed. Mahowald, p. 229.

7. Jean-Jacques Rousseau, *Emile*, trans. Allan Bloom (New York: Basic Books, 1979), pp. 309–364.

8. In using the word *appropriating* I definitely do not mean to imply that women did not actively work and struggle to obtain this education.

9. The material from here to the end of the next section follows closely Jane Roland Martin, "The Contradiction of the Educated Woman," *Forum for Honors 17* (Spring 1987): pp. 6–12.

10. "Women Account for Half of College Enrollment."

11. Roberta M. Hall and Bernice Sandler, "The Classroom Climate: A Chilly One for Women?" (Washington, D.C.: Project on the Status and Education of Women, 1982); "Out of the

Classroom: A Chilly Campus Climate for Women?" (Washington, D.C.: Project on the Status and Education of Women, 1984). Dale Spender, *Invisible Women* (London: Writers and Readers Publishing Cooperative Society, 1982).

12. Spender, *Invisible Women.*

13. For a discussion of Plato as the source of this hypothesis, see Jane Roland Martin, *Reclaiming a Conversation* (New Haven, Conn.: Yale University Press, 1985), Ch. 2.

14. Alexandra G. Kaplan and Mary Anne Sedney, *Psychology and Sex Roles: An Androgynous Perspective* (Boston: Little, Brown, 1980); Rosemary Deem, *Women and Schooling* (London: Routledge and Kegan Paul, 1978); Nancy Frazier and Myra Sadker, *Sexism in School and Society* (New York: Harper and Row, 1972); Ann Oakley, *Sex, Gender and Society* (New York: Harper and Row, 1972).

15. Elizabeth Beardsley, "Traits and Genderization," in *Feminism and Philosophy*, ed. Mary Vetterling-Braggin et al. (Totowa, N.J.: Littlefield, 1977), pp. 117–23. Beardsley uses the term *genderization* to refer to language. I use it to refer to the traits themselves.

16. See, for example, I.K. Broverman, S.R. Vogel, D.M. Broverman, and F.E. and P.S. Rosenkrantz, "Sex Role Stereotypes: A Current Appraisal," *Journal of Social Issues 38* (1972): pp. 59–78.

17. For further development of this idea, see Martin, *Reclaiming a Conversation*, Ch. 7.

18. Alex Zwerdling, *Virginia Woolf and the Real World* (Berkeley: University of California Press, 1986), p. 240.

19. Patricia Jagentowicz Mills, "Hegel and 'The Woman Question': Recognition and Intersubjectivity," in *The Sexism of Social and Political Theory*, ed. Lorenne M.G. Clark and Lynda Lange (Toronto: University of Toronto Press, 1979), p. 94.

20. Anton Chekhov, *Wild Honey*, trans. and adapted by Michael Frayn (London: Methuen, 1984), p. 95.

21. Carolyn Heilbrun, *Toward a Recognition of Androgyny* (New York: Alfred A. Knopf, 1973), p. 138.

22. Anthony Tommasini, *Boston Globe*, October 8, 1988, p. 16.

23. Evelyn Fox Keller, *A Feeling for the Organism* (San Francisco: W.H. Freeman, 1983), p. 141.

24. For further discussion of these separations, see Martin, *Reclaiming a Conversation*, esp. Ch. 7.

25. I borrow this Danish phrase from Kirsten Reisby, who in turn credits Hildur Ve. According to Reisby, *ansvars* can be translated in English as either "caring" or "responsibility." She prefers "responsibility," and I am taking the liberty here of going one step further and interpreting responsibility as responsiveness.

26. For a discussion of programs in moral education having this focus, see Jane Roland Martin, "Transforming Moral Education," *The Journal of Moral Education 16* (October, 1987): pp. 204–13.

27. Lytton Strachey, *Eminent Victorians* (London: Chatto and Windus, 1918), p. 135; cf. Heilbrun, *Toward a Recognition of Androgyny*, pp. 138–42.

28. Strachey, *Eminent Victorians*, p. 157.

29. Peggy McIntosh, "Interactive Phases of Curricular Revision: A Feminist Perspective," Working Paper 124, Wellesley College, Center for Research on Women, 1983; cf. Marilyn R. Schuster and Susan R. Van Dyne, Stages of Curriculum Transformation," *Women's Place in the Academy* (Totowa, N.J.: Roman and Allanheld, 1985).

30. For a fuller discussion of this point, see Martin, *Reclaiming a Conversation*.

31. Zwerdling, *Virginia Woolf*, pp. 211–12.

CHAPTER 6

A Professorship and an Office of One's Own

I can think of no more fitting conclusion to a set of essays on the entrance of women into the educational landscape than the paper I wrote for a symposium that Maxine Greene, Nel Noddings, and I took part in at the 1991 meeting of the Philosophy of Education Society. Although I accepted the invitation to participate with alacrity, our assigned topic—"Women Doing Philosophy of Education"—and the fact that it was the Society's fiftieth anniversary gave me pause. I was delighted that there were now enough women in the field to make the event possible yet deeply troubled that such a symposium was needed. "A Professorship and an Office of One's Own," the one unpublished paper included in this collection, represented my way of saying that the panel's very existence signified our still anomalous status.

As a footnote to this essay, I would like to report that Lamont's Market has since closed down. With the publication of Anne Olivier Bell's abridged version of Virginia Woolf's diaries, I have also learned that on March 8, 1941—that would be exactly fifty years before the Washington D.C. symposium and only a matter of weeks before her death—Woolf wrote, "Now to cook the haddock."

I. Leaving Home

When you asked me to participate in a symposium on women doing philosophy of education, I sat down in the room of my own to ponder what the words meant. They might mean a few remarks about Maria Edgeworth; some more about Mary Wollstonecraft; a tribute to Maria Montessori and a sketch of the Casa dei Bambini; a respectful allusion to Emily Davies. But would I then be done? In October 1928 Virginia Woolf did not have to make the case that Jane Austen, the Brontes, George Eliot wrote fiction. In March 1991 members of this Society would be quick to tell me that philosophy of education is a different cup of tea. I thought about having to prove to you that Maria Montessori engaged in the specialty of this house. I thought about spelling out for all to see general criteria for doing philosophy of education—and for being a philosopher of education—and then bringing the three Marys into court to testify in their own behalfs. But I soon saw a fatal drawback. Before they took the witness stand I would have to step up to the bench and present my own qualifications for pleading their cases. You see the difficulty, I am sure. It is not just that each step in the judicial process would be a step away from what had seemed a straightforward narrative task. To rehabilitate these women from the dust-bin of history the Society would first have to agree on what philosophy of education *is*. I do not think it can do this. I do not even think it *should*.

But reading again the invitation I had tucked neatly away in a folder, the words seemed to mean something different. On second sight, "Women Doing Philosophy of Education" might mean how women *do* philosophy of education. You might have had in mind a lecture about our ways of philosophizing in contrast to men's: do we think about education differently? do we argue our points differently? do we analyze and criticize differently? do we analyze and criticize *at all*? I confess that the longer I considered this topic, the more qualms I had. When I thought that I would have to discover which women have done philosophy of education in the past and who is doing it now, and that I would have to accompany each of them to court, I shrank from the task. Besides, it is so large and complicated a topic and there is so little data to go on that, even if the judicial system could be by-passed, I doubted I could come up with the "nugget of pure truth" that Woolf said is "the first duty of a lecturer" (Woolf 1928:3). Knowing that some members of this Society consider talk of women's difference retrograde, I was not sure in any case that my positive conclusions—were I to reach any—would be well-received. I also wondered how I could presume to address a jury of my peers on this topic. Imagining myself saying to you that when a woman does philosophy of education she does thus and so, I could hear the post-modernist murmur—which women does *a woman* represent? when did *she* live? in what country was *she* born? what color is *she*? where do *you*—that is to say I—stand when I speak about her? and who am *I*, anyway?

The chorus of disapproval drove me out of the house. As I headed down the hill toward the bridge that links our small neighborhood to what Woolf called the city of professions, I found myself envying her. I thought how lucky she was to have an audience that agreed with her that Austen and the rest wrote fiction and that did not reprimand her for talking about women. Were I to speak about "us" without first modifying my nouns, qualifying my main clauses, tempering my conclusions, I could expect trouble. I envied Woolf her escape from another kind of trouble too. Only women came to hear what she had to say about women and fiction. I, in contrast, would be addressing a "mixed" audience.

In January 1991 a *Boston Globe* article reported, "Social psychologists now have hard evidence for what many working women already know: If you want to wield influence in a man's world, you have to play dumb." The *Globe* went on to say:

> A new study has found that men are much more likely to have their minds changed by women who speak in a tentative, self-deprecating manner than by women who

sound like they know what they're talking about.

The same study also found that while men are threatened by assertive women, other women prefer them. Women, in fact, are more likely to be swayed by women who speak directly than by those who start their sentences by saying 'I really don't know much about this but . . . ' (Bass 1991).

You can see why I considered Woolf fortunate. Linda Carli, the psychologist who conducted the study, put it well when she said, "It's kind of sad." In some contexts, she added—and I trust I am being neither too self-deprecating nor too assertive when I say that this may be one of them—"women are damned if they do and damned if they don't. If you're trying to reach an audience of both men and women, you're really in trouble."

Envy aside, here was I, walking down an Auburndale street on one of those sunny September days that lifts New Englanders out of the doldrums, struggling with temptation. The invitation to autobiography was practically irresistible. I saw myself starting today's talk by answering the question Carol Gilligan and her associates (Gilligan 1982) used in their first interviews: "How would you describe yourself to yourself?" I listened as I spoke at length about the progressive school I attended as a child, my three years of school teaching, the students of UMassBoston, my 28 years as a mother of sons. Just as I was reminding myself to exercise some self-restraint, I realized that the information I wanted to give you would not be considered germane. As the boy Jake in Gilligan's sample responded to the question of who he was by citing facts about himself—his age, the town he lived in, his father's occupation—I would be expected to cite my race, class, ethnicity, and sexual orientation. In this moment of revelation, it dawned on me that feminist scholarship has placed feminist scholars in a brand new double-bind—the psychologists saying that females think like Amy, the methodologists telling us to sound like Jake.

At the precise instant when what had looked like harmless self-indulgence took on a more threatening aspect, I passed Lamont's Market. Putting temptation behind me I began to wonder, as I did every day, how this relic of another age had managed to survive. "Fresh fish available on Thursdays and Fridays" a new sign in the window said and, with the memory of Woolf sitting on that riverbank letting thought cast its line down into the stream fresh in my mind, I stepped in and ordered a piece of haddock for supper. Remembering how the small idea she hauled in went into hiding when a college officer chased her off his turf, I gave thanks for the progress that has been made in the world on the other side of that bridge I was about to cross. No more Beadles in cut-away coats telling women to keep off the grassy plots of colleges and universities. No more gentlemen librarians in black gowns informing ladies that they must be accompanied by a Fellow. We walk on the men's turf and burrow in their stacks as to the manner born.

Yet a nagging question tugged at my mind as I turned the bend past Lamont's and approached the broad thoroughfare that leads to the bridge. I found myself asking myself: In the fifty years of this Society's existence has there ever been a Symposium entitled "Men Doing Philosophy of Education"? Why, I continued sub rosa, should it seem "fitting that three noted senior women in the society reflect about their work as women philosophers"—here I was quoting verbatim the rationale for this symposium. Why does it not seem fitting for three noted senior men to reflect about their work? the analyst in me asked. It does, I replied with as much tentativeness as I could muster; so fitting that some men have had the platform all to themselves. Not *as men philosophers*, that stickler for detail retorted. Marveling at how appropriate it had seemed to me upon first receiving your invitation to call the three of us *women* philosophers but how ludicrous it would be to call Benne and Broudy and Beck—or, for that matter, Soltis and Scheffler and Schrag or Price and Peters and Pratte—*men* philosophers, I began to wonder if the joke was on me. It is not the case that the expression "a man philosopher" is laughable because a man philosopher is laughable, my resident analyst persisted. There is nothing funny about a man philosopher; his is a solemn calling and he is a highly respected individual. Does the oddity, supposing there is one—and I was beginning to suspect that there is—by any chance reside in the reality corresponding to that solemn expression "a woman philosopher," I asked no one in particular. Is it possible that the English language and the North American world send opposite signals: that the phrase "men doing philosophy of education" is funny precisely because actual flesh and blood philosophers of education are expected to be men, whereas the fact that we three living and breathing philosophers of education are rare birds, if not actually human contradictions, makes the phrase "women doing philosophy of education" unfunny? Stopping in my tracks to let pass the tall woman one sees shuffling her way through this village each day with a bag of empty soda cans in her arms, I asked myself why the rationale cited our "status of retirement or near retirement" and expressed concern about when we three would meet again. "There must be a question in people's minds about whether there will ever again be thunder, lightning or rain," I muttered, catching up with her. Turning to me she said, "Walk across that bridge and look for yourself. The hurly burly's not yet done. The battle's neither lost nor won."

II. In the City of the Professions

"Ladies are welcome on this turf," the Beadle's successor told me many years ago. As I trudged up the hill to the university I could see that he had been true to his word. The great bells were chiming the hour and a mixed group of undergraduates poured into the quadrangle. Stopping for a moment to sit on the steps of a chapel very like the one whose doors were closed to Woolf in 1928, I watched young men and women bow and curtsy and promenade forward and back before scurrying off in opposite directions to their next classes. "How I envy their mentors," I said to myself upon seeing women graduate students walk across the grass. "How exciting it must be to work with people who are writing about what matters to them," I remarked to the pleasant looking tweedy man who had joined me. "I do not quite know how to say this," the Beadle's successor replied in that confidential tone of voice he employs when he has something difficult to tell one. "Perhaps you as a woman doing philosophy of education can explain to me," he began again—this time in the professional tones I knew so well—"why the interests of so many of the women we have allowed on our turf are not quite in the ball park." "Ball park?" I murmured, surprised that he could mistake such different turfs. "One young woman," he said with amusement, "told me she wanted to do an independent study on Virginia Woolf." "What did you reply?" I asked with what I must admit was bated breath. "I had to tell her the obvious: she would never find a thesis topic that way." Wondering if I should break the news to him that on this selfsame day Woolf had been very much on my mind, I started to say that although I did not know a great deal about it, as a woman philosopher of education I thought it possible that Woolf might have had some interesting ideas on women's education. I need not have worried about my wording. Quite forgetting his audience, this nice man continued his recital of female misdemeanors. "Another woman told me that she wanted to write a thesis on Jane Addams," he said in a tone of what almost sounded like sorrow. "And what did you say to her?" "What anyone would have said: that if she were a candidate in the history of education this would of course be an acceptable topic but that for a philosopher of education it was out of the question. You are not going to believe this," he went on warming to his subject, "but an older student of mine wanted to follow women school teachers around to see how they conceptualized teaching. Naturally, I pointed out to her that participant observation is not a method of philosophical inquiry. And then there was the one who wanted to analyze the concept of coeducation. What did I say to her? I told her the truth: there was not enough to say on this topic to sustain a thesis."

As you might imagine, this tale of woe left me with a question or two, but before I could put them into speech my companion picked up his books, excused himself, and with the bells beginning to toll the next hour, went to meet his class. "I would like to hear your opinions on this strange business some time," he said as he strode across the turf. Keeping to the gravel paths, I in turn repaired to the coffeehouse where I had been invited to lunch, wondering as I did so how that busy man could have found the time to read the writings of Addams and Woolf, why the concept of coeducation was so philosophically thin, and what effects his polite denials must have had on those women students—or if not on them, on the small quivering idea each had pulled in on her line.

But now it was time to dine and I was at my destination. Shaking off the melancholy that for some reason had overtaken me on the chapel steps, I opened the heavy door of my cellar cave and walked in. No plain gravy soup; no beef, greens and potatos; no prunes and custard were served on these premises. What Woolf would have thought about the gazpacho, ham and cheese on French bread, rich pastries and espresso coffee I trembled to think. Deciding on the soup, I settled in to watch the young woman across from me devour a hearty meal. "I have been wanting to tell you about the discovery I made," she said between bites. "You will not know his name, but in my country he is a famous man. And what do you think? I just discovered that he wrote a long treatise on women's education and I am going to do my dissertation on it. I wish I could describe to you how I feel. There I was in a closet where everything was dark. I could not even see my hands in front of me. And then, suddenly, everything became lit up. Someone gave me a torch—a flashlight—and now I can find my way out. You cannot imagine what a wonderful feeling it is. I am going to see my advisor this afternoon and tell him. He will be so happy that I finally see my way through to the end. I can hardly wait to go back to my people and give them this brand new work." Thinking to myself as she plotted aloud the structure of her dissertation and the course of her future how gratifying it must be to direct the thesis of a person whose voice is animated and whose eyes sparkle when she talks about her topic, I bade her meet me later on for tea to tell me how the pleasant looking tweedy man had suggested she proceed. Feeling relieved that one woman, at least, had managed to keep the ball inside the park, I walked out the door, up the stairs, and over to the library.

For Woolf the inevitable sequel to lunching at Oxbridge was a visit to the British Museum. For me the postscript to dining in a smoke filled basement whose windows looked out onto pedestrian boots and automobile tires was a trip to the philosophy of education shelves. "Where is the book on gender and education by Dr. X, that woman who was a candidate last year for a position in this university?" I asked the librarian once I found my way into the catacombs. "I do not see it on your shelves." "We have been advised that it is sociology not philosophy," she said. "What about the treatise on past women philosophers of education by Dr. Y who was on the short list the year before? Is it on loan?" "For that one, you will have to go to the history library," she told me. "May I venture to inquire as to the whereabouts of the slim volume on the education of girls and women by Professor Z, the woman whose tenure decision is still in limbo?" This query seemed to stump her but gaining confidence from a short computer search she announced, as if she had seen just about enough of me, that for this one you will have to go the women's studies shelves. Feeling a good deal less exhilarated than I had when I walked in, I muttered that it looked to me as if women doing philosophy of education were not doing philosophy of education. "We put the books where we are told," she protested as I stomped out. "Who tells you?" I stuck my head back in the door to ask but I did not wait for an answer. Years ago the Beadle's successor had said to me, "Ladies are welcome on this turf provided they obey the rules." Being a law abiding citizen myself, I had often wondered why he had thought the proviso necessary. Knowing that my sister Fellows would not wittingly break the rules followed in this ball park either, I had been equally puzzled by the warnings they reported having received from time to time. In the elevator that took me back to the main floor I recalled a friendly young man cautioning one of my sisters about the risks she was taking—"What risks?" she had asked him—and a kindly older gentleman advising another that she seemed to be going off the track. I had no time to sort out my thoughts, however, for as I emerged once more into the daylight, the bells were ringing for tea and I had to make my way quickly if I was going to toast that happy young woman who was waiting to tell me that she, at any rate, was on the right track.

This cannot be the person I lunched with earlier I thought to myself when I entered the cave and spied a young woman sitting in a dark corner staring vacantly ahead. Ordering two small pots of Earl Grey from the young man in tuxedo pants and a white shirt who greeted me, I sat down opposite her and waited to hear what the Beadle's

successor had said. "Was your mentor as pleased as we were?" Never once looking up
from the small paper napkin she was tearing into bits, she told me the saga of that
afternoon. The story does not bear repeating in full. In brief, while I was searching the
library shelves and reading an occasional journal article, the tweedy man turned out
the light. It was not possible for him to direct work on such a narrow topic, he had
informed my young acquaintance. It would, of course, be acceptable for her to write
in the most general terms on the famous author's theory of education but the man's
views on girls were best put in an appendix; that is, if she really felt it necessary to
include them at all. "I am sure he knows best," she said, finally looking me in the eye.
"He is such a kind man and I am so lucky to be his student." Getting up from her chair
she stood quite still for a moment before adding, "In his office I felt good about my
decision. He's right, you know. The general picture is what counts and I can always
write about women later on, if I want. The only trouble is that when I sat down to wait
for you, everything turned dark again." Apologizing for being such poor company and
assuring me that she could write the thesis her advisor wanted without any difficulty,
she fled the restaurant. Finishing my second cup of tea, I paid the bill and left our
gloomy hideout determined, on my way home, to try to put two and two together.

III. Going Home Again

There is a wooden sign planted in a far corner of the grassy plot to remind those
who walk there of the rules. Deciding that it was time for me to read the small print,
I took the long way home. When the sun lies low in the sky, no place in the world can
match this city on the hillside, I thought as I took out my reading glasses. "No
Trespassing. Do not litter," the large print proclaimed to all and sundry. The small
type was directed specifically to the ladies. "You are welcome to walk on our turf," it
said, "but kindly obey the rules: (1) Keep within its borders. (2) Do not alter its shape.
(3) Do not plant your own ideas. (4) Do not leave your mark." Retracing my steps,
I found a notice tacked unceremoniously onto a post in front of the library: "Ladies,
you can enter the philosophy of education stacks at any time and can even write books
for their shelves, but kindly follow instructions: (1) Do not discuss gender—that is
sociology. (2) Do not write prescriptions for the education of girls—that is ideology.
(3) Do not talk about mothers or the family—that is socialization. (4) In fact, do not
mention girls or women at all." "I thought how unpleasant it is to be locked out; and
I thought how it is worse perhaps to be locked in" (Woolf 1928:24), Woolf said when
she went back to her inn on the day she was chased off the grass, turned away from
the library, and served prunes and custard for dinner at Oxbridge. Heading home, I
wondered why my young friend had locked herself in.

She had no choice, the realist who suddenly took charge of me said. A woman today
may be let into the library without a Fellow at her side but a graduate student cannot
walk on the grass without a mentor. She should have argued her case better, I coun-
tered, quite forgetting that the Beadle's successor was her lifeline. "It would have needed

a very stalwart young woman in 1828 to disregard all those snubs and chidings and promises of prizes," Woolf had thought to herself (Woolf 1928:78). Thinking to myself about the progress the world had made in the last hundred and sixty years or so—how women were now permitted to walk on the grass—I tried to estimate just how stalwart a young woman would have to be to try to strike a bargain with the man who was going to escort her into the company of Fellows and onto the nearest tenure track. Woolf thought that "one must have been something of a firebrand to say to oneself, Oh, but they can't buy literature too. Literature is open to everybody. I refuse to allow you, Beadle though you are, to turn me off the grass. Lock up your libraries if you like; but there is no gate, no lock, no bolt that you can set upon the freedom of my mind" (Woolf 1928:78–9). To say this, a woman doing philosophy of education today would have to be something more than a firebrand, I thought—a mad woman, perhaps, or an ascetic. One or the other or both I murmured for, as I now realized, although she might be able to defy the Beadle's successor and retain her freedom of mind, she would automatically sacrifice the professorship and office of her own which every person doing philosophy of education must have.

Putting two and two together is obviously not always a simple matter and as I stepped onto the bridge, I could see that I had a lot of arithmetic to do before I reached home. Go back to the very beginning, my calculating self advised. Did those warnings to my sisters and the denials to the younger generation add up to our being in short supply or did they not? I guarantee that a month from now your young friend will not remember that she ever cast her line and pulled in a small quivering fish of her own, the realist interjected. She will most likely do her thesis but I wager that when she goes home, she will not have the faith in her own abilities that she needs in order to claim the professorship she told you she wanted because she has experienced no sense of authorship—because she has thought and written in another's voice. Will the others forsake the turf, remove themselves from the field, too? I asked. A realist cannot read the future, my realist said piously. All I know is what I overheard the Beadle's successor say. In the last crop of women whose interests were not in the ball park, he confided to a colleague he met on his way to class, one did not finish her dissertation, another did not even start, a third got her doctorate and immediately left the field, and the woman he had put securely on the tenure track had just telephoned him to say she was jumping off.

We three will certainly be rare birds if this keeps up, I concluded, thinking how sad it was that women who do philosophy of education find it so difficult to obey the rules. Not all of us have this trouble, I reminded myself, but I had to admit that many members of our gender did seem to arrive at the office that the Beadle had so generously bequeathed to his successor with the wrong interests. Taking out the small note pad I carried in my purse for occasions like this, I jotted down:

mothers as educators—
teachers as nurturers—
settlement houses as schools—
violence and virility—

> domesticity and curriculum—
> Rousseau's Sophie—
> Pestalozzi's Gertrude—
> Dewey's friend Jane Addams.

Reserving for another day the task of compiling with proper subheadings a complete list of topics the Beadle's successor would consider unimportant, imprudent, inappropriate, aphilosophical or all of the above, I began to ponder why these items were forbidden fruits and whether women are disobedient by nature. Are women doing philosophy of education true daughters of Eve, I wondered, or could it be—here my own boldness startled me—could it just possibly be that our interests fall outside the park not because we do not care to follow the rules, but because the rules do not follow our interests? By any chance did the Beadle gerrymander the turf, I asked myself feeling quite carried away by this different train of thought.

The idea that the fault lies not in ourselves but in the shape of the turf propelled me some distance across the bridge but when I turned for a last look at the sun setting behind the city of professions, I could see our troubles multiplying. Had not Woolf said after visiting Oxbridge, "A woman writing thinks back through her mothers" (Woolf 1928:101; cf.79)? How I longed to speak to her about just that, if only for a few minutes. "Women writing fiction can think through Fanny Burney and Aphra Behn as well as the big four—Austen, the Brontes, and Eliot," I would say to her, "but a woman doing philosophy of education does not have this luxury. With the gerrymandering having divided us from the works of our mothers, we have no choice but to think through our fathers." She would reply, "It is useless to go to the great men writers for help," for Thackeray or Dickens or "whoever it may be—never helped a woman yet, though she may have learnt a few tricks of them and adapted them to her use." I would admire her assertive manner but press for a justification of this claim. "My dear, you shall have one," she would say: "The weight, the pace, the stride of a man's mind are too unlike her own for her to lift anything substantial from him successfully" (Woolf 1928:79). "Philosophy of education is different," would be my heated retort. "Plato, Rousseau, Dewey—whoever it may be—can help men *and* women." "You are right of course," she would say with a dazzling smile. "The question for women doing philosophy of education is not, Can you think through your fathers, but What is your thinking like when you are divided from your mothers?" "Explain, please," I would demand as we stepped off the bridge together onto the broad avenue that would take me back to Lamont's Market. Woolf would then remind me of the flaw at the center of many nineteenth century women's novels that "rotted them" and she would trace its source to the authors having altered their values "in deference to the opinion of others" (Woolf 1928:77). Just before we went our separate ways, she would put to me the question, "Can you think through—I mean to say, only through—your fathers without forsaking your values and opinions?"

The conversation can never take place, I thought with regret. Then, checking my watch to see how much time I had before Lamont's Market closed and my piece of haddock went into hiding, I told myself that, having had a rather fatiguing day and being too close to the matter to be objective in any case, I was in no position to judge if the works of women philosophers of education have a fatal flaw. No matter how much I wanted to, however, I could not hide from myself that I had just seen one woman after another alter her values and defer in her opinions to others. Could I deny that the young woman who wanted to read Woolf forsook her for Rawls? that the one who wanted to write on Addams abandoned her for Kant? that my young friend cut herself off that very afternoon from what mattered most to herself? I wish I knew what this adds up to, I said going into the store to collect my fish.

"I have come for my haddock," I told the young man behind the counter. "I ordered it this morning." While he searched for the tightly wrapped package with my name on it, I thought about the double binds that had exercised me a few hours earlier and how they did not hold a candle to the predicament in which women doing philosophy of education find themselves. "Young man," I said as he reached into a bin, "do you realize that to acquire a professorship and office of one's own we must forsake our values and opinions and that to hold onto these precious commodities we must give up our ambitions?" "Are you telling me that your interests and ambitions cancel each other out?" he asked, handing me my fish with a flourish. "Come to think of it," I smiled, "I need a lemon." Then, thanking him for my nugget of pure truth, I marched out the door and up the hill to my house. Of course, women doing philosophy of education need a professorship and an office of their own, I thought as I opened my front door and went back into the room of my own. But we need something else too—newly cut turf. And do you know something, I said to myself and will now say to you. What with the mayhem at home, the war abroad, the environmental risks to the earth, and the five year olds carrying guns to school, men doing philosophy of education need newly cut turf, too, because no one who thinks only through their fathers can hope to solve the problems that face education today.

Notes

I wish to thank Ann Diller, Susan Franzosa, Barbara Houston, Susan Laird, Michael Martin, Jennifer Radden, and Janet Farrell Smith for helpful criticisms of a draft of this paper.

PART II
Newly Cut Turf

CHAPTER 7

The Disciplines and the Curriculum

In citing love, friendship, marriage, divorce, child rearing and family living as impor-
tant activities of life that children should study from both the "outside" and "within,"
"The Disciplines and the Curriculum," the earliest published paper in this collection, links
Parts One and Two of the volume. The essay also introduces the work that follows. Even
when I did not explicitly cite it in my later writings on curriculum, my thinking was
affected by its explication of the knowledge-curriculum connection, its distinction between
school subjects and subject matter, its metaphor of curriculum space, its account of the
educational force of the Doctrine of Verstehen.

I would like to inquire here into the relationship between the disciplines and the
school curriculum. In particular, I would like to examine a prevalent view of this
relationship, one which gives the disciplines the ruling hand in what is and what is
not to be taught. It will be necessary to clarify this view and to place it in context. I
will then criticize it for I believe it to be mistaken. I will propose in conclusion that
educational considerations should take precedence where the choice of school subjects and subject matter is concerned and I will attempt to sketch in briefly some
implications of this revised view of the nature of the relationship between the
disciplines and the curriculum.

The Principle 'Teach The Disciplines'

One dominant theme of curriculum theorizing today is that the disciplines should
be taught. On the face of it this is unexceptionable. Who would ever dream of deny-

This essay was originally published in *Educational Philosophy and Theory*, Vol.1 (1969).
Reprinted by permission.

ing that they should be taught? We must distinguish, however, between the moderate claim, 'Disciplines, among other things, should be taught,' and the claim that *only* the disciplines should be taught. The latter is anything but moderate. It is this latter sort of claim about the disciplines that I believe to be implicit in a good deal of the current thinking about curriculum and it is just this sort of claim that I believe to be misguided. I will consider the proposal 'Teach the disciplines' to be equivalent to 'Only the disciplines should be taught.'

Now I suppose no one would hold that in vocational or professional or some other sort of special education only the disciplines should be taught. I will take the claim, therefore, to apply to non-technical or what is frequently called general education. Perhaps I should make it clear, however, that I am less concerned with whether or not anyone today really makes this claim than I am with the validity of the claim; that I am less concerned with the way it has in fact been formulated and hedged around with qualifications than I am with exploring its consequences when it is construed as being quite general. For this reason I will discuss the view that the disciplines should be taught quite apart from any particular person's writings on the topic.[1]

When we are advised to teach the disciplines, granted that this advice tells us to teach only the disciplines, we are being advised to do one of two things. On the one hand we are being advised to select our school subjects from among the disciplines and only from among them; on the other hand we are being advised to select our school subject matter from the disciplines and only from among them. That is to say, 'Teach the disciplines' may be interpreted as a principle governing school subject selection or as a principle governing school subject matter selection. Let us call the principle when interpreted in the former way Discipline Principle S and let us call the principle when interpreted in the latter way Discipline Principle SM.[2]

Consider first Discipline Principle S. It does not by itself determine what specific subjects will be included in a school curriculum. Rather, it distinguishes the class of legitimate candidates for school subject. 'Teach the disciplines' on this interpretation in effect requires that for every school subject there must be a corresponding discipline, but it does not require that for every discipline there must be a corresponding school subject. Unless unprincipled selection from within the class of legitimate candidates for school subject is sanctioned, other principles of subject selection besides Discipline Principle S would have to be invoked. Various principles have been singled out in this regard although I am not sure that any has received general acceptance. Sometimes we are advised to choose the most advanced or disciplined of the disciplines. Frequently the disciplines are grouped in families and we are advised to choose one from each family, perhaps the most representative.[3] But whatever principles are held to govern selection of disciplines, their status is subordinate to Discipline Principle S: the overriding consideration is that each school subject be a discipline.

Discipline Principle SM is weaker than Discipline Principle S. For when 'Teach the disciplines' is construed as governing the selection of subject matter rather than subjects we are being told that all the subject matter we teach must come from the disciplines but not that our subjects must. The disciplines rather than being the source of our school subjects and hence of our school subject matter are here viewed simply as the source of our school subject matter. How the subject matter being taught is to be organized into school subjects is not at issue. Thus, whereas on Discipline Principle S for every school subject there must be a corresponding discipline, on Discipline Principle SM there need not be. A school subject could be interdisciplinary in that it drew its subject matter from more than one discipline—something Discipline Principle S rules out.[4]

Now we must not overlook the fact that in current curriculum theorizing the Discipline Principle functions together with other principles, in particular with the Principles of Structure and Inquiry. Thus we are not merely advised to teach the disciplines; we are advised to teach structure and to teach inquiry. When the Discipline Principle is taken together with the Principles 'Teach structure' and 'Teach inquiry' we may be said to be advised to teach the structure of the disciplines as inquiry. It is worth noting that there is no necessary connection between the Discipline Principle and the Principles of Structure and Inquiry. One could teach the disciplines without viewing them as inquiry: one could, for example, view them as social phenomena or as bodies of knowledge. And one could teach the disciplines without teaching their structure: one could, for example, teach isolated and relatively unimportant bits of information. Conversely, one could teach inquiry without teaching the disciplines: one could, for example, teach students to inquire into social problems—presumably something quite different from teaching one or more of the disciplines.[5] And one could teach structure without teaching the disciplines: one could, for example, teach students the structure of an argument—again something quite different from teaching the structure of a discipline. Yet as a matter of fact the Discipline Principle has been closely connected with the Principles of Structure and Inquiry and we will therefore discuss it in this context.[6]

Our course will be to evaluate the Discipline Principle on the two interpretations discussed here by considering what the consequences of following it would be. The gap between curriculum theorizing and actual school practice is a notable one. That there is a gap between curriculum theorizing and those recommendations for curriculum that are not quite theory yet not actual practice may not be as notable but ought not to be ignored. Advocates of the Discipline Principle do not always recommend courses or school subjects which accord with that principle. Our concern is not with these lapses—which may from the standpoint of educational practice be a godsend—but with the implications of the principle when it is taken seriously and as applying quite generally.

When curriculum theorists say 'Teach the disciplines,' they seem to have in mind what have been called the theoretical disciplines rather than the practical disciplines, that is to say disciplines like physics and economics and geology rather than disciplines like sculpture, the dance and teaching.[7] Thus they speak of the disciplines of *knowledge*, they want the modes of *inquiry* of various disciplines to be taught, they conceive of disciplines as having basic *concepts*, as making *discoveries*, as formulating *laws* and *theories*. This sort of talk is quite out of place where the practical disciplines are concerned but very much to the point in connection with the theoretical disciplines.

Now the proper definition of a theoretical discipline is a matter of controversy.[8] But this does not mean that we do not know a good deal about theoretical disciplines or that we cannot recognize clear cases, such as physics, and clear non-cases, such as chairs, when we meet them. We know, for example, that a theoretical discipline has some realm of study and tries to give a systematic account of it; that it has some vocabulary in which this account is expressed and that it has some methods.[9] This characterization falls short of a definition of a theoretical discipline but it nonetheless gives an idea of the sort of thing advocates of the Discipline Principle are talking about. To be sure, in their concrete proposals these curriculum theorists sometimes forget that they have been construing disciplines in this way and they assign to the rank of school subject a variety of things which, if they are disciplines at all, would come under the heading of practical disciplines. But as I have already noted these lapses should not lead us astray. The sort of thing the Discipline Principle legitimizes as a school subject or the source of school subject matter is a theoretical discipline where this is to be contrasted both with a practical discipline and also with a whole host of things which do not warrant the label 'discipline' at all—things such as chairs, the Far East, and Shakespeare's tragedies.

There is a temptation nowadays to call everything a discipline. This must be guarded against. Some things, such as those just mentioned, are not, never were, and never will be disciplines and some things are not now disciplines although they might conceivably one day become disciplines. Thus to apply the term "discipline" indiscriminately is at the very least to depart from our ordinary conceptions and to do so without warning, where a curriculum principle is concerned, is to mislead. But an unduly generous application of the label 'discipline' does more than mislead. If everything is considered a discipline, then the Discipline Principle gives no guidance and we may as well dispense with it. For a principle to function as it is supposed to, for it to have any practical value, it must not embrace everything; it must rule out certain things. A principle of subject or subject matter selection which legitimizes everything as a school subject or as a source of school subject matter is vacuous.

There is another temptation and that is to call everything one values, although not everything at all, a discipline. But if succumbing to this temptation does not make the Discipline Principle vacuous, it nonetheless undermines it. The Discipline Principle as well as the other principles I mentioned have, or at least are intended to have, normative force; that is to say, they tell us what we *ought* to select or not select. In effect, the Discipline Principle tells us that certain things are worthy of being selected because they are disciplines or because they come from disciplines and that certain things are not worthy of being selected because they are not disciplines or do not come from disciplines. If, however, 'discipline' becomes an honorific term, the Discipline Principle is turned on its head. Instead of something being worthy of being selected because it is a discipline or is a part of a discipline, something is a discipline because it or some part of it is worthy of being selected. But if being a discipline is not what makes something worthy of being selected—and on this view it is not—what *does* make a thing worthy of being selected? Unless we know this, the Discipline Principle is useless for we cannot apply it to new cases. And if we do know this, there is no need to use the Discipline Principle for we will be able to decide new cases without it.

Apart from the fact that misuse of the term 'discipline' tends to vitiate the Discipline Principle, when the term is misused we lose sight of the whole point of the curriculum theory to which the Discipline Principle belongs. Curriculum theorists who hold that the disciplines and only the disciplines should be taught believe that the methods, key concepts and theories of fields like physics, biology, mathematics and economics have great value; that one who masters these will understand and be able to do a great deal more on his own than one who does not. In effect, they justify the Discipline Principle by an appeal to certain characteristics of the standard theoretical disciplines and to the values which they think accrue from studying them. If 'discipline' now refers to things which do not share these characteristics and do not yield these values when studied the whole reason for advocating the Discipline Principle disappears.

Let us grant, then, that the Discipline Principle has to do with theoretical disciplines and that this notion is to be construed in such a way that it accords with ordinary usage. There are then two very basic criticisms that can be made of it. Both criticisms amount in the final analysis to the same thing: the Discipline Principle rules out of the curriculum subjects or subject matter which ought not to be ruled out. They are best viewed as distinct, however, because two rather different sorts of argument are involved. Even supposing that the first argument could one day be met because of changes in the disciplines, the second would still hold.

The Argument From Relevance

Whatever may be the proper definition of a theoretical discipline, there is no doubt that each theoretical discipline involves *some* methods of inquiry and *some* vocabulary in which it formulates *some* laws, theories, principles, or the like. It is just these things—the mode or method of inquiry of a discipline, the key terms or concepts of a discipline, and the most important laws or theories or principles—that the theory of curriculum to which the Discipline Principle belongs singles out for attention. The notion of structure is by no means clear but those who want the structure of the disciplines to be taught seem to be recommending that the basic ideas of a discipline be taught, that is to say the basic concepts of a discipline and the relationships among them.[10] Sometimes the methods of a discipline are considered part of its structure.[11] Even if they are not, when the principle 'Teach inquiry' is combined with the principle 'Teach the disciplines,' the methods of a discipline are put on a par, educationally speaking, with the basic ideas of that discipline. For the two principles together tell us to view the disciplines as fields of inquiry, and methods are surely central to inquiry even if inquiry is not reducible to method.

The fact that the notions of discipline and structure and inquiry themselves are in need of clarification does not stand in the way, then, of evaluating the Discipline Principle. For in the context of the Structure of the Disciplines as Inquiry theory of curriculum it is clear that Discipline Principle S rules out of the curriculum many things which have long been part of it, some of which, at least, ought not to be ruled out. It rules out as school subjects such things as music and art and the dance; reading and writing and literature; French and German and Spanish; physical education, carpentry and typing; the Far East and problems of democracy. No doubt advocates of the Principle want to rule out some of these; but that anyone wants to rule out all is doubtful. In any case all ought not to be ruled out.

Now I can imagine an advocate of Discipline Principle S objecting to this criticism of it. He might argue that the things I say are ruled out by the Principle are in fact disciplines, hence are not ruled out. If the Principle is to retain its normative force and be neither vacuous nor trivial, however, this objection cannot be sustained. On no significant interpretation of 'discipline' is French or the Far East a discipline of any sort; some of the other things listed here might be able to qualify as practical disciplines, but they certainly would not qualify as theoretical disciplines. But, the objection will continue, are there not basic concepts of music, such as harmony? Of literature, such as metaphor? Of language, such as noun? Are not the concepts belonging to each one of these related in significant ways, as in the case of harmony and melody? Do not these fields consist of principles, theories, laws? Are they not theoretical disciplines after all?

There is such a thing as theory of music, there is such a thing as grammar, there is such a thing as literary criticism, and all of these may, perhaps, qualify as theoretical disciplines. But theory of music is not music; grammar, even French grammar, is not French; and literary criticism is not literature.[12] It is true that courses in theory of music are listed in school catalogues under music, that French courses all too frequently turn out to be grammar courses, and that courses in literary criticism fall under literature. But at most this indicates that the school subject *music* encompasses theory, that the school subject *French* encompasses grammar, and that the school subject *literature* encompasses literary criticism. To argue that music, French and literature are theoretical disciplines and therefore do qualify as potential school subjects according to Discipline Principle S because music theory, grammar and literary criticism are theoretical disciplines, as our imaginary objector is in effect doing, is either to commit the fallacy of composition or to deny the facts of the case. That is to say, it is either to argue invalidly from a characteristic of one part of a whole to a characteristic of the whole itself, or it is to deny that there is more to music than its theory, more to French than its grammar, more to literature than criticisms of it.

At this point our imaginary objector may suggest a compromise: he will grant that some parts or aspects of things like music, French and literature are excluded from the pool of potential school subjects by Discipline Principle S provided we grant that some parts or aspects of things like music, French and literature do fall in the pool on that Principle. We may accept this compromise without giving up our initial criticism of Discipline Principle S. For even if some parts or aspects of things like music, French and literature can qualify as school subjects according to the Principle, other parts or aspects of these things cannot. Yet they surely ought to qualify as such. As long as 'music,' 'French,' and 'literature' are retained as labels of school subjects by advocates of Discipline Principle S the compromise has its dangers, however. For it is all too easy to forget that on this principle the school subjects called music, French and literature consist respectively in theorizing *about* music, *about* French, *about* literature and that other sorts of study—study *in* music, French and literature as opposed to study *about* these—are ruled out.

In general, when we view the disciplines as sets of theories, laws, principles and the like arrived at through inquiry, we take them to be asserting things *about* something, be it music, language, literature, falling bodies, living organisms or abnormal behaviour. Now it may as a matter of fact be the case that music theory has something significant to say about music and that literary criticism has something significant to say about literature. There is no guarantee, however, that the theoretical disciplines have something significant to say about all those things which on independent grounds can be shown to be the things our students ought to learn about. How much light can the disciplines shed, for example, on war and peace, marriage and divorce, violence and poverty, love and friendship? Nor is there any reason to think that everything worth teaching must *say* something *about* something. Music, apart from music theory, does not say or assert things about things—at least not in any literal interpretation of 'say' or 'assert'—yet it has great educational significance. A great deal may be said *in* French about things yet French itself does not say or assert things.

The educational importance of things which do not say something about something will be discussed in the next section. For now let us consider the question of whether the disciplines do have something to say about the things we believe our students should learn about. In the face of the criticism of non-relevance an advocate of Discipline Principle S can take one of two tacks. He can argue that the disciplines do in fact have something significant to say about important things, e.g. war and peace, violence and poverty, which on independent grounds can be shown to be of educational significance; or he can argue that those things the disciplines do not in fact shed light on are not concerns of education, at least not formal education which is, after all, the realm in which the Discipline Principle is intended to apply.[13]

This latter tack, it seems to me, is a desperate one. In order to save the Discipline Principle we are, in effect, asked to relinquish our responsibilities as educators. Given a world which does not cooperate with the disciplines or, perhaps, disciplines which do not keep up with the world, our Discipline Principle advocate is saying 'So much the worse for the world' whereas he should be saying 'So much the worse for the disciplines.' I can imagine holding on to Discipline Principle S given that the disciplines did not illuminate the sorts of things I have mentioned only if there were good reason to think that nothing else illuminated them either. If there were nothing outside the disciplines for our students to learn about things like these—things which vitally affect their lives and their times—then, I suppose, the failure of the disciplines to speak to these issues would not count against Discipline Principle S. I doubt very much, however, that there is nothing outside the disciplines worth teaching and learning about things of this sort. In any case, to show that there is nothing is a difficult, if not impossible, task; one which Discipline Principle advocates have not to my knowledge undertaken.

A more promising tack, it seems to me, is to argue that the disciplines do in fact have something to say about those things educators believe students ought to learn about. A sophisticated advocate of Discipline Principle S would, I think, grant that the disciplines do not in all cases talk *directly* about these things; that 'marriage' and 'divorce' are not terms belonging to physics or biology or even to psychology or sociology; that statements such as 'One out of every four marriages ends in divorce' do not belong to any discipline. He would grant this but maintain that the disciplines speak *indirectly* about these things; that they are relevant or applicable to our everyday concerns, although their own vocabularies are technical and their theoretical statements are in many instances quite abstract and are perhaps not obviously related to these concerns. He might also argue that two disciplines, namely history and philosophy, do talk directly about these things.[14]

Now in principle this is certainly true: the theoretical disciplines can speak to concrete, everyday affairs even if they do not speak directly about them. There are no laws or theories of cracking automobile radiators yet supposing that an automobile radiator has cracked during a cold night certain laws of physics will apply to this event and will figure prominently in an explanation of it.[15] History, moreover, does talk directly about war and peace and philosophy talks about the good society. It is an open question, however, if at the present time the theoretical disciplines do in fact have significant things to say to those common, ordinary, everyday but important things our students ought to learn about. No doubt some disciplines do speak right now to some of the vital issues with which education should be concerned; that all of them do or that all the things that from the educational point of view need to be illuminated are illuminated by the disciplines seems to me to be quite problematic. It is also an open question if at the present time history and philosophy talk directly about all the things our students should learn about.

It is one thing to say that the disciplines can in principle apply to the important things in life and it is another thing to say that they do as a matter of fact apply. To say that we recognize exactly what their relevance is for these things, given that they are in fact relevant, is something else again. There is no reason to suppose that a discipline as a whole is relevant to some particular problem or issue; on the contrary, we must expect that some parts of the discipline will be relevant and that other parts will not be. But then it is necessary to decide which parts of a discipline shed light on which problems or issues. This may at times be determined quite easily but it must be remembered that laws and theories and principles wear no badges of relevance and that the task of determining what is relevant to what is itself a task of inquiry with success by no means guaranteed.

Suppose now that the disciplines, or at least some of them, are relevant to those things which our students should learn about and that the respects in which they are relevant are known. Their relevance will not normally be obvious to the student, but will have to be made obvious to him in the course of his education. Granted that the cracking of a radiator can be explained in terms of some laws of physics, it does not follow that a student who has learned the relevant laws will automatically see their relevance to the case at hand. If the disciplines are to shed light for him on the problems and issues in question, they must be taught in such a way that their relevance for these problems and issues becomes clear. No doubt it is possible to do this: physics and the other theoretical disciplines can be taught so that their applicability to such things as war and peace, violence and poverty can be grasped by the student. The question we must ask, however, is if the curriculum theory to which the Discipline Principle belongs sanctions teaching the disciplines in this way.

When the Discipline Principle is conjoined with the Structure Principle and the Inquiry Principle there is no doubt about the way in which the disciplines are to be viewed for purposes of education: they are to be viewed in the way in which practitioners of the discipline themselves view it. To be sure, the three principles when taken together do not require that the student actually engage in inquiry; they do not demand that he learn to be an inquirer or even learn how to inquire. Teaching the structure of the disciplines as inquiry is compatible with simply teaching and learning *about* inquiry.[16] But whether the student learns to inquire or simply learns about inquiry, the intent of the theory is that he see the disciplines from the 'inside.' He is not merely to become acquainted in one way or another with the methods of the practitioner of a discipline—with his conceptual apparatus, with his findings, with his aspirations and general orientation—but to view them from the standpoint of that practitioner. [17]

Now the practitioner—certainly the practitioner advocates of this theory have in mind—typically is not concerned *qua* practitioner with the question of the practical relevance of his work.[18] One mark of a theoretical discipline is its theoretical orientation and its remoteness from practical, everyday concerns. To teach a discipline in such a way that the relevance of its various parts or aspects to particular everyday issues and problems became clear would, I should think, subvert the whole point of the curriculum theory at issue. Quite simply, to teach the disciplines as relevant to practical concerns is not to teach them as inquiry. This is not to say that their methods of inquiry may not be one of the things about them having relevance for practical concerns. Nor is it to say that there is anything intrinsically wrong with viewing them in this way. Rather it is to say that to focus on their relevance for such concerns is in effect to view them from the 'outside,' hence in a way which is not sanctioned by the Structure of the Disciplines as Inquiry theory of curriculum.[19]

History and philosophy are in much the same boat as the other disciplines: even if they do not talk directly *about* the things we have in mind, they may speak *to* them. To the extent that this is the case, however, the points just made apply to history and philosophy as well as to the other disciplines. Moreover, on the theory of curriculum under consideration, even when history and philosophy talk directly about important, everyday things, what they have to say about some particular topic is considered to be of much less importance than their methods, their key concepts and the like. We must also take into account the possibility that neither history nor philosophy illuminates important things in the proper way. The concerns of philosophy are very general and there is a real question as to the illumination philosophy can give directly to particular questions and issues. History, on the other hand, is concerned with particular problems and issues, and it would seem, therefore, to be able to illuminate well the things it does talk directly about. One wonders, however, if historians in talking about topics such as war and peace, do in fact single out for attention the things our students ought to know about these topics. History is notable for its discussions of rulers and generals and politicians and for its lack of attention to the life and point of view of the ordinary man.

Whatever the fate of history and philosophy on this theory of curriculum, I would not be surprised if at this point in our discussion an advocate of the Discipline Principles retreated from Discipline Principle S to Discipline Principle SM. Surely, he will say, the latter principle gets over this argument from relevance even if the former principle does not. For Discipline Principle SM requires only that our school subject matter come from the disciplines; it allows for the organization of subject matter around topics which do not themselves belong to some discipline. Thus those things which educators hold on independent grounds to be worth learning about can on Discipline Principle SM be learned about even if Discipline Principle S does in fact rule them out of the curriculum. For example, Discipline Principle SM allows as school subjects the Far East, poverty, war and peace. What is required is that the subject matter to be learned come from the disciplines. But the issue of relevance is in a sense taken care of: elements from the various disciplines relevant to the topic at hand are incorporated into the one interdisciplinary subject. Thus, in the case of the Far East for example, the subject matter may include findings from history, geography, economics, and so on insofar as they have to do with the Far East.

Without doubt Discipline Principle SM is to be preferred to Discipline Principle S: it allows disciplines to be school subjects but makes it possible for other things to qualify as well. Yet Discipline Principle SM does not satisfactorily get over the objection raised here initially in relation to Discipline Principle S. Discipline Principle SM does not function in isolation. The Principles of Structure and Inquiry do not lose their force when Discipline Principle SM is substituted for Discipline Principle S. It is still the case that the disciplines are to be viewed from the inside; their structure and methods are still the primary focus.

The main concern of the Structure of the Disciplines as Inquiry theory of curriculum is that the student come to understand the disciplines—understand them by getting 'inside' them. The disciplines can be understood from the 'outside'—by looking around them rather than looking into them; for example, by seeing how they came to be the way they are or by seeing how they function in society as a whole. But the theory at issue does not place value on this sort of understanding. Thus, in an important sense it makes no difference whether the Discipline Principle is given a strong or a weak interpretation. For whether the disciplines constitute our school subjects or our school subject matter, the educator must focus on certain internal features of the disciplines. Subject matter from various disciplines may be organized around some topic to which these disciplines are applicable, but interest nonetheless must be on the methods and basic ideas of these disciplines. So long as it is possible to stress these and at the same time illuminate some topic outside the disciplines our objection amounts to very little. But the Discipline Principle in the context of this theory does not allow for illumination of things, no matter how important, to which the disciplines are not relevant, nor does it allow us to focus on a topic if in doing so the structural and methodological aspects of the disciplines are slighted. Given a conflict of interests—to illuminate some vital everyday sort of topic or to illuminate the methods and structure of the disciplines—the outcome is never in doubt: the methods and structure of the disciplines have priority.[20]

Now I have been discussing up to this point the relevance of the disciplines, and in particular their relevance as they are conceived by the Structure of the Disciplines as Inquiry theory of curriculum, for learning about all sorts of important things. We must not forget, however, that the Discipline Principle as we are interpreting it here holds not merely that the disciplines should be taught but that *only* the disciplines should be taught. In evaluating the principle we must not forget then that it rules out subject matter which does not belong to any discipline. Yet there is no guarantee that such subject matter might not be very illuminating. If we are willing to grant, as I think we must, that topics such as war and peace, poverty and violence, love and friendship are educationally important, then we ignore at our peril subject matter which does not belong to the disciplines. Literature and art, and I am not speaking here about literary criticism or aesthetics, are not theoretical disciplines yet they may illuminate these topics. Commonsense knowledge may be quite relevant.[21] Practical wisdom is not to be sneered at, especially when theoretical wisdom is scarce. The Discipline Principle would have us believe that non-disciplinary knowledge is not worth having. Yet surely non-disciplinary knowledge of a thing is in some cases at least better than no knowledge of that thing; moreover, it is difficult to imagine our disciplinary knowledge ever bearing fruit in our everyday life if it were not supplemented with non-disciplinary knowledge.

The Argument From *Verstehen*

There is more to education than advocates of the Discipline Principle seem ever to have dreamed of. Thus far we have simply questioned the adequacy of the Principle in relation to one educational objective, namely that our students *learn about* those things we consider important enough to be learned about. But education is not and ought not to be limited to learning about: there are skills to be acquired, techniques to be mastered, activities to be learned, works of art to be appreciated; there are emotions to be fostered, attitudes to be developed, convictions to be encouraged, ways of acting to be promoted. The Discipline Principle and, indeed, the curriculum theory to which it belongs, must be condemned for ignoring all these things—that is to say, ignoring them except as they enter into one particular context.

When we are told to teach the disciplines (and only the disciplines) one human context is given special status insofar as education is concerned. Whether students are taught to inquire in the manner of the practitioner of the discipline or simply taught *about* this mode of inquiry, the activity of one who engages in a discipline is to be studied in a way that no other activity is to be studied, namely from the standpoint of the actor. Whether students learn the skills and techniques which enter into disciplinary inquiry and acquire the attitudes and convictions of an inquirer or whether they simply learn about these things and learn to appreciate them, the disciplines are seen from the 'inside.' Other human activities or contexts, if they are studied at all, are studied through the study of one or another discipline. But to the extent that the disciplines illuminate human conduct they do so from the 'outside': they take the standpoint of a spectator toward the activity in question, not the standpoint of an actor. Thus, for example, the activities and practices of the consumer and the manufacturer may be studied in the course of studying the discipline of economics. But if they are, they are studied not from the standpoint of an actual consumer or manufacturer but from the standpoint of an economist looking at a consumer or manufacturer. If the economist is interested at all in seeing the world as the consumer or manufacturer does, he is interested only to the extent that it aids his theorizing about their activities and practices.

Philosophers and historians have sometimes maintained that the historian must explain and understand human behaviour in a special way. They have argued that because we are human we must put ourselves in the position of the people we are studying; we must look at things through their eyes, think their thoughts, feel their feelings. William Dray, one of the most influential contemporary advocates of this position, argues that where actions are concerned the historian's task is to take the actor's standpoint and to set forth his reasons for acting as he did.[22] If this account of history is correct, then perhaps the present criticism of the Discipline Principle loses part of its force. For on this view of history, to take the point of view of the practitioner of history, that is, of the historian, would in turn require that one look at the actions of historical figures from the standpoint of the actor. History could then be taught in the way advocates of the Discipline Principle want, namely as a field of inquiry, and at the same time students would see things other than the disciplines from the 'inside.'

For reasons that will become apparent shortly, even if this account of history is correct, much if not all the force of the criticism I am making of the Discipline Principle remains. I myself am very sceptical of this doctrine, sometimes called the Doctrine of *Verstehen*, as it is usually presented.[23] But whatever its claims as an account of history, I do think there is an important moral to be drawn from it for education. It may not be the case that because we are human we must put ourselves in the actor's position if we are to explain and understand what he has done, but it surely is the case that we must put ourselves in the actor's position if we are to learn to act as he does and if we are to come to see the world as he does. The Doctrine of *Verstehen* has educational force, then, independent of any logical or methodological force it may have in history and the social sciences.

There are human contexts and activities over and above that of the disciplines which our students should study from the 'inside.' I do not for a moment mean to suggest that inquiry as it is carried on in the disciplines ought not to be studied from the standpoint of the inquirer himself; on the contrary, I think there are very good reasons for holding that it should be so studied. What is objectionable about the Structure of the Disciplines as Inquiry theory of curriculum is not that it tells us to teach inquiry from this standpoint but that it prevents us from teaching other activities from this standpoint. No matter how much value one places on the disciplines and their modes of inquiry, they are not the whole of life nor ought they to be the whole of education. Artistic practice and appreciation may contain elements of inquiry within them but neither one is reducible to inquiry any more than is professional practice, such as of medicine or law. Political, social, and individual moral problems can be inquired into, but right political and social action is no more reducible to inquiry than is moral behaviour. Yet these things, along with many others—child rearing, family living, community action, to name just a few— ought at the very least to be candidates for study from within.

In maintaining that the Doctrine of *Verstehen* has educational force I do not want to be misunderstood. I am not suggesting that every human context, that every human activity, that all human behaviour, ought to be studied from the actor's standpoint. I am not advocating that we teach pickpocketing and lynching, sadism and character assassination. My point is not that education should embrace the teaching of anything at all but simply that the Discipline Principle and its accompanying theory rule out too much. It is by no means easy to say in any general sort of way which activities, which human contexts ought to be looked at from the 'inside' in the course of a person's education. We may point without too much difficulty to particular cases which seem quite obviously to belong in the curriculum or at least in the pool of potential subjects or subject matter and others which seem just as obviously not to belong in it. But a general principle which would function as the Discipline Principle is intended to function—that is to say, a principle which although it would not by itself determine what is to be our school subjects or at least our school subject matter, would differentiate between those things which ought not to enter into the curriculum in these ways and those which may—is not easily found. Fortunately for us it is not necessary to come up with an alternative to the Discipline Principle in order to show that principle to be inadequate.

One alternative to the Discipline Principle which seems peculiarly relevant to the present discussion may be abstracted from the writings of R.S. Peters. Peters' account of education merits closer examination than we can possibly give it here, yet we would be remiss if we did not consider a portion of it at least briefly for Peters appears to take seriously the very argument we have just been levelling against the Discipline Principle. Peters proposes that we view education as initiation into worthwhile activities and modes of conduct and I think we may fairly construe him as offering an alternative to the Discipline Principle which we will call the Worthwhile Activities Principle.[24] Now in one respect the Principle 'Teach worthwhile activities and modes of conduct' is clearly superior to the Discipline Principle: it allows for activities besides the disciplines and their attendant modes of inquiry to be included in the curriculum for study from within. Thus Peters mentions as a worthwhile activity literary appreciation as well as science, philosophy, and history. Yet in another respect the Worthwhile Activities Principle, at least when taken in the context of Peters' Initiation Theory, is unduly restrictive. Students are to be initiated into worthwhile activities, that is to say they are to learn them by studying them from the 'inside.'[25] While this allows them, as the Discipline Principle does not, to take the actor's point of view and to engage in activities other than inquiry, it does not allow them to study *about* objects of educational significance unless such study is, as it were, accidentally accomplished while being initiated into the various worthwhile activities. Yet as I have already argued, there are any number of things students ought to learn about and there is no more guarantee that they will learn about them given this principle, than that they will learn about them given the Discipline Principle.

There is, however, a more important point to be brought out in connection with Peters' Initiation Theory. When Peters talks about getting inside worthwhile activities he is concerned that the student become committed to them and in some sense or other make them his own. In claiming that the Doctrine of *Verstehen* has pedagogical force, that is, in arguing that students ought in the course of their education to get 'inside' human activities and contexts other than the disciplines and their modes of inquiry, l have not been saying that they must necessarily stay inside; that they must necessarily adopt these activities and contexts or make them their own. When the historian is told to look at things from the point of view of the actor, be it because it will help him to explain and understand human actions or because he must do so to explain and understand them, he is surely not being told to turn into or become that sort of actor. Nor must the student in the course of his education become the sort of person whose point of view he is made to see or whose activity he has come to participate in.

There surely are a number of activities and contexts the student ought to get 'inside' of with a view toward making them his own in the course of his education. Presumably these will be worthwhile activities. But there is a place in the curriculum for activities and modes of conduct which are not worthwhile: activities and modes of conduct which the student views from the 'inside' in order to reject, in order to improve upon, in order to do away with, in order to learn to cope with. Racial discrimination is not a worthwhile activity; neither is living in poverty and despair in a ghetto. Yet there may be good reason for having students take the actor's point of view in cases of this sort. It may be true that education ought to 'pass on' worthwhile activities only, but even if it is, it does not follow that the *only* thing it ought to do is pass things on.

A curriculum is needed which introduces the student to a wide range of human activities and human contexts—wider than either the Discipline Principle or the Worthwhile Activities Principle distinguishes—and allows him to study such activities and contexts from a variety of points of view including that of the actor. This is not to say that every sort of human conduct ought to be studied or that any sort at all ought to be studied. Nor is it to say that every sort that should be and is studied ought to be viewed from the 'inside.' To reject the Discipline Principle and even the Worthwhile Activities Principle as too restrictive is not necessarily to advocate anarchy. The moral to be drawn from our discussion is not that anything goes where curriculum is concerned, but rather that educational considerations ought not to be lost sight of. Indeed I want to urge that they take precedence and that where they conflict with some general rule or principle, the rule or principle, not the educational considerations, must give way.

Had we taken the Discipline Principle to be making the moderate claim 'Teach the disciplines among other things' I would not have objected to it. As a matter of fact the disciplines constitute one very important sort of human activity, one which I have no doubt should at some point in the course of non-technical education be studied from the 'inside'—although not only from the inside. But non-technical or general education surely ought to be viewed in a broader framework than that provided by the Discipline Principle. Some have suggested that we conceive of the curriculum in terms of 'the forms of knowledge' and perhaps this does provide a broader base than does the Discipline Principle.[26] Yet much the same arguments can be adduced against the Forms of Knowledge Principle 'Teach only the forms of knowledge' as have been directed here at the Discipline Principle. If the forms of knowledge include other things besides the disciplines, they still do not include enough; that is to say, they do not unless the notion of a form of knowledge is made so weak that anything—or else anything one wishes—counts as such in which case the Forms of Knowledge Principle loses its force.[27]

When the curriculum is conceived of in terms of the disciplines or, for that matter, in terms of the 'forms of knowledge,' the disciplines loom large: they take up all or almost all 'curriculum space.' Now there surely are advantages to this. When they are spread out across the whole curriculum it is possible to dwell on the special characteristics of each discipline, or at least of each group or family of disciplines. Each one, or each group, is seen as unique; studying history from the 'inside' is as far removed as one can possibly imagine from studying physics or mathematics from the 'inside.'[28] It will be argued that if the disciplines are allotted a relatively modest part of the 'curriculum space,' justice cannot be done them.

It is true that the tendency to dwell on the special characteristics of each distinct discipline may have to be curtailed if curriculum space is redistributed. There is not possibly time to teach the disciplines or forms of knowledge in the way advocates of the relevant principles want them taught if those disciplines or forms of knowledge are given what seems to me to be their fair share, but no more than their fair share, of room in the curriculum.[29] But it must not be forgotten that the separate disciplines, although without doubt distinct and in some respects unique, do have common characteristics. Were the common elements rather than the non-common elements stressed, justice could be done the disciplines, although probably not the sort of justice many advocates of the Discipline Principle have in mind.

Compare a curriculum whose school subjects are history, physics, economics and the like with one whose school subjects are the humanities, the natural sciences, the social sciences.[30] A curriculum of the first sort enables the student to study distinct disciplines in detail and to luxuriate, if he or his teachers wish, in those aspects of a discipline that separate it from all the others. A curriculum of the second sort need not do away with all study of the separate disciplines as such, but it must surely dwell on family resemblances—else why group certain disciplines with certain others for study—and must just as surely overlook much of the rich detail which goes into making each discipline appear unique. In effect, the scale to which the different disciplines are drawn shifts as the school subject shifts. Given the school subject *history*, the discipline history can be drawn to a large-scale; given the school subject *the humanities* (or would it be *the social sciences?*) the discipline history must necessarily be drawn to a smaller scale with many of the characteristics missing which were so prominent in the large-scale drawing.

Consider now a curriculum conceived as embracing a wide and varied range of human activities and conduct—as encompassing forms of living or activity and not just forms of knowledge. Such a curriculum would have to give ample space to the arts and to the professions and to various sorts of work and to all sorts of other practical activities; it would have also to leave room for a variety of social activities and roles—not just the role of inquirer and the one time favourite role of citizen—and it would not be able to ignore things in what for want of a better designation l will call the personal realm, things such as character development. A curriculum so conceived might well have space for neither distinct disciplines nor families of such disciplines as separate school subjects but might only have space for the theoretical disciplines as a *single* school subject. Here, not merely family resemblances, but resemblances holding across families would be brought into focus. Details about families, indeed details about distinct disciplines, might not be totally ignored but elements common to the various disciplines would surely be singled out for attention. The scale to which any one particular discipline was drawn would be small; indeed, the separate disciplines might not be portrayed at all. It would be possible, of course, to present one particular discipline to the student as a sort of paradigm of a discipline. But in this case the special characteristics of the particular discipline would be sacrificed to the paradigmatic aspects of it. We would in effect have a large-scale drawing of the disciplines as a group presented by means of a particular example, rather than a large-scale drawing of the particular discipline.

There are, indeed, many ways in which the school subject *the disciplines* could be taught. It is not my purpose to list them, let alone settle on any one here. I merely wish to point out that when the disciplines are assigned a limited place in the curriculum, as l think they should be, it may be necessary to think more than we have been thinking about the things that make them alike and less about the things that make each one so special. I have no doubt that there are educational dangers in approaching the disciplines en masse rather than individually. One obvious danger is that students will be misled and will come away from their study of the disciplines thinking that one discipline is no different from another. But this need not happen any more than it need happen that a student of music comes away thinking that all music sounds alike. Another danger is that the substantive matter of the disciplines—the key concepts and basic ideas and their relationships—will be lost to view. How can even the most important findings of the disciplines be taught if all the disciplines are relegated to a single school subject? There is nothing, however, in the present view of the place of the disciplines in the curriculum which prevents the findings of the various separate disciplines from entering into any or all the subjects of the curriculum as subject matter to be taught and learned. Where various social roles are studied, for example, findings of sociology, psychology, anthropology and history could all come into play. And the substantive content of the natural sciences, or at least some of it, would surely find its proper home as well.

The smaller the curriculum space allotted the disciplines, the more room there will be in the curriculum for all the other human contexts worthy of study from within and without. There is one grave difficulty with the present attempt to put the disciplines in educational perspective, however. If we grant that students ought to see the disciplines from the standpoint of the actor, we must wonder how this can be accomplished if individual disciplines are not taught as such. There are no practitioners of the disciplines in general in the way that there are practitioners of history and physics and economics. l do not want to hold that it therefore makes no sense to talk about taking the actor's point of view, for we might be able to give sufficient content to the construct 'practitioner of the disciplines in general' to allow us to talk intelligently about his point of view and about putting oneself in his position. But if we want our students to get 'inside' *actual* human contexts—to engage in actual disciplinary activity or simply to get the feel of what it is like—they must engage in or get the feel of some *particular* discipline.

Let the student get 'inside' at least one particular discipline, by all means; let him gain the know-how of the practitioner; let him feel first-hand the pull of inquiry into some particular set of questions asked with a particular conceptual framework. But let us not suppose that he must get inside each discipline now fighting for a position in the curriculum in the course of his general education. I see no more reason to suppose that he should, than to suppose that he must get inside each art. To be sure a myth has developed among educators that one cannot understand a particular discipline or art unless one has some competence in that discipline or art. There are any number of ways to understand any given thing and although it may be the case that an artist can understand art in a way that a non-artist cannot, it does not follow that a non-artist cannot understand art at all. Similarly with the disciplines. There may be good educational reasons for including in a curriculum which assigns limited space to the disciplines the study of some discipline from within with the hope that the student will gain some competence in it, but we need not worry that those disciplines which are not studied from the "inside" cannot be understood.[31]

If we acknowledge that the disciplines constitute one way of life or form of human activity among many and that the many deserve a place in the educational scheme of things, we will have to look for ways to do educational justice by the disciplines both from the 'inside' and from the 'outside' without doing injustice to everything else. Advocates of the Discipline Principle are of course in part reacting against what they consider to have been the utter disregard or misunderstanding of the disciplines by educators. The very thing I advocated above—namely, bringing in disciplinary findings insofar as they relate to important topics—is the very thing they have found to be horrifying. Mathematics, they will remind us, simply cannot be learned in the way it should be learned by bringing it into a unit on mining. I hope l will not be construed as recommending a return to the pre-structure of the disciplines days where subject matter from the disciplines was, or at least is said to have been, diluted and distorted and schooling in general was, or at least is said to have been, soft-headed. I do not think that the disciplines must have a ruling hand over what goes into the curriculum in order for educational justice to be done them. What is important, it seems to me, is that at some point in the curriculum they are taken as important objects to be learned about and as important human contexts to be studied and entered into. Over and above this, it is important that they serve, along with other things, as sources of subject matter insofar as they bear on whatever is being studied. I fully agree with advocates of the Discipline Principle that education ought not to misunderstand or distort the disciplines; my purpose here has been simply to urge that advocates of the disciplines ought not be allowed to misunderstand or distort education.

Notes

1. I should point out, however, that the view of the relationship between the disciplines and the curriculum to be discussed here is widely held. For explicit formulations of it I refer the reader to, among others, Philip Phenix, *Realms of Meaning* (New York: McGraw-Hill, 1964); Arthur R. King, Jr. and John A. Brownell, *The Curriculum and the Disciplines of Knowledge* (New York: John Wiley, 1966); Paul H. Hirst, 'Liberal Education and the Nature of Knowledge,' in Reginald D. Archambault, *Philosophical Analysis and Education* (London: Routledge and Kegan Paul, 1965). This view is implicit, moreover, in Jerome S. Bruner's, *The Process of Education* (Cambridge: Harvard University Press, 1961), surely the most influential book of the last decade in curriculum circles. King and Brownell provide us with an example of the sort of hedging I am referring to; see p. 120 where they allow the school a 'nondiscipline curriculum' as a sort of minor and somewhat disreputable adjunct to the liberal (i.e. discipline) curriculum which is its main business. Note also that of the authors cited here only Hirst is talking solely about higher education.

2. This distinction between principles presupposes a distinction between the notion of a school subject and the notion of school subject matter. Very roughly, a school subject consists of subject matter—some might prefer to use the term 'content'—organized in some way. To say what subject matter should be taught is not in itself to say how it should be organized, hence it is not to say what the school subject should be. And to select school subjects is not in itself to say what subject matter should be taught, since different selections of subject matter can be consistent with a given school subject.

3. E.g., Phenix, P. *op. cit.*, distinguishes what he calls realms of meaning, classifies the disciplines under these realms, and asks us to choose from the different realms; Hirst, P.H. *op. cit.*, suggests (but does not require) that 'paradigm' examples of the various forms of knowledge (the disciplines) be selected.

4. Of the authors cited in note 1, Phenix quite clearly advocates Discipline Principle SM, rather than Discipline Principle S, *op. cit.* p. 319; Hirst is committed only to Discipline Principle SM, *op. cit.* p. 136ff; King and Brownell seem to be committed to Discipline

Principle S, op. cit. p. 120. Bruner would seem to be committed only to Discipline Principle SM; in this connection see his 'Man: A Course of Study,' *Toward a Theory of Instruction* (Cambridge: Harvard University Press, 1966).

5. For an approach to social studies education which rejects the Discipline Principle and the Structure Principle but not the Inquiry Principle see Donald W. Oliver and James P. Shaver, *Teaching Public Issues in the High School* (Boston: Houghton Mifflin, 1966).

6. See P. Phenix, *op. cit.* Chap. 26, 27; A.R. King, and J.A. Brownell, *op. cit.* Ch. III where they characterize a discipline in terms of a mode of inquiry and a conceptual structure; P.H. Hirst, *op. cit.* p. 132ff.

7. See Kingsley Price, 'Discipline in Teaching, In Its Study and Its Theory,' Israel Scheffler, 'Is Education a Discipline?', Max Black, 'Education as Art and Discipline,' in Scheffler, *Philosophy and Education*, 2nd ed. (Boston: Allyn and Bacon, 1966), for discussions of practical disciplines, theoretical disciplines and the disciplinary value of disciplines and other things.

8. For a thoughtful analysis of the notion of a theoretical discipline see I. Scheffler, 'Is Education a Discipline?' However, see King and Brownell, *op. cit.* Ch. III and Phenix, *op. cit.* Ch. 25, for rather different accounts of the notion. Fred M. Newmann has an interesting discussion of the problem of the definition of the term 'discipline' in the course of a criticism of the theory of curriculum under examination here as it applies to social studies education in his 'Questioning the Place of Social Science Disciplines in Education,' *The Record-Teachers College* 69 (1967), pp. 69–74.

9. Note that in saying this I am leaving open the question of whether each discipline has a unique method, a unique vocabulary, etc.

10. Bruner, *op. cit.*.

11. Joseph J. Schwab seems to take this tack when he distinguishes between the substantive and the syntactic structures of the disciplines. See, for example, his essay 'Problems, Topics and Issues' in Stanley Elam, *Education and the Structure of Knowledge* (Chicago: Rand McNally, 1964). King and Brownell, *op. cit.* p. 77, follow Schwab in this.

12. To be sure, by its very nature literary criticism, or at least some of it, qualifies as literature in a way that music theory does not qualify as music and French grammar does not qualify as French. Yet insofar as literary criticism constitutes a theoretical discipline it does so not because it itself is literature but because it provides an account of literature.

13. I suppose there is a third possibility. He can acknowledge the educational significance of the sorts of things under discussion here, admit that the disciplines do not shed light on them, yet refuse to recognize that this has any bearing on the Discipline Principle. We are assuming, however, that our Discipline Principle advocate is rational.

14. Although advocates of the Discipline Principle invariably consider history to be a theoretical discipline it is not at all obvious that it is in fact one or that it meets the criteria these writers themselves set up for a discipline. For example, they conceive of a discipline as having some central concepts peculiar to it and it is questionable that history meets this condition.

15. The cracked radiator example is taken from Carl G. Hempel's essay 'The Function of General Laws in History,' *Journal of Philosophy XXXIX* (1942), pp. 35–48. Reprinted in

Hempel, *Aspects of Scientific Explanation* (New York: The Free Press, 1965). Hempel uses it for a different purpose. See, Scheffler, 'Is Education a Discipline?' Section VI, for a discussion of the relevance of the disciplines to everyday affairs.

16. What is at stake is that the disciplines be shown as fields of inquiry and that students come to see them as such. This can be accomplished in a number of ways. I do not want to suggest that advocates of these principles do not also advocate that students engage in inquiry, indeed that students learn to be inquirers. My point is simply that the three principles under discussion do not by themselves necessitate this.

17. One could study the methods of the practitioner of a discipline without looking at that discipline from the 'inside'. For example, one could become acquainted with the methods of physics through a study of philosophy of science.

18. I have said that the task of determining exactly which parts or aspects of a discipline are relevant to any given thing outside the discipline is itself a task of inquiry. Inquiry into the relevance of a discipline for our practical, everyday affairs must, however, be distinguished from the inquiry carried on within that discipline.

19. Arno A. Bellack in his discussions of the curriculum has invoked a distinction similar to the inside-outside distinction l am introducing here, namely the distinction between a participant's language and an onlooker's language; see, for example, Bellack's 'What Knowledge is of Most Worth?' in William M. Alexander, *The Changing Secondary School Curriculum* (New York: Holt, Rinehart & Winston, 1967). If I understand him correctly, Bellack wants students to learn both sorts of languages; in effect, then, he advocates their viewing the disciplines from the outside as well as the inside. He is, moreover, concerned about some of the problems with the Discipline Principle I am raising here.

20. Hirst, *op. cit.*, for one, makes this crystal clear.

21. For an interesting discussion of commonsense knowledge and its relation to disciplinary knowledge see L.R. Perry, 'Commonsense Thought, Knowledge and Judgement and Their importance for Education,' *British Journal of Educational Studies XIII* (1965), pp. 125–138.

22. *Laws and Explanation in History* (Oxford: Oxford University Press, 1957), Ch. 5.

23. See my 'Another Look at the Doctrine of *Verstehen*,' *British Journal of Educational Studies* 20 (1969), pp. 53–67.

24. See 'Education as Initiation' in Reginald D. Archambault, *Philosophical Analysis and Education* (London: Routledge & Kegan Paul, 1965); also *Ethics and Education*, Ch. 4 (Chicago: Scott, Foresman, 1967). It should be noted that Peters himself speaks throughout of education not teaching.

25. Thus Peters says that the teacher's task is to 'try to get others on the inside of a public form of life that he shares and considers to be worthwhile'; the teacher, having been initiated, is already on the inside according to Peters; see 'Education as Initiation,' pp. 104, 107.

26. Hirst, *op. cit.*, speaks in this way. He seems, however, to have in mind the distinct disciplines. Phenix, *op. cit.* speaks of ways of knowing but again seems to be talking about the disciplines.

27. Hirst may well have left himself open to this criticism when he allowed the arts to qualify as forms of knowledge, *op. cit.* p. 130.

28. Advocates of the Discipline Principle invariably stress the distinctive features of each discipline.

29. One wonders if there is even time to do what advocates of the Discipline Principle want to do when the disciplines are given all the space in the curriculum. Consider: 'What is being sought is, first, sufficient immersion in the concepts, logic and criteria of the discipline for a person to come to know the distinctive way in which it 'works' and then sufficient generalization of these over the whole range of the discipline so that his experience begins to be widely structured in this distinctive manner.' Hirst, *op. cit.* p. 132.

30. See Bellack, *op. cit.* for a 'broad groupings of knowledge' approach to curriculum planning.

31. I would hope that there would be a wide choice of disciplines to be studied from within for it is no more reasonable to suppose that all students will profit from getting 'inside' some particular discipline than that all will from getting 'inside' art or music or the dance.

CHAPTER 8

What Should We Do with a Hidden Curriculum When We Find One?

A manuscript reader for the journal that published "What Should We Do with a Hidden Curriculum When We Find One?" once told me that although in the interests of anonymity my name had been removed from this paper, he knew I had written it. Yet the essay, with its hints of the author's emerging feminist sensibility, bears witness to the fact that in 1976 I was already becoming a different person. I no longer used the generic form of the masculine pronoun, I made reference to school's hidden curriculum in sexism, and—perhaps most telling—I suggested that the feminist practice of consciousness raising be taken as a model of what to do with an objectionable hidden curriculum when you find one. In thinking about the education of girls and women I have come to rely on that advice. Realizing, moreover, that it applies equally to boys and men, in The Schoolhome *I made the transfer of school's hidden curriculum in misogyny and anti-domesticity into the curriculum proper one of the staples of good educational practice.*

At the end of a very interesting article, "Hiding the Hidden Curriculum" (1973/74), Elizabeth Vallance raises the question of what to do with the hidden curriculum now that we have found it. We can embrace it wholeheartedly, she says, or we can attempt to expunge it altogether, or we can do something between these two extremes. Vallance leaves the question open and I have no intention of closing it here; indeed, I am not sure it is one that can or should be closed. I would, however, like to explore some of the things that can be done with a hidden curriculum once it is found and some of the pitfalls of doing those things. But first we need to get clearer than we now are on the nature of the beast.

This essay was originally published in *Curriculum Inquiry*, 6:2 (1976): 135–151. Copyright © 1976 by John Wiley & Sons, Inc. Reprinted by permission.

1. Misleading Labels

Most of the labels we use when talking about hidden curriculum are either singularly unilluminating or highly misleading. To call hidden curriculum "covert" or "latent," as people often do, does no harm, but neither does it promote our understanding. To call hidden curriculum "what schooling does to people," "by-products of schooling," or "nonacademic outcomes of schooling" would seem to promote our understanding but in fact leads us astray.[1] For these last three labels, and others, too, make it seem as if hidden curriculum is necessarily tied to schools and schooling when it is not. Much of our education—and I am talking now of formal education and not simply of the informal education which enters into all aspects of our lives—much of this education has always taken place outside of schools. In an earlier day, apprenticeships to craftsmen prevailed. Presently, there are internships in hospitals, management training programs in industry, fieldwork placements in social agencies; there are private music lessons, group karate lessons, swimming programs at the Y; there are summer camps, Cub Scouts, basic training in the armed forces. I see no reason whatsoever to suppose that schools have a hidden curriculum but that formal educational programs in nonschool settings do not. Labels such as "by-products of schooling" or "what schooling does to people" do no harm if we realize that they refer to one particular class of hidden curricula, namely, the hidden curricula of schools. We must not, however, let them dominate our thinking lest they blind us to the hidden curricula lurking in other habitats.

These labels mislead in another way, too, for they give the impression that everything an educational setting does to people belongs to its hidden curriculum. But while hidden curriculum is not necessarily tied to schools and schooling, it is always and everywhere tied to learning. Both schools and nonschool educational settings do lots of things to people—they have all sorts of by-products. It needs to be stressed, therefore, that only *some* of the things done by a given educational setting constitute its hidden curriculum. Some hospitals because of their location create traffic jams, some swimming programs because of their pools cause earaches, and some schools because of their expenditures produce rising tax rates, but these results or outcomes do not belong to the hidden curriculum of the educational setting in question. They do not because, although they happen, they are not *learned*.

Implicit in hidden curriculum talk, moreover, is a contrast between hidden curriculum and what, for want of a better name, I will call *curriculum proper*—that thing, difficult as it is to define, about which philosophers and educational theorists have long debated and which curriculum specialists have long tried to plan and develop. The contrast is between when it is openly intended that students learn and what, although not openly intended, they do, in fact, learn. Indeed, one important thrust of the critique of contemporary schooling mounted by those who have been called radical school reformers (see Gross 1969) is that curriculum proper is failing while hidden curriculum thrives: students do not learn to read, they do not learn math or science or any of the other subjects and skills endorsed by all parties to the educational enterprise; what they do learn is to be docile and obedient, to value competition over cooperation, to stifle their creative impulses, and to believe in what Ivan Illich calls the Myth of Unending Consumption (Illich 1971, p. 55). Thus, some results or outcomes of school or of nonschool educational settings are not constituents of a hidden curriculum because they are not states that individuals have attained through learning: what I will henceforth call *learning states*. Other results are not because they are openly intended learning states, hidden from neither teacher nor student. In a school which openly acknowledges the goal that students learn to speak French and provides courses to that end, the ability to speak French, if achieved, although a learning state, is not part of its hidden curriculum.

I do not mean to suggest that knowledge of French could never be part of a hidden curriculum. It is tempting to conceive of the contrast with curriculum proper implicit in hidden curriculum talk as one between academic and nonacademic learning states in the manner of one of the labels listed above, but this is a mistake. Curriculum proper can and often does quite directly and openly aim at what is normally taken to be nonacademic learning, be it of moral values, religious attitudes, political preferences, or vocational skills. We are so used to thinking of the academic dimension of curriculum proper that we forget this. And just as a curriculum proper can be nonacademic, so a hidden curriculum can consist of what normally would be considered academic learning, be it learning of addition facts, scientific theories, or French. To be sure, the hidden curriculum of contemporary public schooling discovered to date is what most of us would call nonacademic. But it does not follow from this discovery that a hidden curriculum *could* not consist of academic learning states. A hidden curriculum, like a curriculum proper, has subject matter, but just as there is no particular subject matter which must be present in or absent from every curriculum proper, so there is none which must or cannot belong to every hidden curriculum.

In sum, a hidden curriculum consists of some of the outcomes or byproducts of schools or of nonschool settings, particularly those states which are learned yet are not openly intended. There is no special subject matter which always and everywhere characterizes hidden curriculum, although, of course, a hidden curriculum must have *some* subject matter. It should perhaps be stressed that this neutrality with respect to subject matter means not only that the learning states of a hidden curriculum can be academic as well as nonacademic; it means that the subject matter can be significant as well as trivial, worthwhile as well as worthless.

Actually, when one speaks of learning states one is usually speaking of two things at once: some *state* a learner is in (for example, a state of knowing or believing or being interested or being cautious), and something which may be called the *object* of that state—provided "object" is construed broadly enough to include not just physical objects but such things as the theory of relativity, *David Copperfield*, the free enterprise system, and love. Thus, a learning state is not 2 + 3 = 5, but believing or remembering that 2 + 3 = 5; it is not the free enterprise system as such, but being committed to or, perhaps, being adamantly opposed to the system.[2] When I said just now that there is no special subject matter necessarily associated with hidden curriculum,

I meant that the learning states which constitute a hidden curriculum are not limited to one sort of object. But they are not limited to one sort of state either. The learning states of a hidden curriculum can be states which we think of as character traits—for example, docility or conformity. They can also be cognitive states such as believing or knowing, states of readiness or of skill, emotional states, attitudinal states, or some combination of those and other sorts of states.[3]

2. The Hidden Curriculum

Those who describe the hidden curriculum of contemporary schooling talk of the hidden curriculum as if there is and can be only one, as if hidden curriculum is everywhere the same. But of course it is not. A hidden curriculum is always *of* some setting, and there is no reason to suppose that different settings will have identical hidden curricula. Actually, a hidden curriculum is not only of some setting but is *at* some time; therefore, we cannot even assume that a single setting will have identical hidden curricula at different times. Settings change, and as they do some learning states may become extinct as new ones emerge.

It is sometimes said that learning states must occur systematically if they are to belong to a hidden curriculum.[4] I am not sure what this means. True, they must *be* results of the setting. However, the learning states of a hidden curriculum need not be systematic in the sense that they are mass products—learning states for all or even most learners in that setting. If John is the only one of his classmates who comes to appreciate good art as a result of the teacher's putting Picasso prints on the classroom walls, the teacher in this instance wanting to make the room more attractive and having no thought of learning states, this learning state of John's belongs to the hidden curriculum of his school, at least for him. A hidden curriculum, like a curriculum proper, is *of* some setting, *at* some time, and *for* some learner.

In view of this relativity to context, talk of *the* hidden curriculum is normally elliptical. Those who speak in this way usually have a particular setting in mind—often, but not always, public schooling in the United States—and they have a particular time, usually the present, in mind. From the standpoint of the learner, moreover, *the* hidden curriculum is an abstraction, for it is neither the set of learning states attained by anyone in particular nor the set attained by all the learners in a given setting. Idiosyncratic learning states are overlooked when a portrait of *the* hidden curriculum is painted, and rightly so, for *the* hidden curriculum of a setting consists not in all the learning states therein attained, but rather in the dominant ones. An account of *the* hidden curriculum of a setting, like an account of *the* history of an era, is selective. Attention is directed to common themes running through the learning states, presumably themes of some importance. Learning states which seem insignificant or which do not fit readily into the general pattern will be shunned, even though they are in fact produced by the setting.

The learning states of *the* hidden curriculum of a setting do, then, occur systematically in the sense that idiosyncratic states are ignored. But what is considered idiosyncratic will depend on one's interest. Learning states which are legitimately ignored when *the* hidden curriculum of some setting is the focus of attention may require attention when *the* hidden curriculum for some learner is at issue. Suppose what is unlikely, namely, that Mary is the only person in her school in the last twenty years who has come to believe as an unintended result of her schooling that women cannot be doctors. This idiosyncratic learning state is rightly ignored by those trying to determine *the* hidden curriculum *of Mary's school.* But those trying to discover *the* hidden curriculum of that school *for* Mary would be remiss if they did not take it seriously, since it might well play a very significant role in Mary's life.

I want to emphasize here, because I think it too often forgotten, that our interest can be in hidden curricula for learners as well as of settings. And just as *the* hidden curriculum of a setting is an abstraction from the standpoint of learners, so *the* hidden curriculum for a learner is an abstraction from the standpoint of settings. *The* hidden curriculum for Mary "cuts across" settings, so that to discover it we must look not simply at Mary's schooling, but at the other settings having hidden curricula in which Mary is a participant—or perhaps is simply an unwilling victim. Once again, *the* hidden curriculum is a selection from among the relevant learning states: it is a set of learning states thought to be dominant for Mary.

3. Finding a Hidden Curriculum

A hidden curriculum is not something one just finds; one must go hunting for it. Since a hidden curriculum is a set of learning states, ultimately one must find out what is learned as a result of the practices, procedures, rules, relationships, structures, and physical characteristic which constitute a given setting. But one can begin by spotting learning states and making sure they can be traced back to the setting, or by examining aspects of the setting and discovering what learning states they produce. Motivations for the search can, of course, vary. Some investigators may simply want to know what is learned in school, others will want to make their teaching methods more efficient, and still others will be intent on revealing connections between education and the larger social order. But whatever the motivation may be, a full-blown theory of curriculum cannot afford to neglect the hunt for hidden curricula, for the quarry plays a central role in the education of each one of us.

One consequence of the relativity of hidden curriculum to setting, time, and learner is that investigative work on it is never done. New settings with their own hidden curricula are forever being created and old ones are forever changing. Information gathered yesterday on the hidden curriculum of a given setting may not accurately portray that setting's hidden curriculum today. Thus, the scope of the search for hidden curricula needs to be extended beyond schools to nonschool settings, and at the same time the searchers must continually retrace their steps.

Even if hidden curricula did not change over time, there would be reason to revisit the old haunts, for the information gathered at any time is never the whole story.

Regardless of setting or time, what we find when we investigate hidden curricula is a function of what we look for and what we look at. The literature describing the hidden curriculum of public schooling in the United States published in the mid to late 1960s provides an interesting case in point. It draws our attention to learning states having class and racial overtones, but it overlooks those having sexist implications (e.g., Henry 1963, Herndon 1968, Kozol 1967). Yet no one who has seen the film *High School* or read even a sampling of the articles in *And Jill Came Tumbling After* (Stacey et al. 1974) can doubt that public schooling in the 1960s included a wide range of sexist practices and that its hidden curriculum included sexist beliefs, attitudes, and values. If sexist learning states were not found it is not because they did not exist, but because they were not seen or—if they were seen—because they were not recognized for what they were.

A description of the hidden curriculum of public schooling of the 1960s, or for that matter of the 1970s, written today would most likely draw our attention to its sexist component. But who knows what other components it might overlook! Christian doctrine? Heterosexual bias? Speciesism? The search for hidden curricula needs to retrace its steps, then, because even if a hidden curriculum does not change over time, we change. Our interests shift, our knowledge of the world is enlarged, our consciousness is raised, and we therefore come to see and care about things in a hidden curriculum we did not care about, indeed perhaps could not see, before.

One way to determine if we have overlooked important parts of a hidden curriculum is to examine the different aspects or elements of the relevant setting or settings to see what learning states they produce. In other words, look beyond learning states to sources![5] Thanks to a variety of inquiries, many of which Vallance cites in her article, we have an idea of some of the sources of important elements of hidden curricula of schools. Vallance mentions, for example, the social structure of the classroom, the teacher's exercise of authority, the rules governing the relationship between teacher and student (1973/74, pp. 6–7). Standard learning activities are also sources. Who can forget Jules Henry's description of a classroom game of Spelling Baseball or John Holt's account of Twenty Questions (Henry 1963, Holt 1964). In a somewhat different vein, Joanne Bronars (1970) has drawn our attention to dissecting frogs and catching insects. Another source of hidden curricula is the teacher's use of language (Gayer 1970). And, of course, there are textbooks and audiovisual aids, furnishings and architecture, disciplinary measures, timetables, tracking systems, and curricular priorities.

The problem in looking to sources is that it is not clear that a list of sources of the learning states which constitute hidden curricula will have an end, for as new practices, procedures, environments and the like are introduced into educational settings, they become potential generators of hidden curricula. Can anyone doubt that the new classification of students as learning-disabled and the practices which accompany it are generating a hidden curriculum, or rather elements of one? As pocket calculators begin to be used in math and science classes, will they not generate hidden learning states? Just as there are no limits on the subject matter of the learning outcomes which can constitute a hidden curriculum, I think we must conclude that there are none on the elements or aspects of educational settings which can be sources of those states.

There is, of course, a good reason for looking to sources and for recognizing that when limits are placed on the sorts of things within a setting which can generate elements of hidden curricula, they are arbitrary. If our concern is not simply to discover hidden curricula but to do something about them, we must find out which elements or aspects of a given setting help bring about which components of that setting's hidden curriculum. For if we do not know the sources of the learning states belonging to a hidden curriculum, we must either let that hidden curriculum be or do away with the whole setting. But some hidden curricula or parts thereof quite clearly ought not to be left as they are; and on the other hand, if we do away with whole settings, we may be doing away with practices, procedures, physical environments and the like which on balance generate desirable learning outcomes.

Rational intervention requires that we know sources. It requires also that we return to the scene of our interventions to make sure we have not done more harm than good. There is no guarantee that, when we change an educational setting so as to do away with a portion of its hidden curriculum we find abhorrent, we will succeed; indeed, if we are not careful, the changes we make can generate the very learning states we are trying to banish or, for that matter, ones even more unsavory. The learning disabilities movement purports to be trying to end the practice of labeling students because of the hidden curriculum resulting from it, but one wonders if the movement is not in fact promoting the very learning states it claims to reject (see Schrag and Divoky 1975).

Once we recognize that any aspect of an educational setting can have learning states which are not openly intended, that changes in settings can produce such states, that the learning states produced by a setting may be different for every learner and that new learners constantly enter educational settings, then I think we must acknowledge that for any given setting hidden curricula cannot be avoided. We can get rid of a particular hidden curriculum of a setting, but in principle we cannot avoid some hidden curriculum or other unless we abolish the setting itself. I stress this point because educators often suppose that if their reforms are put into practice we will never again have to worry about hidden curricula. As the documentary film *Infants School* unwittingly testifies, this is a terrible mistake, for the most enlightened practices can carry with them an undesirable hidden curriculum.[6] In many ways, the British infants school of the film is a model of school reform, yet if one looks closely one sees traditional sex roles and stereotypes being transmitted. Those of us concerned with educational settings cannot rest on our laurels. It is impossible to do away with all hidden curricula; hence for any given setting, we must always be on our guard.

4. Two Kinds of Hiddenness

That *some* hidden curriculum or other for any given setting is inevitable, ought not to be taken as grounds for maintaining the status quo in education.

To say that some hidden curriculum or other is inevitable for any given setting is not to say that a hidden curriculum consisting in learning states we take to be undesirable is inevitable. We need to guard against replacing an objectionable hidden curriculum with a worse one, but although there is always the possibility of our ending up with a worse one, there is no necessity at work here. And there is always the possibility that we will end up with a better one.

I realize that an important part of the message of Illich's *Deschooling Society* is that the hidden curriculum of contemporary public schooling cannot be changed—at least not for the better—by changes in the setting. Hence the need for deschooling. Illich has been attacked on this score by critics speaking from very different points on the educational spectrum. It is all too easy, however, to do less than justice to his claim. He is surely *not* saying that *none* of the hidden learning states produced by contemporary public schooling can be banished or that *no* changes for the better can be produced by changes in the setting. His view of *the* hidden curriculum of public schooling is highly selective, and his claim about the resistance of public schooling to reform that makes a real difference must be understood as holding only for the learning outcomes with which he is concerned. Exactly what these are and whether he is right about them is a topic for another occasion. But whether or not he is right, there is certainly nothing in his remarks which shows reform of hidden curricula to be *in general* impossible. His claim applies only to school settings, and he is the first to point out that nonschool settings also have hidden curricula (1971, p. 48). Some of these latter might be as resistant to real reform as he says schools are, but there is no reason to suppose that all would be.

The inevitability thesis is not a counsel for inaction. Yet inaction is, in fact, one viable alternative when we find a hidden curriculum and wonder what we ought to do with it. I indicated above that we may be forced to let a hidden curriculum be when we find it because we do not know its exact sources. It should be clear, however, that even if we know its sources, we can nonetheless choose not to abolish or even alter them in any way. It may be wondered, however, if a hidden curriculum, once it is found, *can* be left as is. Once we find a hidden curriculum doesn't it stop being hidden, hence being a hidden curriculum?

Our discussion has for too long avoided the question of the hiddenness of the learning states belonging to a hidden curriculum. Suppose a sociologist studies a school or school system and finds elements of its hidden curriculum. Is that hidden curriculum, simply by virtue of being known to the sociologist, no longer a *hidden* curriculum? Surely not. Being hidden, like being north of, is a relation: just as Boston is north of Miami but not north of Montreal, so something can be hidden from one person or group but not from another. When we speak of something as hidden, moreover, we usually have some context in mind in relation to which we make our judgments of hiddenness. In the game Hide and Seek, a player is hidden just so long as the one who is It has not found him or her; that others know where the player is has no bearing on the player's hiddenness from the standpoint of the game; and when the player is found, that others do not know where the player is also has no bearing on the player's hiddenness.

Education is no game, but nonetheless a hidden curriculum is in this respect like a hidden player in Hide and Seek. Once the learners in a setting are aware of the learning states they are acquiring or are supposed to acquire, these learning outcomes no longer belong to the hidden curriculum of that setting. Indeed, once learning states are openly acknowledged so that the learners can readily become aware of them even if they do not, the learning states can no longer be considered hidden. Until learning states are acknowledged or the learners are aware of them, however, they remain hidden even if sociologists, bureaucrats, and teachers are all aware of them. Thus, a hidden curriculum can be found yet remain hidden, for finding is one thing and telling is another.

There are, in effect, two kinds of hiddenness, and an account of hidden curriculum needs to come to terms with both. Something can be hidden in the sense in which a cure for cancer is hidden or in the sense in which a penny in the game Hide the Penny is hidden. Both academicians who investigate the hidden curriculum of public schooling today and radical school reformers who decry it vacillate on this issue. Some make it sound as if a hidden curriculum is hidden by someone or some group in the manner of the penny in the children's game. Others seem to assume that the learning states of a hidden curriculum have not been hidden by anyone: they just happen to be unknown to us, much as the cure for cancer is unknown to us at the present time.

Whether we are trying to explain why the hidden curriculum of a given setting is what it is or to change a hidden curriculum, we need to take into account this basic ambiguity in the notion of hidden curriculum. For any set of hidden learning states which interests us, we must try to settle the question of intent. It makes no sense to explain a hidden curriculum by means of a conspiracy theory, as some of those writers who point out that the hidden curriculum of public schooling in the United States serves capitalism do, and at the same time describe its learning states as the unintended by-products of schooling. Nor does it make sense simply to tinker with school practices and procedures in order to do away with a given hidden curriculum if it is really the product of intent.

Some readers would doubtless prefer that I characterize hidden curriculum solely in terms of unintended learning states. To introduce intention muddies the waters, they will say. Yet I do not think we have any choice here. It is not only that those writers most concerned with hidden curricula move back and forth between the two kinds of hiddenness. The relevant research on intent has not all been done. We may assume that all the elements of the hidden curricula discovered to date are unintended, but we certainly do not know for sure that they are. A characterization which accommodates the descriptions of hidden curricula we now have is surely to be preferred over one which may require us when the evidence is in to reject some on the grounds that the learning states they describe were intended although we did not realize it.

Earlier I characterized hidden curriculum in terms of learning states which are not openly intended. The point of that negative formulation was to accommodate the two kinds of hiddenness. That characterization did not, however, take into account the learner's point of view. Although a learning state of a setting is not openly intended a learner can be aware of it, in which case it will not belong to the hidden curriculum of that setting for that learner. Thus, my earlier characterization must be amended. A hidden curriculum consists of those learning states of a setting which are either unintended or intended but not openly acknowledged to the learners in the setting unless the learners are aware of them.

5. Out of the Frying Pan

What then can we do with a hidden curriculum once we have found it? This depends, of course, on who "we" are. Assuming we are the educators in a setting and have found both hidden curriculum and sources, there are a number of alternatives open to us.

(1) We can do nothing: we can leave the setting alone rather than try to change it, in which case the relevant learning states become foreseen by us, whereas previously they were not, but they do not otherwise change; in particular, the hidden curriculum remains hidden. This may seem to be the alternative of despair but that is not necessarily the case, for there may be some hidden curricula, or elements thereof, with respect to which we are neutral—we do not positively value them but we do not consider them undesirable either. In relation to such learning states, doing nothing is a reasonable alternative.

(2) We can change our practices, procedures, environments, rules and the like in an effort to root out those learning states we consider undesirable. The radical school-reform movement known as open education has tried to do just this. It has opposed tracking, grading, and examinations, changed the physical environment of classrooms, introduced new learning activities and educational materials, and tried to alter both teacher-pupil and pupil-pupil relationships in order to avoid the hidden curriculum of contemporary public schooling. The free-school movement, while varying in its details from open education, can be understood in this same light.

(3) Instead of changing a setting, we can simply abolish it. This, of course, is the alternative those in the deschooling movement recommend. I say "simply" abolish, but for some educational settings, notably the public school systems of modern industrial societies, abolition is not a simple matter. Abolition of a setting does, however, guarantee abolition of that setting's hidden curriculum, but not of all hidden curricula like it.

(4) It is always possible that we will want to embrace rather than abolish the hidden curriculum we find. There are many today who applaud the learning states of neatness and competitiveness, docility and obedience to authority attributed to the hidden curriculum of our public schools (e.g., Pursell 1976). They actually have two alternatives: (*a*) they can openly acknowledge these learning states, thereby shifting them from hidden curriculum to curriculum proper, or (*b*) they can intend these learning states but not openly, in which case they remain part of the hidden curriculum.[7]

What *should* we do with a hidden curriculum when we find it? The significance of the question is a function of the quality of the hidden curriculum we find. If a hidden curriculum is harmless, what we do with it will not matter very much. It is when the one we find is not harmless—when it instills beliefs, attitudes, values, or patterns of behavior which are undesirable—that our question takes on urgency. And it becomes more urgent the more undesirable the learning states are. There can be no doubt that when the hidden curriculum we find contains harmful learning states, we must try to root them out. But this is sometimes easier said than done. A teacher can stop using the game of Spelling Baseball as a learning activity, but this will be but a small step toward rooting out learning states such as competitiveness, self-hatred, and hostility toward one's peers. Attitudes and traits such as these seldom have a single, easily isolated source; indeed, those which are most offensive, because very basic, are likely to be products of a complex set of interrelated and entrenched practices and structures. To give up or modify one of these may well accomplish very little.

Large-scale changes, perhaps even total destruction, of a setting may be necessary if a hidden curriculum or some central part thereof is to be abolished. And this, of course, is what the radical school-reform movement in all its variations has been about.[8] The hidden curriculum of contemporary public schooling in the United States has been held to be abhorrent—and rightly so. Drastic changes have been seen—again rightly in my view—as the only hope if its highly undesirable and very deep seated learning outcomes are to be banished. This is not the place to catalog or assess those proposals, although they need to be assessed in a way they have not yet been. I do, however, want to draw attention to a problem which confronts anyone who tries to change drastically or abolish altogether an educational setting in order to do away with it hidden curriculum—a problem too many radical school reformers have ignored.

Some changes in educational settings involve the deliberate placing of the learners of that setting in other settings so as to break down the barriers between the setting and the "real" world, meanwhile enhancing learning. Thus, for example, schools are encouraged to put students in nonschool settings where they will learn through being apprenticed to master craftsmen and women, through working at a job, through helping others do their jobs or, perhaps, simply through watching and observing. Other changes in educational settings involve restricting its function so as to reduce its power over its participants. It has been proposed, for example, that schools be limited to giving basic skill training (e.g. Bereiter 1973, Katz 1974). In this case, even if participants in the setting are not deliberately placed in other settings, the likelihood of their drifting into them is great. And of course there is the total abolition of a setting, in which case the participants may simply be abandoned to other settings. In all three sorts of reform, the risk is real that those on the receiving end of the offending learning states will be taken out of the frying pan only to be sent or allowed to leap into the fire.

It is not just formal educational settings which have hidden curricula. Any setting can have one and most do. When I argued initially that hidden curricula can exist in nonschool settings, I limited the discussion to formal educational settings such as teaching hospitals, private piano lessons, and basic training in the armed services. But learning states occur in settings which are not usually considered educational at all. At IBM and Bell Telephone, at one's local gas station and City Hall, workers learn more than their jobs: attitudes, values, and patterns of behavior are as much the product of these settings as of formal educational ones. It seems not only legitimate, therefore, but theoretically important that we recognize explicitly that hidden curricula can be found anywhere learning states are found. IBM and Bell Telephone are not exempt;

neither are one's neighborhood streets, one's church, or the national book club one joins. And what is important to remember is that there is no good reason at all to suppose that the hidden curricula of these and kindred settings are significantly better than the one which is the target of school reforms.

Radical school reformers have been called romantics—this label, needless to say, having derogatory connotations. The source of their romanticism is seen as lying in their view of the child as by nature a happy, curious, creative, and good being who is ruined by school. Perhaps some radical school reformers do romanticize the child, but in general this is a caricature of their position. If the reformers are romantics it is not in their beliefs about human nature, but in their beliefs about the world outside schools. It is as if they bracket their critique of contemporary society, when they begin to theorize about education. I am sure that they are as aware as anyone of the sorry state of the outside world. Indeed, they were probably aware of the sorry state of *it* long before they perceived the sorry state of schools. But they forget it in their excitement upon discovering the hidden curriculum of contemporary public schooling. Make the outside world, not schools, the dominant educational setting, they say, and all will be well—as if the world out there were a benign setting, one in which there either are no hidden curricula or in which only worthwhile ones thrive.[9]

A mistake we all tend to make—except perhaps when we are thinking of our own children—is to concentrate on the hidden curriculum *of* a given setting when what matters is the hidden curriculum *for* a given individual or group. To do away with the complex network of practices and structures which in a given setting produce highly undesirable learning outcomes—assuming this is possible, and to some extent I think it is—may leave the learning states *for someone* unchanged. This may be so because our very reforms send a person, or allow the person to drift, into settings having hidden curricula similar to the one we have been trying to abolish. Or it may be so because the learning states in question were all along the result of more than one setting. Settings can combine to produce learning states. And they surely do. The learning states of docility and conformity, competitiveness and unending consumption, which are said to belong to the hidden curriculum of public schooling in the United States today, are certainly not the products of that schooling alone. Who can doubt that family, church, community organizations, place of work, and the media have all combined to produce them?

The problem I spoke of is really two problems, both hinging on the obvious point that different settings can but need not have significantly different hidden curricula. The one problem is that some educational reforms designed to rid us of undesirable hidden curricula can be self-defeating, because they substitute for the old setting new ones producing essentially the same learning states. The other problem is that the reform of a given educational setting may simply not be enough to do the job if other settings having the same old hidden curriculum survive. It has been pointed out that radical school reform can only succeed if it goes hand in hand with radical societal reform (e.g., by Graubard 1972). That this is so becomes especially clear once we shift our attention from the hidden curriculum of schooling to the hidden curriculum for those being schooled. For it is not just that wide-scale basic reform of public schooling—that is, reform of the whole system as opposed to small units within or alongside it—may not be possible without concomitant societal reform. Supposing it to be possible, it is not at all obvious that the hidden curriculum for those being schooled will be materially improved if the other dominant educational settings in their lives remain the same.

6. Knowledge Can be Power

I am not as optimistic as some about the prospects of radical societal reform. But whether one takes these prospects to be good or not, there are two courses of action open to us when we find a hidden curriculum we abhor which we still need to consider. One is part and parcel of many radical school-reform programs. The other is not.

Radical school reformers do not all take learners out of the frying pan and, with no thought of the fire outside, send them to get burned. Both those who advocate open classrooms and those in the free-school movement try to provide their learners with insulation so that the fire, even if it singes, will not burn. They do this by advocating practices and structures which have a dual function: they are intended to do away with the hidden curriculum of public schooling and at the same time to substitute for the attitudes and values of that hidden curriculum ones considered to be admirable. Thus, competition is to be replaced by cooperation while conformity is to be replaced by creativity and initiative. The attitudes and values espoused by radical school reformers are openly acknowledged by some and embraced not so openly by others. But be they part of the curriculum proper of radical school reform or of its hidden curriculum, they are expected to take hold not just while the learner is in school and until graduation, but in nonschool settings too and for life. If any policy can successfully protect learners from the hidden curricula of the larger unreconstructed society, surely the policy of fostering learning states in conflict with those fostered by the larger society can.

It should be noted that some radical school reformers deplore this aspect of the reform movement. In their view, schools should get out of the business of forming attitudes and values altogether (see, e.g., Bereiter 1973, Katz 1971). It is not clear, however, that schools *can* get out of the business. Even schools whose functions are pared away and minimized through reform will have hidden curricula, hidden curricula which may or may not themselves be minimal so far as attitudes and values are concerned. I am afraid that those who condemn the hidden curriculum of public schooling today, yet want to preserve schools in some form or other without substituting better values and attitudes for the ones to be abolished, are being unrealistic. The question they should be asking of those who try to insulate learners from the fires outside is not whether the schools should do the insulating, but whether schools alone can do it. If the larger society remains as it is, will schools be allowed to foster values and attitudes counter to those of surrounding institutions? And if so, will these values and attitudes "take"; will they really provide the needed protection?

I do not know the answer to these questions, but I am pessimistic enough to want to consider one more thing that can be done with a hidden curriculum when we find it, something which, although independent of the course of action just described, is compatible with it and, indeed, could be used to buttress it. When we find a hidden curriculum, we can show it to those destined to be its recipients. Consciousness raising, if you will, with a view to counteracting the hidden curricula of settings we are not now in a position to change or abolish. Not that consciousness raising is any guarantee that a person will not succumb to a hidden curriculum. But still, one is in a better position to resist if one knows what is going on. Resistance to what one does not know is difficult, if not impossible.

The raising to consciousness of hidden curricula can proceed in many different ways. It can take place in informal rap sessions or formal seminars, and can be aimed at those in a setting, those about to enter it, or those who once were in it. But whatever form it takes, it will consist in transforming the learning states of the hidden curriculum of a setting into the subject matter of a person's curriculum proper. I do not mean by this that the hidden curricula we find abhorrent are to be openly embraced. Quite the contrary. The point of raising a hidden curriculum to consciousness is not to *foster* but to *prevent* the acquisition of the learning states belonging to it. The method of prevention is to make these learning states themselves the objects of new and very different learning states.

Most of us never stop to think that the settings we enter have hidden curricula, let alone what those hidden curricula might be. A program of consciousness raising would aim at such simple yet not at all obvious learning states as realizing that a given setting has a hidden curriculum, knowing what that hidden curriculum is, knowing which practices of the setting are responsible for the various learning states of its hidden curriculum, and understanding the significance of these learning states for one's own life and for the larger society. It would aim not only at making the hidden curriculum of a setting an object of a cognitive state such as these, but of skill states, too—for example, being able to spot a hidden curriculum, being able to recognize heretofore undiscovered sources, and knowing how to avoid the learning outcomes one does not want to acquire.

Having knowledge and skill concerning hidden curricula can be a form of self-defense against the onslaught of unasked-for learning states. But consciousness raising, as I understand it, aims at the acquisition of attitudes and values too. Certainly consciousness raising in the women's movement is not thought to be successful if a woman in coming to know the facts about sexist practices in modern society also comes to approve of them. Knowledge of hidden curricula will not provide a defense against them if those subject to hidden curricula do not *want* to resist.

To do its job, consciousness raising with respect to hidden curricula must tend to attitudes and values and feelings while imparting knowledge and skill. In this respect it resembles the program of those who want to substitute cooperativeness for competitiveness and creativity for conformity. But if it, too, is in the business of forming attitudes and values there is a difference, for in consciousness raising the attitudes and values acquired are, or at least are supposed to be, the result of a direct confrontation between learner and hidden curriculum: to see it is to despise it, to want to resist it, perhaps even to want to go out in the world and try to change it. The attitudes and values honored by radical school reformers have perhaps been chosen by them because of their own confrontation with a hidden curriculum, but the students who are to acquire them do not do so as a result of such confrontation.

The consciousness raising I am suggesting would seem to require a knowledge of the hidden curricula of nonschool settings which is not now available. Am I not then proposing a course of action for which we are not ready, one which would require an investment of funds and scholarly energy which is not likely to be forthcoming? Again, we must look to consciousness raising in the women's movement for our model. It has generated knowledge even while relying on it, for much if not all of the important research on women being done now is surely a direct result of it. I would expect the consciousness raising I am recommending to have a similar effect on our knowledge: that it would generate research into hidden curricula, research which in turn produced new subject matter for it. Thus, although knowledge of hidden curricula in nonschool settings is surely needed, consciousness raising can begin with the little we have, in the expectation that we will soon have more.

Lest there be any doubt, we do have some with which to begin—if nothing else, our own experiences in these settings. We may, however, have more knowledge now than we realize. Our knowledge of the hidden curricula of schools comes primarily from two sources: from those who have worked in schools and those who have done research on schools. To discover the hidden curricula of other institutions we must turn to those who study them: to medical sociologists and to sociologists of family, church, science, sports, and business. We must turn also to those who have taken or given management training courses at Gulf and those who have worked the switchboard at the telephone company. Perceptive practitioners are not the monopoly of schools. Hospitals, businesses, even city halls have their James Herndons and John Holts who see and record hidden curriculum for us.

Who should conduct this consciousness raising? Insofar as schools send their students into nonschool settings to learn, one would hope that they would do their own consciousness raising: that medical schools would do it for prospective interns, social work schools for students doing fieldwork, education schools for practice teachers, and high schools for those sent out to learn on the job. One would hope that schools trying to abolish their own hidden curriculum while keeping students within their walls would conduct consciousness-raising sessions about the hidden curricula in the larger society, too. Schools that did this would, in effect, become centers for the critique of social institutions. I believe strongly that schools should serve this function, but perhaps only an optimist would think they could or would serve it as long as they remain public and society remains the way it is. Schools are not the only possible forum for consciousness-raising with respect to hidden curricula, however. Victims of a given hidden curriculum can do it for themselves as women have done and Blacks have done.

As I have said, there is no guarantee that consciousness raising will insulate us successfully against learning states we do not want and should not acquire. Certainly we must not view it as a substitute for institutional and societal reform. Yet, as the women's movement has shown, knowledge about what has happened or is happening to one can have powerful effects. I would not count on a single individual whose consciousness had been raised in private, so to speak, to withstand the hidden curriculum of a setting in which he or she is put. But when knowledge is shared and there is strong peer support, consciousness raising may be the best weapon individuals who are subject to hidden curricula have.

Notes

I wish to thank the reviewers for *Curriculum Inquiry* and especially the editor, Leonard Berk, for their helpful comments and criticisms of this paper.

1. I have taken these labels from Vallance (1973/74, p. 6).

2. It is possible that some states of an individual have no object—for example, a generalized state of despair. Normally, however, the states that constitute learning states will have objects, albeit very complex ones at times. Thus, although the state of being competitive may seem to have no object, an individual will in fact be competitive with respect to certain situations or types of situations, and those would constitute the object of the state.

3. It will be noted that I have characterized hidden curriculum as what happens (and curriculum proper as what is intended to happen), rather than as statements about what happens (or is intended to happen). Should the reader prefer the linguistic level—that is, a characterization of hidden curriculum is a set of statements about learning states rather than as the learning states themselves—the present account can readily be translated into it.

4. Vallance suggests as much (1973/74, p. 7).

5. As I have characterized hidden curriculum, the sources of the learning states of a hidden curriculum do not themselves belong to that curriculum. Should the reader prefer a broader characterization, one that includes the practices that produce the relevant learning states, the necessary adjustments in my formulation of the problem of finding hidden curricula can readily be made.

6. *Infants School,* by Lillian Weber, is distributed by Education Development Center, Newton, Massachusetts.

7. It should be noted that learning outcomes unintended by us could all along have been intended by others, e.g., by those who hired us.

8. For purposes of this discussion I take the radical school-reform movement to include not just open-classroom advocates, free-school proponents, and those wanting to decentralize the control of schools, but also deschoolers and those who advocate minimal schooling.

9. I do not mean to suggest that all radical school reformers romanticize the world outside the schools. Illich does not. Nor does Allen Graubard (1972).

CHAPTER 9

Needed: A New Paradigm
For Liberal Education

"Needed: A New Paradigm for Liberal Education" was written for the 1981 Yearbook of The National Society for the Study of Education. In the spirit of the volume's title, Philosophy and Education, *the editor, Jonas Soltis, structured the book so that each chapter would discuss a different "subarea" of philosophy—logic, metaphysics, ethics, and the like. Authors would then be expected to show how their chapter's area illuminated an educationally important topic. As a member of the Yearbook's editorial committee, I took part in long conference calls in which the problem of what to do about teaching and curriculum was debated. Would we wait and see if an author chose to illuminate these topics or were they too educationally important to be left to chance? When it was finally decided that they deserved chapters in their own right, I jumped at the opportunity to write one of the two chapters in the volume that fell outside its main scheme.*

As a footnote to this essay, I should report that I have it on good authority—that of Paul Hirst, himself—that he no longer holds the theory of liberal education discussed herein.

The Forms of Knowledge Theory

Curriculum, in the sense of decision making about what should be learned, is here to stay. There was a time in the late 1960s and early 1970s when its disappearance was momentarily expected. But in fact, even if the educational reforms proposed during those years had been generally adopted, curriculum would not have vanished. It was thought that it would disappear if students were in charge of their own learning; it was not realized that curriculum need not be compulsory and does not require for

This essay was originally published in *Philosophy and Education 1981*, the Eightieth Yearbook Part I, edited by Jonas P. Soltis. Reprinted by permission of The National Society for the Study of Education.

its survival that some knowledge be essential for all. It was thought that it would disappear once we deschooled society; it was not realized that curriculum can outlive schools. So long as people try to educate one another, or even simply themselves, decisions about what is to be learned will remain a central fact of life.

I draw attention to the persistent character of curriculum because educational fashions change so quickly. As I write, discussions of the basics, of liberal education, of minimal competency testing—all of them in large part discussions of curriculum— are in the news. By the time this is read, educational issues with less obvious ties to curriculum may have replaced these in the public consciousness. If so, curriculum will still demand our serious consideration.

Sad to say, contemporary philosophers of education have not given curriculum its due. I am not sure why. They have not, in the manner of the radical school reformers, expected curriculum to disappear. Perhaps they have taken it for granted, perhaps they have underestimated its importance, perhaps they have found it too hot to handle. Whatever the reason, contemporary philosophical investigation of curriculum has for some time been in a rut: it has focused on a very limited range of curricular questions and has endorsed a theory of curriculum that is seriously deficient.

The curricular theory to which I refer was first expounded by Hirst in a widely read article.[1] It has since been elaborated by Dearden,[2] by Peters in collaboration with Hirst,[3] and by Hirst himself in a number of papers in his volume *Knowledge and the Curriculum*.[4] Anyone who remembers the movement for curricular reform of the post-Sputnik era and Bruner's popular book entitled *The Process of Education*, or is acquainted with the curriculum theory set forth by Phenix, or with that presented by Broudy, Smith, and Burnett will find the broad outlines, if not all the details, of Hirst's "forms of knowledge" theory familiar.[5] I have chosen to discuss Hirst's theory here, rather than one of these others, because his is the one that has come to dominate the thinking of philosophers of education. To use Kuhn's language, Hirst's theory has become one of the paradigms in the field of philosophy of education. Just as scientists articulate the paradigms of what Kuhn calls "normal science,"[6] so Hirst with the help of both colleagues and critics has clarified and modified his forms of knowledge theory of liberal education.

Behind Hirst's theory lies a conception of liberal education as the development of mind and the identification of the achievement of knowledge with that development. Upon this foundation rests Hirst's thesis that a liberal education is an initiation into the forms of knowledge.

In his original statement of the theory Hirst distinguished seven forms of knowledge: mathematics, physical sciences, human sciences, history, religion, literature and the fine arts, philosophy (p. 46). He has since taken history and the human sciences off the list, replacing them with moral judgment and understanding of our own and other people's minds. In doing so he has made clear what some readers did not realize, namely that the original list did not refer to disciplines, but that the forms of knowledge are to be understood as classes of true propositions. Thus, history and the human sciences have been dropped from the list not because Hirst now questions their disciplinary status, but because he has come to believe that their statements are not *sui generis*: some of them are truths about the physical world, some are truths of a mental or personal kind, and some presumably are moral or even aesthetic judgments (pp. 86–87).

Hirst takes the seven forms to embrace commonsense as well as technical knowledge (p. 90). He also takes the forms to be irreducible (pp. 84, 89–90). He does not mean by this that they have nothing in common, that they share no concepts and logical rules with one another; his claim seems simply to be that each form has *some* unique concepts *and some* distinctive network of relations between concepts. The forms are not, however, eternal and immutable in Hirst's view (p. 92). They are human creations and as such are open to change; indeed, Hirst holds not only that each form can change, but that new forms can be created (p. 95).

Hirst makes it very clear that the forms of knowledge theory is compatible with different patterns of curriculum organization: for example, a curriculum with subjects like mathematics, physics, literature, and philosophy; or a curriculum organized around what he calls fields (as opposed to forms) of knowledge such as geography and engineering; or even a curriculum involving practical projects of design and building. Decisions about the organization of a curriculum are to be made on a variety of practical grounds, which he does not attempt to specify. For these decisions to be in accord with Hirst's theory of liberal education, it is essential that the curriculum organization in question serve to initiate students into each of the seven forms (p. 51).

Initiation must not be confused with the acquisition of encyclopedic information or the expertise of a specialist. A liberal education, in Hirst's view, is neither a technical nor a specialized one. Hirst characterizes initiation as sufficient immersion in the concepts, logic, and criteria of a form of knowledge for a person to come to know the distinctive way in which it works; a coming to look at things in a certain way is what is wanted, and along with this an outline of the major achievements in each area so as to grasp the range and scope of experience that it has made intelligible (pp. 47–48).

The many critics of Hirst's theory of liberal education have concentrated on his analysis of knowledge. Thus, they have questioned his classification of art, religion, and morality as forms of knowledge;[7] they have challenged the criteria he uses to differentiate the various forms;[8] they have taken him to task for claiming that the forms can change;[9] they have argued that common sense should be recognized as a distinct form.[10] Important as criticisms of this sort are, they do not get at the heart of the matter, in part because so many of them seem to share Hirst's basic and mistaken assumption that the nature and structure of knowledge determines the nature and structure of a liberal education and in part because the form in which he presents his theory makes deeper criticism seem inappropriate.[11] Hirst's assumption about knowledge will be examined in the third section of this chapter, and in the fourth section the implications of the sharp separation between mind and body implicit in the forms of knowledge theory will be discussed. First, however, I want to make clear the extent to which that theory is narrow and intolerant.

Kuhn has shown us that when a scientific paradigm faces serious problems the time for scientific revolution has come. I hope to show here that Hirst's theory has major flaws that no modification or clarification will remedy. It is a paradigm in need of a revolution. The object of this chapter, then, is to get philosophical investigation of curriculum out of its rut by challenging the existing paradigm, thereby extending the range of questions to which philosophers should devote attention. In the last sections I will sketch in the bare outlines of an alternative paradigm and will argue, even as I do so, that philosophical investigation of curriculum must go beyond liberal education.

Ivory Tower People

The forms of knowledge theory conceives of liberal education as the acquisition of knowledge and understanding. In so doing it ignores feelings and emotions and other so-called "noncognitive" states and processes of mind.[12] Except for what Hirst calls "the arts and techniques of different types of reasoning and judgment" (p. 47), it also ignores *procedural knowledge* or *knowledge how.*[13] Complex conceptual schemes are to be acquired, but aside from the "know how" involved in using them, knowing how to do something (for example, playing the violin, riding a bicycle, writing a well-organized essay, or managing a political campaign), is not primarily a matter of having learned concepts, logic, and criteria. Rather, it is a matter of having learned skills and procedures.

Needless to say, as a result of its identification of liberal education with initiation into the forms of knowledge, the received curriculum theory of our day places physical education and vocational training beyond the pale of a liberal education. What is perhaps less apparent, but equally important, is that it also excludes from a liberal education the development of artistic performance, the acquisition of language skills including the learning of a second language, and education for effective moral action as opposed simply to moral judgment.

A natural criticism to make of the forms of knowledge theory is that it is unduly narrow. As Hirst himself has said, it excludes all objectives other than intellectual ones and even the intellectual ends it seeks are limited (p. 96). He has made it clear, however, that his is a theory of liberal education, not the whole of education. Thus, feelings and emotions and procedural knowledge are not barred from a person's education; they simply fall outside the boundaries of a liberal education. When the fact that Hirst calls his concept of liberal education "stipulative" (p. 96) is added to the restricted domain of his theory, he seems to have an airtight defense against the charge of narrowness. We cannot claim that liberal education is not by nature as narrow as he suggests it is, for he is stipulating its nature—making it up, if you will—and he surely has the right to do this in any way he sees fit. We cannot claim that the things the forms of knowledge theory leaves out are important to learn whereas the theory deems them to be unimportant, for Hirst never says they are not important; he simply leaves them for other theorists of education to consider. Small wonder Hirst's critics have focused on his analysis of knowledge. He has left nothing else open to attack.

Still, we ought not to ignore the fact that Hirst has chosen to call the conception of education he has formulated "liberal education," for this label is not neutral. Over the years liberal education has been thought of as an education having great value, indeed as an education having greater value than any other; we look down on education that is illiberal, some of us even refusing to call it education at all. It seems as if we cannot condemn Hirst's theory for being narrow because it is not a theory of all education. Yet as Hirst must realize, "liberal education" is an honorific title. Suppose he had used the label "intellectual education" instead. Would his theory have been taken as seriously as it has been by philosophers of education? Would it have come to dominate thinking in the field so that to all intents and purposes it has become a theory of the whole of education deemed valuable? Surely not.

Philosophers of education today never ask the question, "What is left over when we subtract a liberal education from the whole of education?" Seldom, if ever, do they try to develop theories to supplement Hirst's. Hirst is not to be condemned either for devoting his considerable philosophical talents to elaborating a theory having limited intellectual objectives or for the uses to which others have put that theory. At the same time we should recognize that his theory has taken on a life of its own at least in part because Hirst has traded on the label "liberal education." The forms of knowledge theory has become the received theory not just of intellectual education but of that education deemed valuable, at least in part because Hirst has presented it as a theory of liberal education and liberal education is thought to exhaust that education which is valuable. In judging the forms of knowledge theory, therefore, we need to remember the limited claims Hirst has made for it, but we must also feel free to go beyond Hirst's explicit intentions. Granted he does not claim to be setting forth a theory of education in general, we must still ask if the forms of knowledge theory provides a tenable account of all education deemed valuable. Granted his concept of liberal education is stipulative, we must ask what the programmatic implications of Hirst's stipulations are.[14]

The great irony of Hirst's theory of liberal education is that it is neither tolerant nor generous: it conceives of liberal education as the development of mind, restricts the development of mind to the acquisition of knowledge and understanding, and restricts knowledge to true propositions. Because the gap between liberal education and the whole of education tends to be obscured and liberal education has come to be equated with that education deemed valuable, this series of restrictions has grave practical consequences. The best way to grasp them is to envision the "products" of a liberal education conceived of as an initiation into the forms of knowledge.

The received theory's liberally educated person will be taught to see the world through the lenses of the seven forms of knowledge, if seven there be, but not to act in the world. Nor will that person be encouraged to acquire feelings and emotions. The theory's liberally educated person will be provided with knowledge about others, but will not be taught to care about their welfare, let alone to act kindly toward them. That person will be given some understanding of society, but will not be taught to feel its injustices or even to be concerned over its fate. The received theory conceives of a liberally educated person as an ivory tower person: one who can reason, but has no desire to solve real problems in the real world; one who understands science, but does not worry about the uses to which it is put; one who grasps the concepts of biology, but is not disposed to exercise or eat wisely; one who can reach flawless moral conclusions, but has neither the sensitivity nor the skill to carry them out effectively.

We make fun of ivory tower people—their interests are so narrow, their inability to cope with the realities of life is so pronounced. Yet those who allow the received theory to dominate their thinking about curriculum may be said to encourage that life-style. In fact, there is nothing objectionable about a world in which *some* individuals choose to live in an ivory tower, but imagine a world populated by the people envisioned by Hirst's theory.

It will be said that this portrait of the forms of knowledge theory's liberally educated person depends for its validity on the false assumption that no other education will be received. To be sure, the portrait is a caricature. Some people educated according to the theory will no doubt become competent doers and makers; some will become moral agents and some social reformers. From the standpoint of the theory in its role as paradigm of education deemed valuable, however, this will all be accidental, for what matters is simply that the forms of knowledge be acquired. To be sure, the theory does not require an educated person to live in an ivory tower. Yet by failing to address the question of how best to educate for effective participation in the world, the theory-become-paradigm stands guilty of sanctioning a world filled with ivory tower people.

A supporter of the forms of knowledge theory of liberal education might argue that its "products" will not be ivory tower people because an education in the forms of knowledge sets people on the right track. Given an initiation in Hirst's seven forms of knowledge we can relax, they will say; competent action, moral agency, altruistic feeling will all fall into place. In a society whose dominant institutions fostered virtues such as caring about others, a sense of justice, honesty, and benevolent action, faith in the sufficiency of an initiation in the forms of knowledge might be justified. In a society whose institutions encourage conformity of thought and action, a desire for instant riches and worship of self—that is, in our society—I am afraid that such faith is nothing but a pious dream.

A supporter of the forms of knowledge theory with a rather different orientation might argue that ivory tower people are not to be despised; that, on the contrary, detachment, disinterestedness, and freedom from passion are ideals to be cherished. No doubt they are in some circumstances. However, when a country is fighting an unjust war, there is nothing admirable about a detached citizenry; when a regime is exterminating an ethnic or religious minority, a people free from passion is scarcely the ideal; when a government is caught in a web of corruption, a disinterested electorate is a foolish electorate. There is a time and place for the cool virtues of detachment, disinterestedness, and freedom from passion and also for the warmer ones of feeling, fervor, and taking a stand. The trouble with the ivory tower people of the forms of knowledge theory is that the cool virtues will not have been tempered by any warmer ones.

No theory of education can take everything into account. Does not the fact that the forms of knowledge theory ignores education for feeling, emotion, and effective participation in the world simply mean that it is incomplete? Does it really *sanction* non-participation? It must not be supposed that every theory endorses or sanctions everything it fails to address. This would be absurd. However, when a theory functions as the forms of knowledge theory does, namely, as a theory of that education deemed valuable, it surely must be held responsible for ignoring the development of such central aspects of human existence as action, feeling, and emotion.

The Epistemological Fallacy

Basil Bernstein, the British sociologist of education, has said, "The battle over curricula is also a conflict between different conceptions of social order and is therefore fundamentally moral."[15] He is surely right. Yet Hirst and too many of his colleagues and critics do not see the battle in this way. For them it is fundamentally epistemological: a conflict between different conceptions of knowledge.

According to a sympathetic critic of Hirst's theory, it is a principle of educational theory "that upon one's analysis of the structure of knowledge depends what one will admit into a curriculum and what one will leave out."[16] This critic has fallen victim to a fallacy that preys all too successfully on those who theorize about curriculum. The epistemological fallacy, as I will call it, consists in arguing from a theory of knowledge to conclusions about the full range of what ought or ought not to be taught or studied. Some years ago William Frankena warned against the epistemological fallacy, although he did not call it by that name. "Suppose we hold that music is not knowledge," he said. "Does it follow that it should not be taught? Not unless we also accept the normative premise that only knowledge should be taught."[17] His point was that decisions about curriculum content and objectives necessarily rest on value judgments. Theories of knowledge are relevant to curriculum theory and planning, but they are not in themselves decisive.

Hirst and a number of his critics have paid no heed to Frankena's warning. They seem to think that their respective accounts of knowledge are decisive in determining the broad outlines of curriculum, if not all its details (p. 27).[18] Their approach to curriculum theory is understandable, for it gives them authority in relation to curriculum that otherwise Hirst's own conception of the task of philosophers would deny them. Hirst has argued that philosophy is an analytic pursuit: concerned with the clarification of concepts and propositions, it investigates the meanings of terms and expressions and the logical relations and presuppositions these terms and expressions involve (p. 1). In this view of philosophy there is no place for the making of value judgments. If Frankena is right—if value judgments are an essential ingredient in decisions about what should be taught and studied—then those who accept Hirst's conception of philosophy must also accept a rather limited role for philosophers vis-a-vis curriculum. They can offer analyses of the concept of knowledge, but they will have to do so in the realization that curriculum planners may reject them saying, "Who cares if music is not a form of knowledge. On independent grounds it ought to be part of a liberal education." If, however, value judgments can be circumvented, philosophers can accept Hirst's conception of philosophy and also dictate the broad outlines of curriculum.

By virtue of his definition of liberal education and his conception of mind, Hirst's forms of knowledge theory gives the *appearance* of dispensing with value judgments, but it does not in fact do so. His claim that a liberal education consists in an initiation into the forms of knowledge does not seem to require value judgments because liberal education is defined as the development of mind and the latter is identified with the acquisition of knowledge. Since on Hirst's account there are seven forms of knowledge, the conclusion that a liberal education is an initiation into those forms seems unavoidable.[19] Given his definitions, his claim that all the objectives of a liberal education are intellectual seems unavoidable too.

Definitions and analyses are not sacrosanct, however. Hirst's analysis of knowledge is a description of a certain kind. Like all descriptions it is selective; it singles out some aspects of knowledge to the exclusion of others. Assuming that Hirst has given us a true account of the nature of knowledge, alternative ones singling out different aspects of knowledge can nonetheless be constructed. But if alternative analyses can be given, upon which analysis should curriculum decisions rest? In particular, why should we choose Hirst's analysis of knowledge rather than some other, for example, one that divides knowledge into two forms—empirical and nonempirical?[20] We cannot appeal to epistemology for an answer to this question since the answer will depend on our purposes. Given some purposes, Hirst's account of knowledge will be the one to choose; given others, it will not be. Since our choice of an account of knowledge depends on our aims or purposes, we cannot use an account of knowledge to justify these. Their justification will involve value judgments about the kind of life people should lead and the kind of society they should live in.

Those who commit the epistemological fallacy say that the nature of liberal education is dependent on their analysis of knowledge when, in fact, their analysis of knowledge depends on their views of the nature of liberal education. They decide what a liberal education should consist in and tailor their accounts of knowledge accordingly. It is because they think the arts ought to be part of a liberal education that they take the trouble to argue at such length that they constitute a form of knowledge. It is because they believe that religion and moral judgments ought to belong to a liberal education that they worry about their cognitive status. In effect, being worthy of inclusion in a liberal education is sufficient for something to be knowledge for them.

Hirst assumes that a liberal education consists solely in knowledge. This is why he has to tailor his theory of knowledge to fit the arts and other fields, such as religion, whose cognitive status is in doubt. But this assumption is not required by a conception of liberal education as the development of mind. To be sure, Hirst identifies the development of mind with the acquisition of knowledge, but just as there can be alternative analyses of knowledge so too there can be alternative conceptions of mind. We have feelings and emotions, moods and attitudes. These and other noncognitive states and processes can figure in an account of mind. Thus, when a conception of mind enters into a curriculum theory, once again a choice must be made. Why should Hirst's conception of mind in terms of knowledge alone be adopted, rather than one which, for example, embraces feelings and emotions too? A choice is involved that rests not on the nature and structure of mind, but on one's educational purposes.

Actually, no matter what account of mind is adopted, an education intent on developing mind need not develop only those characteristics thought to define it. So long as noncognitive states and processes of mind exist, educators have the option of developing them. Indeed, even if they did not exist, an education of the mind could try to bring them into existence and develop them. Philosophical analyses are not as powerful as they seem. For Hirst's account of mind to determine curriculum we would have to agree not simply with his conceptions of liberal education and of mind, but with the assumption that liberal education ought to develop only the aspect of mind he singles out as definitive, namely knowledge.

As I have already made clear, Hirst conceives of the forms of knowledge theory as a theory of liberal education, not the whole of education. Liberal education is concerned, he says, with "those elements in a total education that are logically basic" (p. 96). Since in his view noncognitive mental states are dependent on cognitive ones, he concludes that the latter are the most fundamental or basic curriculum objectives.[21] Noncognitive states are not thereby barred from a person's education; as objectives they simply fall outside the boundaries of a liberal education.

Once again, however, we find Hirst in the clutches of the epistemological fallacy. From the fact, if it is one, that noncognitive states are dependent on cognitive ones and hence that cognitive states are logically basic, it does not follow that cognitive educational objectives are logically basic. If it were the case that once mind was developed, feelings and emotions, attitudes and sentiments would take care of themselves, there might be reason to consider cognitive objectives as in some sense primary. As we have seen, however, no such case can be made in relation to our society. Hirst does not himself subscribe to the view that an initiation in the forms of knowledge *simpliciter* makes one a person for all seasons. In his view an education in the forms of knowledge is necessary, not sufficient, for the development of desirable noncognitive states and processes. It lays the groundwork, so to speak. Thus he says, "Only in so far as one understands other people can one come to care about them and actively seek their good."[22] Even this more modest thesis is false, however. Do children first understand their parents and then care about them? Do we not often discover as adults that we cannot understand those we care about? Furthermore, if we grant Hirst his premise, it does not follow that an education in the knowledge required to understand others is therefore more basic or important than an education in caring for others and actively seeking their own good.

In sum, neither curriculum content nor curriculum objectives are determined by the structure we attribute to knowledge. In choosing them we make value judgments about our educational purposes and we set these, in turn, in relation to the moral, social, and political order we believe to be desirable.

An Untenable Dualism

John Dewey spent his life trying to combat the tendency of educators to separate reason from emotion, thought from action, education from life.[23] The forms of knowledge theory of liberal education resurrects the dualisms Dewey thought he was laying to rest. It does so by banishing both knowledge how and noncognitive states and processes from its conception of mind, and hence from the realm of liberal education. But this is just a part of the story. The theory relies on a conception of liberal education that divorces mind from body. It thus makes education of the body nonliberal, thereby denying it value. Since most action involves bodily movement, education of and for action is denied value also.

Ivory tower people are a legacy of the dualisms that Hirst's stipulative concept of liberal education presupposes. Lest it be imagined that the received theory's value judgments stop there, I refer the reader to the work C.B. Macpherson has done on the life and times of liberal democracy.[24] Through the use of historically successive models, Macpherson has revealed the assumptions about people and about the whole society implicit in democratic theory. Thus, the democracy of John Stuart Mill, John Dewey, and A.D. Lindsay viewed people as exerters, developers, and enjoyers of their own capacities. Developmental democracy, as Macpherson calls it, took the good society to be one that permits and encourages all people to act as exerters, developers, and enjoyers of their own capacities. The model that has replaced developmental democracy is quite different. Equilibrium democracy, the democracy of Joseph Schumpeter and Robert Dahl, is not a kind of society or set of moral ends; it is simply a mechanism for choosing governments. The citizen's role is not to decide political issues, but to choose between sets of politicians. Voters are consumers rather than active participants in the political process. Indeed, equilibrium democracy requires and encourages apathy.

Equilibrium democracy is the kind of democracy that prevails in our society. The equilibrium it maintains is one of inequality. The consumer sovereignty it claims to provide is an illusion. Equilibrium democracy, in other words, is not very democratic. Nevertheless, the received theory's liberally educated person is tailor made for equilibrium democracy, since that theory encourages neither the development, enjoyment, and exertion of one's capacities nor participation in political and social life.

The strength of the connection between the forms of knowledge theory and equilibrium democracy must not, of course, be exaggerated. Hirst's theory is compatible with those political models other than equilibrium democracy that also require apathetic citizens. Equilibrium democracy, in turn, is compatible with other curriculum theories that also yield apathetic people. But the ivory tower people of the received theory are *not* compatible with developmental democracy. Nor are they compatible with the participatory democracy, which Macpherson sees as a desirable successor to equilibrium democracy. In short, while the forms of knowledge theory by no stretch of the imagination entails equilibrium democracy, acceptance of it commits one to political models that require, or at least desire, people to be passive rather than active participants in the political process. Ivory tower people are, after all, apathetic people.

Suppose Hirst's conception of mind were broadened to include noncognitive states and processes. A world populated by liberally educated people would then be a slight improvement over the one envisioned earlier: the people in it might care for others even if their caring did not prompt altruistic action; they might be concerned about injustice and the fate of modern society even if they did nothing about either; they might have a desire to solve the problems of the real world even if they had none of the requisite skills. However, as long as a conception of liberal education drives a wedge between mind and body, as Hirst's does, and liberal education is equated with the whole of valuable education, a liberally educated person will be a lopsided person: a thinker but not a doer, an experiencer but not a maker, a feeler but not a moral agent. And consequently a world populated by liberally educated people had better be perfect to begin with for the individuals in it will not act to make it better; even if it occurs to them to do so, they will not know how.

A conception of liberal education as the development of mind is not peculiar to Hirst; many educators conceive of liberal education in precisely this way. So long as the rest of education is slighted, Hirst's or any curriculum theory that singles out mind as the sole focus of liberal education implicitly sanctions a world inhabited by lopsided, apathetic people and, in so doing, a social, economic, and political order that will accommodate them.

Toward a New Paradigm

A conception of liberal education as the development of a person can provide the basis for the much needed curricular revolution. A person consists in reason and emotion. A person is a thinker and an actor. More important, reason and emotion are inextricably bound together in persons and so are thought and action. To be sure, nothing follows about the content and aims of a liberal education from these facts about persons; an analysis of the concept of a person no more determines the general outlines of curriculum than does an analysis of knowledge. One could conceive of liberal education as the development of a person, but define a person in terms of mind alone and identify the development of mind with the acquisition of knowledge. That is to say, one could adopt an alternative starting point to Hirst's yet end up with his forms of knowledge theory of curriculum. However, a conception of liberal education as the development of a person can serve as the bedrock of a curriculum theory quite different from Hirst's.[25]

Begin with a conception of liberal education as the development of a person, add to it an analysis of the concept of a person in which mind and body are inseparable, mix in the value judgment that the purpose of a liberal education ought to be to develop us as persons and not simply as minds. Guidelines for a liberal education that drives no wedge between thought and action, between reason and emotion begin to emerge. In such an education the acquisition of conceptual schemes would play an important role but a limited one. Initiation of the sort Hirst proposes into the forms of knowledge could be one of its components, but it would not be the whole thing. There would be initiation into various forms of skill, for example, artistic and athletic, linguistic and mechanical. In this liberal education there would also be room for feelings, emotions, and attitudes to flourish, for creativity and imagination to develop, for making and doing and moral commitment.[26]

Presumably an education is called liberal because it is thought to free us not only from ignorance, but also from the constraints of habit, custom, and inertia. The standard conception of liberal education would free our minds, but not our selves. Surely if being a victim of ignorance and a slave to habit, custom, and inertia are undesirable, then our whole selves ought to be liberated from them.

An education whose purpose was to liberate us as persons would include within its boundaries a much broader range of things than the classic theory has dreamed of. Some would disapprove of a theory of liberal education developed along these lines for precisely this reason. If anything can go into a curriculum, one commentator on Hirst has said, then the concept of curriculum loses its practical value.[27] But to reject the principle that a liberal education should consist only of knowledge is not to say that anything goes. A theory that countenances more kinds of things than true propositions need not allow everything imaginable into the curriculum.

Others would object to the present proposal on the grounds that most skills and activities, feelings and emotions are picked up in the course of living so that to include them in a liberal education is to devote time and effort to them which could better be spent acquiring knowledge. I do not mean to deny that noncognitive states and processes, as well as skills and ways of acting, will be acquired if they are not included in a liberal education. However, there is no reason to suppose that the attitudes, feelings, and emotions, the skills and ways of acting that are picked up in the course of living will be ones that *ought* to be acquired. If particular skills and ways of acting, attitudes, and emotions are held to be desirable and others are held to be undesirable, then reasons of economy militate against a liberal education that ignores everything but knowledge.

The trouble with this liberalized theory of liberal education is not that it ignores the principle of economy,[28] but that it does not solve a very basic problem confronting the received theory, namely, that it is wedded to an atomistic ideology. Liberal education is supposed to free us from ignorance and the like so that we will be free in the sense of being autonomous individuals. Since autonomy involves action as well as thought, a conception of liberal education as the development of persons is more adequate to this task than Hirst's conception. However, individual autonomy is not the only important value for education to consider. Even as our education develops autonomous thought and action by liberating us from ignorance and the constraints of habit, custom, and inertia, it should bind us to one another and to the natural environment.

The atomistic ideology underlying the received theory of liberal education is reflected not in the fact that the "products" of that theory learn to be apathetic people, but that they learn to be asocial. Because no attempt is made to foster other-directed feelings and emotions, such as caring about the welfare of others and a sense of injustice, or to develop other-directed skills, their social links will at best be weak and their social sensitivity will be nonexistent. Just as the tobacco farmer who, when asked if he experienced any moral conflict about continuing to grow his crop in the face of massive evidence linking cigarette smoking to death, allowed that it never occurred to him to feel guilty because his primary responsibility was to make a living, the liberally educated people of the received theory will see themselves if all goes as planned not as mutually dependent, cooperating members of a society, but as self-sustaining atoms.[29]

A liberal education conceived of as the development of a person can encompass other-directed sentiments and skills. However, so long as a theory of liberal education conceives of persons as self-sustaining atoms who may bump up against one another in passing, but are socially indifferent, it will be deficient for it will ignore the kind of social and natural education everyone should have.

An adequate theory of education needs to go beyond a conception of persons as autonomous individuals not simply because education ought to bind human beings to one another, but because it should bind us to the natural order of which we are a part.[30] Just as education should foster in us a sense of community, so too, in the interests of future generations, if nothing else, it should foster recognition of our solidarity with other living things. A sense of community requires a change in our consciousness so that we see ourselves not as self-sustaining atoms, but as dependent, contributing members of a group. A recognition of our solidarity with nature requires at least as great a shift in consciousness, for we must begin to see the earth as a cooperative endeavor in which "other lives have lives to live,"[31] indeed, to see the earth as part of a larger order in which other "earths" have lives to live. Changes in consciousness are not enough, however. Natural education should foster restraint, so that the natural environment will not be destroyed, and a willingness to share what there is with other species, even while social education fosters other-directed feelings, attitudes, and ways of acting.

Agenda for the Future

Can the kind of social and natural education I have just sketched in be accommodated by a new paradigm of *liberal* education? This question cannot be answered simply by an appeal to the nature of knowledge or mind or a person or liberal education itself for, as we have seen, an account of each of these will depend on one's purposes. I do not mean to suggest that for every purpose some form or other of liberal education is suitable: for some purposes, liberal education of any sort may be inappropriate. An answer to our question will, therefore, rest on value judgments about the worth of the education at issue and on decisions about the relationship of liberal education to the rest of education. If liberal education continues to be equated with that education which is valuable, then a positive answer to our question must be given. If, on the other hand, liberal education is acknowledged to be one valuable part of education but not the only valuable part, then it may not matter very much if social and natural education fall outside its boundaries.

What does matter is that the received theory of our day—the forms of knowledge theory—be replaced by a more general curricular paradigm, whether that be a paradigm of liberal education or not: one that does not ignore the forms of knowledge, but reveals their proper place in the general scheme of things as but one part of a person's education; one that integrates thought and action, reason and emotion, education and life; one that does not divorce persons from their social and natural contexts; one that embraces individual autonomy as but one of many values. What matters, in other words, is that a new paradigm become established that addresses itself, not simply by default, to the whole of that education which is valuable.

With a new paradigm will come new questions for philosophers of education to answer. The nature of social and natural education will have to be explored as will their relationship to education for individual autonomy. The nature of vocational education and its relationship to liberal education will become a respectable concern as will the general problem of the integration of education and life. But this is not all. Because the existing paradigm incorporates the epistemological fallacy, it obscures the links between curriculum theory and social and political theory. A whole range of philosophical questions will become pertinent when that paradigm is discarded: for example, questions about the relationship between philosophy of education on the one hand and social and political philosophy on the other, about the social and political implications of curricular aims and content, about the possibility or impossibility of curricular neutrality.

The epistemological fallacy encourages philosophers to take the structure of knowledge and run. It fosters the illusion that curriculum can be determined without their asking questions about the good life and the good society. It also allows them to ignore the social and historical context of education. Yet to formulate curricular aims and content without taking into account the educational setting and also the practices and beliefs of the larger society is to court disaster. In freeing us from the epistemological fallacy a new paradigm will force us to confront questions about the relationship between a curriculum and both its educational and societal setting. Ultimately, this will lead to questions about hidden curriculum, something philosophers of education have pretended does not exist, and to questions about curriculum, both hidden and otherwise, in nonschool settings.

An agenda for the future cannot be laid out in detail. One thing leads to another in philosophy of education as in any other form of inquiry. It should be clear, however, that the curriculum questions to be addressed come in various guises. Some will call for analysis, some for the making of value judgments. Some will require knowledge of school practices, some will require broader institutional knowledge. Some will lead directly to epistemology, some will lead to ethics and social philosophy. At the outset of this chapter I said that philosophers of education have not given curriculum its due. I trust that once the wide range of relevant topics and variety of questions are recognized—once the philosophical challenge of curriculum is felt—this long standing neglect will disappear.

Notes

I wish to thank Ann Diller, Nancy Glock, Michael Martin, Beatrice Nelson, the editorial committee for this volume, and my colleagues for helpful comments on two drafts of this chapter.

1. Paul H. Hirst, "Liberal Education and the Nature of Knowledge," in *Philosophical Analysis and Education*, ed. Reginald D. Archambault (London: Routledge and Kegan Paul, 1965), pp. 113–38. Reprinted as chapter 3 in Paul H. Hirst, *Knowledge and the Curriculum* (London: Routledge and Kegan Paul, 1974). (All page references to Hirst appearing in parentheses in the text are to this latter volume.)

2. R.F. Dearden, *The Philosophy of Primary Education* (London: Routledge and Kegan Paul, 1968).

3. R.S. Peters and Paul H. Hirst, *The Logic of Education* (London: Routledge and Kegan Paul, 1970).

4. Hirst, *Knowledge and the Curriculum*.

5. Jerome S. Bruner, *The Process of Education* (Cambridge: Harvard University Press, 1961); Philip Phenix, *Realms of Meaning* (New York: McGraw-Hill, 1964); Harry S. Broudy, B. Othanel Smith, and Joe R. Burnett, *Democracy and Excellence in American Secondary Education: A Study in Curriculum Theory* (Chicago: Rand McNally, 1964).

6. Thomas S. Kuhn, *The Structure of Scientific Revolutions* (Chicago: University of Chicago Press, 2d ed., 1970).

7. See, for example, A.J. Watt, "Forms of Knowledge and Norms of Rationality," *Educational Philosophy and Theory* 6 (March 1974): pp. 1–11; Robin Barrow, *Common Sense and the Curriculum* (London: George Allen and Unwin, 1976), Ch. 2; James Gribble, "Forms of Knowledge," *Educational Philosophy and Theory* 2 (March 1970): pp. 3–14. See Hirst's reply to Gribble, "Literature, Criticism, and the Forms of Knowledge," *Educational Philosophy and Theory* 3 (April 1971): pp. 11–18. Reprinted in Hirst, *Knowledge and the Curriculum*, Ch. 10.

8. See, for example, Gribble, "Forms of Knowledge"; D.C. Phillips, "The Distinguishing Features of Forms of Knowledge," *Educational Philosophy and Theory* 3 (October 1971): pp. 27–35; idem, "Perspectives on Structure of Knowledge and the Curriculum" in *Contemporary Studies in the Curriculum*, ed. Peter W. Musgrave (Sydney: Angus and Robertson, 1974).

9. Allen Brent, *Philosophical Foundations for the Curriculum* (London: George Allen and Unwin, 1978), Ch. 3.

10. John P. White, *Towards a Compulsory Curriculum* (London: Routledge and Kegan Paul, 1973), Ch. 6.

11. In *The Marxist Theory of Schooling: A Study of Epistemology and Education* (Brighton: Harvester, 1980), Michael Matthews does get to the heart of the matter after providing an

especially clear, comprehensive account of the development of Hirst's theory. Some of the points to be made here were reached independently by Matthews.

12. I qualify my introduction of the term "noncognitive" in this way to indicate that, although I am following ordinary usage, I do not mean to commit myself to the view that there is a hard and fast distinction between the cognitive and the noncognitive.

13. Hirst himself points this out (p. 57). For a criticism of Hirst based on this point, see Ormond Smythe, "On the Theory of Forms of Knowledge," in *Philosophy of Education 1978*, Proceedings of the Thirty-fourth Annual Meeting of the Philosophy of Education Society (Champaign, Ill.: the Society, 1979), pp. 28–39. For the classic account of knowledge how, see Gilbert Ryle, *The Concept of Mind* (London: Hutchinson's University Library, 1947), Ch. 2.

14. For a discussion of programmatic and stipulative definitions, see Israel Scheffler, *The Language of Education* (Springfield, Ill.: Charles C. Thomas, 1960), Ch. 1. The reader is referred also to Robert H. Ennis, "Rational Thinking and Educational Practice," in *Philosophy and Education 1981*, the Eightieth Yearbook, Part I, ed. J. P. Soltis (Chicago: National Society for the Study of Education); and to Ennis's discussion of impact equivocation in his presidential address to the Philosophy of Education Society in 1979. See *Philosophy of Education 1979*, Proceedings of the Thirty-fifth Annual Meeting of the Philosophy of Education Society (Normal, Ill.: The Society, 1980), pp. 3–30.

15. Basil Bernstein, *Class, Codes, and Control*, vol. 3 (London: Routledge and Kegan Paul, 1975), p. 81.

16. Brent, *Philosophical Foundations of the Curriculum*, p. 31.

17. William K. Frankena, "A Model for Analyzing a Philosophy of Education," in *Readings in the Philosophy of Education: A Study of Curriculum*, ed. Jane R. Martin (Boston: Allyn and Bacon, 1970), pp. 15–22.

18. "The question is simply which account of knowledge is correct, for surely that alone can form the basis of defensible curriculum planning." (Hirst, *Knowledge and the Curriculum*, p. 67.)

19. Even with these definitions the conclusion does not follow unless a premise is added that initiation into all the forms of knowledge, that is, comprehensive initiation, is essential for the development of mind.

20. As, for example, Barrow does in *Common Sense and the Curriculum*.

21. Peters and Hirst, *The Logic of Education*, p. 62.

22. Ibid.

23. See, for example, John Dewey, *Democracy and Education* (New York: Macmillan, 1961).

24. C.B. Macpherson, *The Life and Times of Democracy* (Oxford: Oxford University Press, 1977).

25. Langford claims that to be educated is to learn to be a person. See Glenn Langford, "The Concept of Education," in *New Essays in the Philosophy of Education*, ed. Glenn Langford and D.J. O'Connor (London: Routledge and Kegan Paul, 1973), pp. 3–32. My conception of liberal education does not assume, as Langford's seems to, that those being educated are not already persons.

26. Hirst and Peters argue that the central feature of emotions is cognition and that for creativity to be developed initiation into the forms of knowledge is essential. See Hirst and Peters, *The Logic of Education*, pp. 32, 49ff. Supposing for the sake of argument that they are right, it does not follow that the forms of knowledge and limited intellectual objectives should monopolize a liberal education. Moreover, creativity in practical endeavors such as the arts and politics are not served by this argument.

27. Brent, *Philosophical Foundations of the Curriculum*, p. 31.

28. For discussions of curricular economy see Israel Scheffler, "Justifying Curriculum Decisions," in *Readings in the Philosophy of Education*, ed. Martin, pp. 23–31; White, *Towards a Compulsory Curriculum*, pp. 37, 71–72.

29. For discussions of atomism and education see Elizabeth Cagan, "Individualism, Collectivism, and Radical Education Reform," *Harvard Educational Review* 48 (May 1978): pp. 227–66; Ann Diller and Nancy Glock, "Individualized Instruction: Some Questions," in *Philosophy of Education 1977*, Proceedings of the Thirty-third Annual Meeting of the Philosophy of Education Society (Urbana, Ill.: The Society, 1977), pp. 190–97.

30. On this topic, see Stephen R.L. Clark, *The Moral Status of Animals* (Oxford: Oxford University Press, 1977).

31. Ibid., p. 160.

CHAPTER 10

Two Dogmas Of Curriculum

Although "Two Dogmas of Curriculum" was written for the 1982 special issue of
Synthese, "Questions in the Philosophy of Education," edited by C.J.B. Macmillan, it
draws upon research I did in the 1970s. In those days I tended to think of myself as work-
ing on the logic of curriculum development, but when I told a philosophical colleague
that I was asking what things can be subjects and had introduced the concepts of subject-
entities and subject versions, he told me that my project belonged to metaphysics. Whether
it be logic or metaphysics, this essay's analysis of The Dogma of God Given Subjects uses
material from "The Anatomy of Subjects," written in 1971, and from a working paper I
presented in 1972 at a conference sponsored by the New England Program for Teacher
Education entitled "The Teacher in 1984." Its analysis of The Dogma of the Immutable
Basics was, in turn, developed in the mid 1970s.

A cluster of second order assumptions is so deeply entrenched in our thinking
about curriculum that its existence is seldom recognized and the assumptions themselves are almost never challenged. In this essay I will examine two such assumptions
and will argue that they are untenable. I call the Dogma of God-Given Subjects and
the Dogma of the Immutable Basics *second order* assumptions because they speak
about and analyze curriculum instead of prescribing what it should be. Thus the
Dogma of God-Given Subjects does not tell us what to teach or when. Rather, it tells
us that the subjects of curriculum are "givens," that they are found, not made; in other
words, it speaks about the nature of curriculum itself. Similarly, its special case, the
Dogma of the Immutable Basics, does not tell us how the basics of education should
be taught or to whom, but that they are unchanging and eternal.

The prospects of constructing an adequate theory of curriculum are dim so long
as the dogmas to be discussed here remain intact, and so are the prospects for true

This essay was originally published in *Synthese*, Vol. 51 (1982): 5–20. Reprinted by
permission.

curricular reform. Reform which goes beyond mere tinkering with existing curricula requires that proposals for new subjects be taken seriously and that the present hierarchy of subjects be challenged.[1] These dogmas of curriculum serve as barriers to such change. An adequate theory of curriculum must illuminate clearly the choices confronting those who develop curriculum. To do this it must adopt a generous conception of subjects and acknowledge the fact that our subjects are complex human constructions to which we ourselves attach value. So long as these dogmas of curriculum are allowed to go unexamined, theoretical illumination will continue to elude us.

I. THE DOGMA OF GOD-GIVEN SUBJECTS

What Things Can Be Subjects?

We tend to assume that the subjects we are accustomed to—the 3Rs, the sciences, foreign languages, the humanities, the fine arts—are the only subjects there are. In fact our subjects are not limited in number.[2] We assume they are because we wear blinders and recognize as subjects only those things which in the past have been considered suitable candidates for a general and a liberal education. There is a much greater range to choose from than we realize. Neither Chairs, Hamburgers nor Humphrey Bogart has the ring of a bona fide subject to most of us. Yet if we shed our narrow frame of reference we realize not only that these can be subjects, but that they undoubtedly are—Chairs a subject in a curriculum for furniture makers, Hamburgers a subject in a curriculum for McDonald trainees, Humphrey Bogart a subject in a curriculum for film enthusiasts. Even a brief glance at the wide variety of curricula there are should convince us that anything can be a subject; that French, Mathematics and Physics can give way to Identity, Community and the Reality of Material Objects or to the Rights of Animals, Mary Queen of Scots and Dying.

Anything can be a subject because subjects are made, not found. They are not "out there" waiting for us, but are human constructions. Think for a moment about the subject Physics. From the standpoint of teaching and learning, although not perhaps from that of writing the history of science, the *science* physics is a given. The *subject* Physics is something quite different from the science physics, however. People engage in the science physics, whereas they study the subject Physics. To be sure, physicists study things, but not the identical set of things students of Physics study, for physicists study physical phenomena, while students of Physics study also the laws and theories developed by those who study physical phenomena. The subject Physics is both more and less than the science physics. It depends on the latter for its very existence: were there no science physics there would scarcely be the subject Physics. Yet if the science physics provides the *raison d'être* for the subject Physics, the latter draws its subject matter not merely from the former but from the history and philosophy of science, the sociology and the politics of science and from numerous other sources as well.

Every subject takes as its point of departure something "out there" in the world which for want of a better term I will call a *subject-entity*. The subject-entity of each of the subjects Physics, Chemistry, Biology is a science; of each of the subjects French, Spanish, Latin, a language; of the subject Driving, a practical activity and of the subject Drama, a performing art. The question "What things can be subjects?" is really a question about subject-entities; thus when I said above that anything can be a subject, what I meant was that anything can be a subject-entity. So far as I can see, there are no limits to the kind of thing that can be the subject-entity of a subject. Some things might seem too "small" to serve in that capacity, for example a Chopin Waltz or, better still, one phrase of a Chopin Waltz. However, judgments of the size of a subject-entity are really judgments of importance and these must be assessed in relation to some context of study. If the purpose is to acquaint non-musicians with Western music, it is obviously a mistake to offer as a subject of study something whose subject-entity is a single work or a part thereof, but if the purpose is, e.g., to sensitize accomplished musicians to innovations of the Romantic period, the study of a subject whose subject-entity is a Chopin Waltz or even a phrase of a waltz may not be so far-fetched.

The Dogma of God-Given Subjects addresses the question "What *can* be our subjects?" not the question "What *should* be our subjects?" To say that anything can be a subject-entity is simply to say that those in the curriculum field *can* look far and wide for the points of departure of the subjects they construct. It is not to say that everything in heaven and earth *ought* to be a subject in the curriculum. It is important to recognize, however, that there are all kinds of curricula for all kinds of purposes and that something which seems too trivial to serve as the subject-entity of a subject in relation to one educational purpose might acquire significance in relation to a different educational purpose. There is no reason whatsoever to suppose that everything which can be a subject-entity will or should become the point of departure for a subject in a curriculum. Yet the possibility remains that something which has consistently been overlooked or rejected for that role might one day serve it well.

The distinction between a subject and its subject-entity has been ignored, perhaps because a subject usually takes its name from its subject-entity. It is an important distinction to maintain, for while every subject has a subject-entity, no subject is identical with its subject-entity: on the one hand, the function of a subject is educational; on the other, a subject has not only a subject-entity belonging to it but a body of subject matter which ranges far and wide. Thus, for example, the subject matter which belongs to the subject Cooking comes from the subject-entity of Cooking, namely the practical activity of cooking, but also from a variety of other sources including the disciplines of biology, chemistry, anthropology, history, politics.

Just as the distinction between a subject and its subject-entity is overlooked, so is the distinction between both of these and subject matter. This is perhaps because curriculum theorists tend to assume that except for the so-called interdisciplinary subjects the subject matter of each subject comes from a single source. They assume too that subjects are neat, ready-made bundles of subject matter which one finds on one's doorstep. Thus they worry about content selection—which parts of the bundle should be pulled out and tied together for seniors in high school? which parts for fifth graders?—but they take the initial bundles for granted. Such complacency is not justified: the bundles of subject matter which belong to our subjects are not out there waiting to be recognized, but are themselves human creations. Think of the subject matter of that relative newcomer to curriculum, Women's Studies. It ranges over the social sciences, the natural sciences, the arts, the humanities. Yet there was no ready-made bundle of subject matter out there waiting to be found. Over time a bundle has simply been constructed.

The wisdom of my introducing Women's Studies into a discussion of subjects may be questioned, for it may be doubted that Women's Studies really is a subject. Yet what is Women's Studies if not a subject? It is taught and studied and is an integral part of many college curricula. What property does it lack? The answer most likely to be given to this question is that Women's Studies is not a field of knowledge. What is meant by this, presumably, it that the subject-entity of Women's Studies is not a field of knowledge. This is, of course, true: its subject-entity is women, not some discipline which studies women. But this fact is scarcely relevant to the claim that Women's Studies is not a subject since there are many subjects in the same boat. The subject-entity of the subject the Far East is a geographical location, the subject-entity of the subject French is a language, the subject-entity of the subject Reading is a practical activity. Subjects can take intellectual disciplines as their subject-entities, but they certainly do not have to. As I have already said, anything at all can play that role.

The classic text books on the theory of curriculum development do not recognize this fact.[3] They catalogue several different patterns of curriculum organization, one of which they call the "subject curriculum." That, of course, is the standard liberal curriculum whose subjects are History, Literature, Mathematics, Physics and the like. They fail to recognize that some of the other types of curricula they distinguish are also subject curricula, because they do not realize that what they call "broad fields"—combinations of fields of knowledge such as the natural sciences or the humanities—can themselves be the subject-entities of subjects as can "social processes" such as earning a living or making a home.[4] Although these texts do not distinguish between a subject and its subject-entity, they tacitly assume that the subject-entity of a subject must be a field of knowledge.

Women's Studies really is a subject. However, it does not follow from this fact that it *should* be a subject in a given curriculum. Subject construction no more dictates the makeup of curriculum than does epistemology.[5] The point of the present discussion is not to promote particular subjects, but to make clear the deficiencies of the received view of subjects and to urge that a generous conception of them be incorporated into curriculum theory and practice.

It will perhaps be granted that curriculum theorizing would profit from a broad conception of subjects, yet be denied that such a conception is required for true curricular reform. Members of the radical school reform movement of the late 1960s and early 1970s seemed inclined to reject subjects altogether on the grounds that subjects carry with them rigid teaching methods and institutional structures and hence were not compatible with curricular reform. Does not such reform require that subjects be abandoned rather than that our conception of them be expanded? This suspicion of subjects was based on a confusion between tradition and necessity. To be sure, subjects have in the past been taught by lecture and recitation methods and have been tied to very formal administrative arrangements, but these are not inevitable accompaniments of subjects. Mathematics and French can be taught informally at skill centers of the kind envisioned by Ivan Illich, and Physics can be taught in the laboratory or the kitchen. In sum, there is neither a short list of subjects nor a pre-established pattern of human behavior to which every subject must accommodate itself, and thus there is no reason at all to fear them. Perhaps true curricular reform can occur through the exclusion of subjects in general from the curriculum, but before they are banned it behooves reformers to search for new and better subjects and better patterns for relating them to one another.

Subject Construction

New subjects such as Women's Studies and Black Studies are not the only ones whose legitimacy has been questioned. Well-established subjects such as Social Studies have come under attack for being conglomerations of subjects rather than subjects themselves.[6] The complaints seem to be that "real" subjects like Physics have unity and integrity whereas Social Studies does not because it is made up of history, geography and the various social sciences. Each one of these has unity, it is said, but together they do not form an integrated whole.

Interestingly enough, the criticism of traditional school subjects made by those curriculum reformers of the post-Sputnik era who developed the so-called New Curricula was of just this sort. In their eyes Physics, as taught in the schools, was nothing but a collection of unrelated topics such as heat and light, and History was nothing but a collection of unrelated facts.[7] They did not go so far as to say that these were not school subjects; they simply rejected the way in which they were conceived. Insofar as Social Studies is conceived of and taught as a collection of unrelated disciplines perhaps it deserves to be criticized. But it does not have to be conceived of in that way any more than Physics or History has to be presented as a group of discrete units.

The trouble with this complaint is that it uses a double standard. Subjects have different *versions*. It is quite unfair to compare a well-integrated version of one subject with a badly integrated version of the other and to conclude on this basis that the latter is not a subject at all. Every subject has parts. Their degree of integration depends on whether the parts are conceived of as related to one another in some sensible way or whether they are conceived of in "one thing after another" fashion. To be sure, some sets of parts may lend themselves better than others to attempts at integration. One ought not to assume, however, that because the parts of a subject *are* not well-integrated, that they *cannot* be. A Social Studies in which psychology, sociology and economics are all brought to bear on selected historical events or eras can readily be imagined as can be a Social Studies in which history, geography and the social sciences are all used to illuminate other cultures. Social Studies can have unity although there is no one right way to achieve it.

Actually there is no one right set of parts into which to divide a subject. The New Curricula rejected the topics which had long been considered the proper parts of Physics, Biology, Chemistry, Mathematics and substituted for them the methods, theories and basic concepts of the related discipline. Integration was then easy. Social Studies does not have to be divided up into history, geography, and the social sciences. Its parts could be social institutions such as family, church, government, business or it could be different kinds of cultures. There are any number of ways to divide up a subject and any number of ways to integrate the resultant parts.

Subject construction is in fact a creative activity. In choosing a subject-entity—the science physics, women, the environment—one's work has just begun. There are parts to be chosen and relationships among them to be traced. There is also the question of how the subject-entity is going to be viewed. The New Curricula for the most part took intellectual disciplines as their subject-entities.[8] What distinguished them from earlier efforts at subject construction was that they viewed the disciplines as fields of inquiry rather than as accumulations of knowledge. This was no slight change. Although the aspects under which a subject is viewed does not dictate its parts and the degree to which they are integrated, it surely influences these decisions. One who views history as a field of inquiry will normally be led to a very different version of the subject than one who views history as an account of the past.

Consider the subject English. View its subject-entity, namely English, as a language and one naturally thinks of its structure, its history, its various functions. View it instead as a means of communication and one thinks of composition and literature and speech. This is not to say that either view of English carries with it one and only one set of parts. The point is simply that some things seem to fall into place naturally in relation to one view of English, but not another. The classic texts in curriculum development give the impression that one curriculum decision leads inexorably to the next. In fact, subject construction—something they scarcely touch on—is a creative art. One decision may make certain others seem inappropriate or out of place, but they do not flow from one another in accordance with the rules of deductive logic.

Anything can serve as the subject-entity of a subject and when something does, any number of versions of the subject can be constructed. Some of those versions will have grave flaws, the lack of unity and integrity perhaps being one. But flaws are reasons for improving a particular version of a subject or for selecting a different version. They do not justify the claim that something which people are studying is not "really" a subject at all.

Subjects and Learning Activities

Additions can be made to the list of subjects, yet it would be a mistake to assume that every significant change in education brings with it new subjects. The open classrooms advocated by one wing of the radical school reform movement are a case in point.[9] They embodied a number of significant changes in educational practice, but they were not bearers of serious *curricular* reform, for the standard subjects of the elementary school curriculum were all preserved in open classrooms, albeit in disguised form.

The traditional conception of the classroom had led people to see relatively few things as educational materials: books, maps, pencils, paper, chalk, blackboards. The very different conception of the open classroom encouraged people to see as educational materials things they would previously have overlooked: costumes, wallpaper sample books, old tires, egg cartons, sand, water. It extended radically the range of things acknowledged to be useful in learning. Similarly, it extended the range of activities acknowledged to be promoters of learning. The traditional conception of the classroom limited people's sights to reading and writing and to drill, memorization and recitation. The theory and practice of the open classroom opened their eyes to painting, building robots, dramatizing stories, dancing and countless other activities which engage children's interest.

Open education did not, however, extend radically the range of things people take to be subjects. Visitors to open classrooms looked around in dismay crying "Where have all the subjects gone?" They saw children doing woodwork and messing around with water, but science, spelling and mathematics had apparently vanished. In fact they had simply donned disguises. The vast changes in learning activities and educational materials and the emphasis on informal, incidental learning served as masks for subjects which were, in the main, the subjects of the traditional classroom.

In education, as in life, appearances can be deceptive. To discover what is taking place one must look behind and beyond the overt behavior of both students and teachers for intentions which are not always obvious to the naked eye. One must also differentiate between the point of view of the student and the point of view of the teacher. Had one looked behind the surface goings on of the typical open classroom and examined the teachers' intentions, one would have found the standard school subjects. When the children in an open classroom baked cookies *they* did not take themselves to be learning to multiply fractions, nor did they take themselves to be learning to spell when they ran printing presses or gave titles to their art work. Yet from their *teacher's* standpoint baking cookies was primarily a vehicle for learning arithmetic while running a printing press was a vehicle for learning to spell.

The theory and practice of open classrooms was not concerned with significant *curricular* reform. In such classrooms informal learning—that is learning through engaging in activities one enjoys—was the rule, and the creative energy of teachers was spent devising new and better materials to use and activities to do. One great contribution of open education was its stress on the fact that from a single activity many very different things can be learned. Thus the search for activities and materials was really a search for especially fruitful ones: for activities and materials from which a wide range of results would flow. Nonetheless, the search was one-sided. Perhaps because subjects were considered to be inherently conservative, activities, not subjects, were sought. The traditional subjects were not banned from the classroom, however.

Instead, they were taken as givens and the creative task was seen to be that of discovering how to teach those subjects without doing the kind of psychological and moral damage to children which traditional classrooms were thought to do.

To be sure, activities can themselves serve as subject-entities. The subjects Reading and Writing, Cooking and Sewing, Woodwork and Drama all testify to this fact. However, when students engage in activities, those activities often serve as aids to learning some other subjects and are not themselves subjects of study. Take the activity reading. It is a subject-entity of the subject Reading in grade school, but when a high school student reads a biology textbook, reading functions as a learning activity harnessed to the subject Biology, and not as a subject in its own right. So too with the activity cooking. It can be a subject, but it can also be harnessed to the subject Arithmetic or to the subject Reading or even to Biology and Chemistry in order to make learning more efficient and pleasurable.

To change curriculum radically it is not enough to introduce new ways of learning old subjects as open education did. The old subjects must be abandoned or else made to cede some of the curriculum space they now occupy to new subjects. When true curricular reform is wanted, simply extending the range of learning activities and materials, important as this may be, is not sufficient. Nor is it sufficient simply to give students the freedom to make their own curriculum, as some radical school reformers tended to assume. New subjects must be seen to be chosen and they must be created in order to be seen. Unless the eyes of students are opened to a wide range of alternative subjects, there is no reason at all to suppose that they will see, let alone choose, new ones. The grip of tradition and habit is strong. To make curriculum the province of untutored free choice—be it student, teacher or parental choice—is to minimize the likelihood of significant curricular reform.

II. THE DOGMA OF THE IMMUTABLE BASICS

What Makes Something Basic?

The 3Rs are subjects. In calling them our basics we give them a near monopoly over the curriculum of the early years, but subjects they nonetheless are. Now one of our most deeply entrenched assumptions about curriculum is that the basics are immutable givens. Thus teachers believe that theirs is not to reason why, theirs is but to teach the 3Rs or die in the attempt. However, the 3Rs are not given to us as subjects, but are made by us. We construct them as we do all subjects, and once constructed they become basics by our decision.

It will be protested that we do not choose our basics, they are given to us. To understand that the subjects we call the basics not only are human constructions, but that they serve as basics at our pleasure, it is necessary to ask what qualifies something to be one of the basics of education. What, for example, do Reading, Writing and

Arithmetic have that Cooking and Driving lack? The answer to this question cannot be that Reading, Writing and Arithmetic are essential for everyone to study whereas Cooking and Driving are not, for we take the 3Rs to be essential subjects of study *just because* they are so basic.

One of the directors of the Council for Basic Education has said that the 3Rs are basic because they have "generative power."[10] A consideration of the philosophical notion of a basic action contributes to an understanding of this metaphor.[11] One opens a door by turning the knob, one pushes a stone by kicking it, one signals a right turn by moving one's arm and one nods assent by moving one's head. Compare these acts with those one just does. One turns the knob by moving one's hand, but one just does move one's hand and one just does move one's arm when one signals a right turn. Those acts which require no other act in doing them are called "basic actions" since they are the starting point, the "building blocks" out of which all other acts are formed. Indeed, they have been described as *generating* all other acts.[12]

Of course, from the standpoint of a general theory of human action, reading, writing and arithmetic are not basic at all: one does not just do them; one does them by doing a variety of other actions. Yet from the standpoint of education it makes good sense to call the 3Rs basic. The central concern of education is learning, and learning is one of those acts one does by doing other things, in particular by reading, by writing and by doing arithmetic. Just as moving one's hand is a building block or generator of the act of opening a door, so reading, writing and arithmetic are building blocks or generators of the act of learning.[13]

Learning is not the only action generated by the 3Rs, however. The 3Rs are generators of the acts of living as well as learning—at least of living in modern, industrial society. Reading, writing and arithmetic enter into our work and play, our jobs and recreation. We use them in our roles of consumer and parent, citizen and neighbor. One may vote by pulling a lever and pull the lever by moving one's arm, but one chooses one's candidates by keeping informed about the issues and one does this by reading the appropriate literature. One may buy bread by taking it off the shelf and giving money to the salesperson and one may do this by moving one's arms and legs, but one decides which bread to buy and determines how much money to give by calculating costs and counting coins, both of which one does by doing arithmetic. At home one writes notes to one's children's teachers and reads school announcements, at work one writes and reads memoranda and one does calculations concerning one's income. The list of everyday activities central to living which are done by doing the 3Rs is endless.

The answer to the question "What makes the 3Rs basic?" is that we perform the acts or activities of learning and living by reading, writing and doing arithmetic. To generalize, a subject qualifies as a basic of education if its subject-entity generates those acts. Of course, for some acts of learning and living the 3Rs are all but irrelevant. Moreover, many acts which can be generated by the 3Rs can also be done without their help: one can vote without reading the relevant literature and can buy food without calculating costs. Thus we take the 3Rs to be the basics of education not because they generate all acts of learning and living, but because we believe that so many of the valued acts of learning and living must be done by doing them if those acts are to be done well.

Choosing the Basics

We take the 3Rs to be our basics because we perform many of the activities of learning and living we value by doing them. Yet the 3Rs are by no means the *only* constituents of those activities, nor are they *absolutely fundamental* constituents of them. We do not just read, although once we know how to read it may seem as if we do; rather, we perform this activity by doing a number of other things. Exactly what one does in reading is itself an interesting question. A look at the scholarly literature on the topic gives the strong impression that there are almost as many accounts of its constituents as there are experts in the field of reading.[14] There are competing theories about the constituents of writing too. Indeed, even arithmetic—whose components one might have naively assumed to be addition, subtraction, multiplication and division—is divided up in different ways by different interested parties. The precise nature of the elements of the 3Rs is not the issue, however. The point is that since the 3Rs are done by doing other things, in calling them our basics we make a practical decision. After all, we could have continued our search for the basics past the 3Rs, stopping at their components or perhaps at the components of their components—for there is no reason to suppose that the things we do in reading, writing and arithmetic are themselves unitary activities.

Assuming for the sake of argument that something *can* be absolutely uncomplex, we do not make this a requirement which our educational basics must meet for the very good reason that our basics play a central role in curriculum. Were we to push our search for them too far back, we would find ourselves in the absurd position of designing educational programs around such things as eye movements or perhaps even brain waves. That we call the 3Rs *rather than their components* our basics is, then, a matter of practical decision. That we consider the 3Rs *rather than some other components* of the activities of learning and living our basics is a matter of decision too. One may learn science, history, literature and mathematics by reading, writing and doing arithmetic, but one does not learn them by the performance of these skills alone. One learns them by doing a host of things including listening and speaking, by asking questions and testing assumptions, by using one's imagination to conjecture about what might be the case and inventing ways of testing hypotheses. When one performs the activities of living by reading, writing and doing arithmetic, these skills are not exercised in isolation either, but are done in conjunction with other skills as well as with attitudes, values and numerous character traits. We could call some of these other things our basics, but we do not. Instead we single out the 3Rs for this honor.

Of course not everything which is a constituent of living and learning is a qualified candidate for the office of educational basic. Thus the 3Rs are not in competition with things which cannot be taught or learned. Some of us have blue eyes and some of us do not, but none of us has learned to have blue eyes and it is quite futile to try to teach someone to have blue eyes. In choosing our basics from among the many constituents of learning and living, we are limited to the kind of thing over which students and teachers can exercise some control. We are limited also to the kind of thing which would not develop in any case as human beings mature. Walking can no doubt be taught, but except in unusual circumstances it would be unnecessary to make it a basic of education since it is learned anyway. Finally, the 3Rs face no competition from those constituents of living and learning which lack generative power. To choose as the basics of education things such as the inside and outside edges of figure skating, or major scales on the piano, which have very specific application, would be foolhardy.

In choosing basics a grasp of the larger picture is essential. If mastery of figure skating is the goal, skating on one's edges in indeed basic. If mastery of the piano is the goal, playing the major scales is certainly a strong candidate for that office. When the activities of learning and living are at stake, however, neither of these skills has sufficient generative power, whereas the 3Rs seem to fit the bill. Yet generative power is not a constant. As the world changes and we change, the activities of learning and living generated by the 3Rs can fall into disuse or disfavor, and other activities, ones not generated by the 3Rs, can come to overshadow those we once held to be especially valuable. Even if the activities the 3Rs generate remain important to us, substitute ways of doing them can become available and, if they do, the generative power of other constituents of those activities may increase, for generative power can grow as well as diminish over time.[15]

The generative power of the 3Rs is neither universal nor eternal. Given a training program in figure skating, skating on one's inside and outside edges, not the 3Rs, has wide ranging application; given a program designed to teach the 3Rs, some components of reading, writing and arithmetic, rather than the 3Rs themselves, will have great generative power. Even when one's primary concern is learning and living, the generative power of the 3Rs will not everywhere be the same. For the Ntsetlik Eskimos portrayed in the social studies curriculum, 'Man: A Course of Study,' the generative power of fishing and hunting will be far greater than that of the 3Rs.[16]

Since we choose our basics—since they are a matter of decision, not discovery—we must make quite sure that the special status we thereby confer upon them is deserved. There is no doubt about the fact that rank and privilege attach themselves to the basics of education. No one would ever call one of the basics a "frill"; no one would try to push a basic subject out of the curriculum in favor of some non-basic subject. Programs are designed around the basics; for better or worse the basics are never far from the thoughts of curriculum planners and designers.

It might seem that the decisions of what to make our basics could depend in a straightforward way on the facts of the case. Just do a survey of the activities of learning and living and see what things generate them, then select the ones with the greatest generative power. This method is not adequate however, because it begs the important question of *which* activities of learning and living people *should* perform. In this regard it is important to remember that the decision of what to make the basics of

198 / NEWLY CUT TURF

education, like every major curriculum decision, depends not simply on the way the world is but on the way we think it should be, on the kind of life we believe to be worth living, and on the kind of society we believe to be worth living in.

Notes

1. For an example of the kind of reform I have in mind see "Needed: A New Paradigm for Liberal Education," Chapter 9 in this volume.

2. The next few paragraphs draw on Jane R. Martin. "Toward an Open Curriculum," *Futurist Working Papers: The Teacher in 1984,* New England Program for Teacher Education, 1972.

3. See, for example, Hilda Taba, *Curriculum Development* (New York: Harcourt, Brace & World, 1962); B. Othanel Smith, William O. Stanley, J. Harlan Shores, *Fundamentals of Curriculum Development* (New York: Harcourt, Brace & World, 1957), Rev. Ed.

4. The typologies of the classic texts differ. Thus, for example, Smith, Stanley and Shores, *op. cit.,* isolate the subject, the activity and the core curriculum while Taba, *op. cit.,* isolates the subject, the activity and the social processes curriculum. Smith, Stanley and Shores call the broad fields curriculum a modified subject curriculum (pp. 255 ff.). Taba lists it separately but then refers to it as a "type of subject organization" (p. 395).

5. On the role of epistemology in relation to curriculum decisions see "Needed: A New Paradigm for Liberal Education," Chapter 9 in this volume.

6. For a more detailed discussion of this topic see Jane R. Martin, "The Anatomy of Subjects," *Educational Theory* (Spring 1977), pp. 85–95.

7. The classic formulation of the theory behind the New Curricula is to be found in Jerome S. Bruner, *The Process of Education* (Cambridge: Harvard University Press, 1961).

8. For a discussion of the role of the disciplines in curriculum decisions see "The Disciplines and Curriculum," Chapter 7 in this volume.

9. For an account of these classrooms see Joseph Featherstone, "The British Infant Schools" in Ronald and Beatrice Gross (eds.) *Radical School Reform* (New York: Simon & Schuster, 1969); Charles Rathbone (ed.) *Open Education* (New York: Citation Press, 1971); Ewald B. Nyquist and Gene R. Hawes (eds.) *Open Education* (New York: Bantam Books, 1972).

10. Clifton Fadiman, "The Case for Basic Education" in James D. Koerner (ed.) *The Case for Basic Education* (Boston: Little, Brown, 1959), p. 6.

11. The classic work on this topic is Arthur C. Danto, "Basic Actions," *American Philosophical Quarterly 2* (1965), pp. 141–148. For criticisms of Danto's account see Frederick Stoutland, "Basic Actions and Causality," *The Journal of Philosophy 65* (1969), pp. 467–475; Myles Brand, "Danto on Basic Actions," *Nous 2* (1968), pp. 187–190.

12. Alvin I. Goldman, *A Theory of Human Action* (Englewood Cliffs, N. J.: Prentice-Hall, 1970).

13. The analogy to the standard account of basic actions breaks down at several points: (1) the 3Rs must be learned; (2) they are themselves done by doing other actions; (3) the

action generated does not necessarily have the same time boundaries as the generating action. Still, the analogy serves to illuminate the reasons for calling certain subjects rather than others the basics of education.

14. For one theory of the component skills of reading see Magdelen D. Vernon, "Varieties of Deficiency in the Reading Processes," *Harvard Educational Review 47* (1977), pp. 396–410.

15. In "Literacy and Learning," an address given to the New England Philosophy of Education Society, October, 1980, I have treated this topic in greater depth.

16. See Jerome S. Bruner, *Toward a Theory of Instruction* (Cambridge: Harvard University Press, 1966), pp. 73–101.

CHAPTER 11

Becoming Educated: A Journey of Alienation or Integration?

"Becoming Educated: A Journey of Alienation or Integration?" began life as a guest lecture in a curriculum course offered by the Harvard Graduate School of Education. The problem I set myself for that occasion was to show, using Richard Rodriguez's Hunger of Memory *as a case study, not just that received accounts of both education and curriculum were unacceptable, but that to remedy the situation it was necessary to take into account the workings of gender. In its next incarnation the essay was my contribution to the November 1983 Symposium on Excellence and the Curriculum in honor of Mauritz Johnson at SUNY Albany. I then gave an invited address based on it to Division B of the American Educational Research Association at its 1984 meeting, after which I worked much of the material into the last chapter of* Reclaiming a Conversation.

In his educational autobiography *Hunger of Memory*, Richard Rodriguez (1982) tells of growing up in Sacramento, California, the third of four children in a Spanish-speaking family. Upon entering first grade he could understand perhaps 50 English words. Within the year his teachers convinced his parents to speak only English at home and Rodriguez soon became fluent in the language. By the time he graduated from elementary school with citations galore and entered high school, he had read hundreds of books. He went on to attend Stanford University and, 20 years after his parents' decision to abandon their native tongue, he sat in the British Museum writing a PhD dissertation in English literature.

Rodriguez learned to speak English and went on to acquire a liberal education. History, literature, science, mathematics, philosophy: these he studied and made his own. Rodriguez's story is of the cultural assimilation of a Mexican-American, but it is more than this, for by no means do all assimilated Americans conform to our image of a well-educated person. Rodriguez does because, to use the terms the philosopher R.S. Peters (1966, 1972) employs in his analysis of the concept of the educated man, he did not simply acquire knowledge and skill. He acquired conceptual schemes to raise his knowledge beyond the level of a collection of disjointed facts and to enable him to understand the "reason why" of things. Moreover, the knowledge he acquired is not "inert": It characterizes the way he looks at the world and it involves the kind of commitment to the standards of evidence and canons of proof of the various disciplines that comes from "getting on the inside of a form of thought and awareness" (Peters, 1961, p. 9).

Quite a success story, yet *Hunger of Memory* is notable primarily as a narrative of loss. In becoming an educated person Rodriguez loses his fluency in Spanish, but that is the least of it. As soon as English becomes the language of the Rodriguez family, the special feeling of closeness at home is diminished. Furthermore, as his days are increasingly devoted to understanding the meaning of words, it becomes difficult for Rodriguez to hear intimate family voices. When it is Spanish-speaking, his home is a noisy, playful, warm, emotionally charged environment; with the advent of English the atmosphere becomes quiet and restrained. There is no acrimony. The family remains loving. But the experience of "feeling individualized" by family members is now rare, and occasions for intimacy are infrequent.

Rodriguez tells a story of alienation: from his parents, for whom he soon has no names; from the Spanish language, in which he loses his childhood fluency; from his Mexican roots, in which he shows no interest; from his own feelings and emotions, which all but disappear as he learns to control them; from his body itself, as he discovers when he takes a construction job after his senior year in college.

John Dewey spent his life trying to combat the tendency of educators to divorce mind from body and reason from emotion. Rodriguez's educational autobiography documents these divorces, and another one Dewey deplored, that of self from other. Above all, *Hunger of Memory* depicts a journey from intimacy to isolation. Close ties with family members are dissolved as public anonymity replaces private attention. Rodriguez becomes a spectator in his own home as noise gives way to silence and connection to distance. School, says Rodriguez, bade him trust "lonely" reason primarily. And there is enough time and "silence," he adds, "to think about ideas (big ideas)" (p. 47).

What is the significance of this narrative of loss ? Not every American has Rodriguez's good fortune of being born into a loving home filled with the warm sounds of intimacy, yet the separation and distance he ultimately experienced are not unique to him. On the contrary, they represent the natural end point of the educational journey Rodriguez took.

Dewey repeatedly pointed out that the distinction educators draw between liberal and vocational education represents a separation of mind from body, head from hand, thought from action. Since we define an educated person as one who has had and has profited from a liberal education, these splits are built into our ideal of the educated person. Since most definitions of excellence in education derive from that ideal, these splits are built into them as well. A split between reason and emotion is built into our definitions of excellence too, for we take the aim of a liberal education to be the development not of mind as a whole, but of rational mind. We define this in terms of the acquisition of knowledge and understanding, construed narrowly (Ch. 9, this volume). It is not surprising that Rodriguez acquires habits of quiet reflection rather than noisy activity, reasoned deliberation rather than spontaneous reaction, dispassionate inquiry rather than emotional response, abstract analytic theorizing rather than concrete storytelling. These are integral to the ideal of the educated person that has come down to us from Plato.

Upon completion of his educational journey Rodriguez bears a remarkable resemblance to the guardians of the Just State that Plato constructs in the *Republic*. Those worthies are to acquire through their education a wide range of theoretical knowledge, highly developed powers of reasoning, and the qualities of objectivity and emotional distance. To be sure, not one of Plato's guardians will be the "disembodied mind" Rodriguez becomes, for Plato believed that a strong mind requires a strong body. But Plato designed for his guardians an education of heads, not hands. (Presumably the artisans of the Just State would serve as their hands.)Moreover, considering the passions to be unruly and untrustworthy, Plato held up for the guardians an ideal of self-discipline and self-government in which reason keeps feeling and emotion under tight control. As a consequence, although he wanted the guardians of the Just State to be so connected to one another that they would feel each other's pains and pleasures, the educational ideal he developed emphasizes "inner" harmony at the expense of "outward" connection. If his guardians do not begin their lives in intimacy, as Rodriguez did, their education, like his, is intended to confirm in them a sense of self in isolation from others.

Do the separations bequeathed to us by Plato matter? The great irony of the liberal education that comes down to us from Plato and still today is the mark of an educated person is that it is neither tolerant nor generous (Ch.9, this volume). As Richard Rodriguez discovered, there is no place in it for education of the body, and since most action involves bodily movement, this means there is little room in it for education of action. Nor is there room for education of other-regarding feelings and emotions. The liberally educated person will be provided with knowledge about others, but will not be taught to care about their welfare or to act kindly toward them. That person will be given some understanding of society, but will not be taught to feel its injustices or even to be concerned over its fate. The liberally educated person will be an ivory tower person—one who can reason but has no desire to solve real problems in the real world—or else a technical person who likes to solve real problems but does not care about the solutions' consequences for real people and for the earth itself.

The case of Rodriguez illuminates several unhappy aspects of our Platonic heritage, while concealing another. No one who has seen Frederick Wiseman's film *High School* can forget the woman who reads to the assembled students a letter she has received from a pupil now in Vietnam. But for a few teachers who cared, she tells her audience, Bob Walters, a sub-average student academically, "might have been a nobody." Instead, while awaiting a plane that is to drop him behind the DMZ, he has written her to say that he has made the school the beneficiary of his life insurance policy. "I am a little jittery right now," she reads. She is not to worry about him, however, because "I am only a body doing a job." Measuring his worth as a human being by his provision for the school, she overlooks the fact that Bob Walters was not merely participating in a war of dubious morality but was taking pride in being an automaton.

High School was made in 1968, but Bob Walters's words were echoed many times over by 18- and 19-year-old Marine recruits in the days immediately following the Grenada invasion. Readers of *Hunger of Memory* will not be surprised. The underside of a liberal education devoted to the development of "disembodied minds" is a vocational education whose business is the production of "mindless bodies." In Plato's Just State, where, because of their rational powers, the specially educated few will rule the many, a young man's image of himself as "only a body doing a job" is the desired one. That the educational theory and practice of a democracy derives from Plato's explicitly undemocratic philosophical vision is disturbing. We are not supposed to have two classes of people, those who think and those who do not. We are not supposed to have two kinds of people, those who rule and those who obey.

The Council for Basic Education has long recommended, and some people concerned with excellence in education now suggest, that a liberal education at least through high school be extended to all. For the sake of argument let us suppose that this program can be carried out without making more acute the inequities it is meant to erase. We would then presumably have a world in which no one thinks of him- or herself as simply a body doing a job. We would, however, have a world filled with unconnected, uncaring, emotionally impoverished people. Even if it were egalitarian, it would be a sorry place in which to live. Nor would the world be better if somehow we combined Rodriguez's liberal education with a vocational one. For assuming it to be peopled by individuals who joined head and hand, reason would still be divorced from feeling and emotion, and each individual cut off from others.

The world we live in is just such a place. It is a world of child abuse and family violence (Breines & Gordon, 1983), a world in which one out of every four women will be raped at some time in her life (Johnson, 1980, Lott, Reilly & Howard, 1982). Our world is on the brink of nuclear and/or ecological disaster. Efforts to overcome these problems, as well as the related ones of poverty and economic scarcity, flounder today under the direction of people who try hard to be rational, objective, autonomous agents but, like Plato's guardians, do not know how to sustain human relationships or respond directly to human needs. Indeed, they do not even see the value of trying to do so. Of course, it is a mistake to suppose that education alone can solve this world's problems. Yet if there is to be hope of the continuation of life on earth, let alone of a good life for all, as educators we must strive to do more than join mind and body, head and hand, thought and action.

Redefining Education

For Rodriguez, the English language is a metaphor. In the literal sense of the term he had to learn English to become an educated *American,* yet, in his narrative the learning of English represents the acquisition not so much of a new natural language as of new ways of thinking, acting, and being that he associates with the public world. Rodriguez makes it clear that the transition from Spanish to English represented for him the transition almost every child in our society makes from the "private world" of home to the "public world" of business, politics, and culture. He realizes that Spanish is not intrinsically a private language and English a public one, although his own experiences made it seem this way. He knows that the larger significance of his story lies in the fact that education inducts one into new activities and processes.

In my research on the place of women in educational thought (Ch. 1, this volume; Martin 1985) I have invoked a distinction between the productive and the reproductive processes of society and have argued that both historians of educational thought and contemporary philosophers of education define the educational realm in relation to society's productive processes only. Briefly, the reproductive processes include not simply the biological reproduction of the species, but the rearing of children to maturity and the related activities of keeping house, managing a household, and serving the needs and purposes of family members. In turn, the productive processes include political, social, and cultural activities as well as economic ones. This distinction is related to the one Rodriguez repeatedly draws between public and private worlds, for in our society reproductive processes are for the most part carried on in the private world of the home and domesticity, and productive processes in the public world of politics and work. Rodriguez's autobiography reveals that the definition of education as preparation solely for carrying on the productive processes of society is not a figment of the academic imagination.

Needless to say, the liberal education Rodriguez received did not fit him to carry on all productive processes of society. Aiming at the development of rational mind, his liberal education prepared him to be a consumer and creator of ideas, not an auto mechanic or factory worker. A vocational education, had he received one, would have prepared him to work with his hands and use procedures designed by others. They are very different kinds of education, yet both are designed to fit students to carry on productive, not reproductive, societal processes.

Why do I stress the connection between the definition of education and the productive processes of society? *Hunger of Memory* contains a wonderful account of Rodriguez's grandmother telling him stories of her life. He is moved by the sounds she makes and by the message of intimacy her person transmits. The words themselves are not important to him, for he perceives the private world in which she moves—the world of childrearing and homemaking—to be one of feeling and emotion, intimacy and connection, and hence a realm of the nonrational. In contrast, he sees the public world—the world of productive processes for which his education fit him—as the realm of the rational. Feeling and emotion have no place in it, and neither do intimacy and connection. Instead, analysis, critical thinking, and self-sufficiency are the dominant values.

Rodriguez's assumption that feeling and emotion, intimacy and connection are naturally related to the home and society's reproductive processes and that these qualities are irrelevant to carrying on the productive processes is commonly accepted. But then, it is to be expected that their development is ignored by education in general and by liberal education in particular. Since education is supposed to equip people for carrying on productive societal processes, from a practical standpoint would it not be foolhardy for liberal or vocational studies to foster these traits?

Only in light of the fact that education turns its back on the reproductive processes of society and the private world of the home can Rodriguez's story of alienation be understood. His alienation from his body will reoccur so long as we equate being an educated person with having a liberal education. His journey of isolation and divorce from his emotions will be repeated so long as we define education exclusively in relation to the productive processes of society. But the assumption of inevitability underlying *Hunger of Memory* is mistaken. Education need not separate mind from body and thought from action, for it need not draw a sharp line between liberal and vocational education. More to the point, it need not separate reason from emotion and self from other. The reproductive processes *can* be brought into the educational realm thereby overriding the theoretical and practical grounds for ignoring feeling and emotion, intimacy and connection.

If we define education in relation to *both* kinds of societal processes and act upon our redefinition, future generations will not have to experience Rodriguez's pain. He never questions the fundamental dichotomies upon which his education rests. We must question them so that we can effect the reconciliation of reason and emotion, self and other, that Dewey sought. There are, moreover, two overwhelming reasons for favoring such a redefinition, both of which take us beyond Dewey.

All of us—male and female—participate in the reproductive processes of society. In the past, many have thought that education for carrying them on was not necessary: These processes were assumed to be the responsibility of women and it was supposed that by instinct a woman would automatically acquire the traits or qualities associated with them. The contemporary statistics on child abuse are enough by themselves to put to rest the doctrine of maternal instinct. Furthermore, both sexes have responsibility for making the reproductive processes of society work well. Family living and childrearing are not today, if they ever were, solely in the hands of women. Nor should they be. Thus, both sexes need to learn to carry on the reproductive processes of society just as in the 1980s both sexes need to learn to carry on the productive ones.

The reproductive processes are of central importance to society, yet it would be a terrible mistake to suppose that the traits and qualities traditionally associated with these processes have no relevance beyond them. Jonathan Schell (1982, p. 175) has said, "The nuclear peril makes all of us, whether we happen to have children of our own or not, the parents of all future generations" and that the will we must have to

save the human species is a form of love resembling "the generative love of parents."
He is speaking of what Nancy Chodorow (1978) calls nurturing capacities and Carol
Gilligan (1982) calls an "ethic of care." Schell is right. The fate of the earth depends
on all of us possessing these qualities. Thus, although these qualities are associated in
our minds with the reproductive processes of society, they have the broadest moral,
social, and political significance. Care, concern, connectedness, nurturance are as
important for carrying on society's economic, political, and social processes as its
reproductive ones. If education is to help us acquire them, it must be redefined.

The Workings of Gender

It is no accident that in *Hunger of Memory* the person who embodies nurturing
capacities and an ethic of care is a woman—Rodriguez's grandmother. The two kinds
of societal processes are gender-related and so are the traits our culture associates with
them. According to our cultural stereotypes, males are objective, analytical, rational,
interested in ideas and things. They have no interpersonal orientation; they are not
nurturant or supportive, empathetic or sensitive. Women, on the other hand, possess
the traits men lack (Kaplan & Bean, 1976; Kaplan & Sedney, 1980).

Education is also gender-related. Our definition of its function makes it so. For if
education is viewed as preparation for carrying on processes historically associated
with males, it will inculcate traits the culture considers masculine. If the concept of
education is tied by definition to the productive processes of society, our ideal of the
educated person will coincide with the cultural stereotype of a male human being, and
our definitions of excellence in education will embody "masculine" traits.

Of course, it is possible for members of one sex to acquire personal traits or qualities our cultural stereotypes attribute to the other. Thus, females can and do acquire
traits incorporated in our educational ideal. However, it must be understood that
these traits are *genderized*; that is, they are appraised differentially when they are
possessed by males and females (Beardsley, 1977; Ch. 3, this volume; Martin 1985).
For example, whereas a male will be admired for his rational powers, a woman who
is analytical and critical will be derided or shunned or will be told that she thinks
like a man. Even if this latter is intended as a compliment, since we take masculinity and femininity to lie at opposite ends of a single continuum, she will thereby be
judged as lacking in femininity and, as a consequence, judged abnormal or unnatural. Elizabeth Janeway (1971, p. 96) has said, and I am afraid she is right, that
"unnatural" and "abnormal" are the equivalent for our age of what "damned" meant
to our ancestors.

Because his hands were soft Rodriguez worried that his education was making him
effeminate.[1] Imagine his anxieties on that score if he had been educated in those sup-
posedly feminine virtues of caring and concern and had been taught to sustain intimate
relationships and value connection. To be sure, had his education fostered these qualities, Rodriguez would not have had to travel a road from intimacy to isolation. I do

not mean to suggest that there would have been no alienation at all; his is a complex case involving class, ethnicity, and color. But an education in which reason was joined to feeling and emotion and self to other would have yielded a very different life story. Had his education fostered these qualities, however, Rodriguez would have experienced another kind of hardship.

The pain Rodriguez suffers is a consequence of the loss of intimacy and the stunting of emotional growth that are themselves consequences of education. Now it is possible that Rodriguez's experience is more representative of males than of females. But if it be the case that females tend to maintain emotional growth and intimate connections better than males do, one thing is certain: educated girls are penalized for what Rodriguez considers his *gains*. If they become analytic, objective thinkers and autonomous agents, they are judged less feminine than they should be. Thus, for them the essential myth of childhood is every bit as painful as it was for Rodriguez, for they are alienated from their own identity as females.

When education is defined so as to give the reproductive processes of society their due, and the virtues of nurturance and care associated with those processes are fostered in both males and females, educated men can expect to suffer for possessing traits genderized in favor of females as educated women now do for possessing traits genderized in favor of males. This is not to say that males will be placed in the double bind educated females find themselves in now, for males will acquire traits genderized in their own favor as well as ones genderized in favor of females, whereas the traits educated females must acquire today are *all* genderized in favor of males. On the other hand, since traits genderized in favor of females are considered lesser virtues, if virtues at all (Blum, 1980), and the societal processes with which they are associated are thought to be relatively unimportant, males will be placed in the position of having to acquire traits both they and their society consider inferior.

One of the most important findings of contemporary scholarship is that our culture embraces a hierarchy of values that places the productive processes of society and their associated traits above society's reproductive processes and the associated traits of care and nurturance. There is nothing new about this. We are the inheritors of a tradition of Western thought according to which the functions, tasks, and traits associated with females are deemed less valuable than those associated with males. In view of these findings, the difficulties facing those of us who would transform Rodriguez's educational journey from one of alienation to one of the integration of reason and emotion, of self and other, become apparent.

It is important to understand the magnitude of the changes to be wrought by an education that takes the integration of reason and emotion, self and other, seriously. Granted, when girls today embark on Rodriguez's journey they acquire traits genderized in favor of the "opposite' sex; but if on account of trait genderization they experience hardships Rodriguez did not, they can at least console themselves that their newly acquired traits, along with the societal processes to which the traits are attached, are considered valuable. Were we to attempt to change the nature of our educational ideal without also changing our value hierarchy, boys and men would have no such consolation. Without this consolation, however, we can be quite sure that the change we desire would not come to pass.

Toward an Integrated Curriculum

Just as the value structure I have been describing is reflected in our ideal of the educated person, so too it is reflected in the curriculum such a person is supposed to study. A large body of scholarship documents the extent to which the academic fields constituting the subjects of the liberal curriculum exclude women's lives, works, and experiences from their subject matter or else distort them by projecting the cultural stereotype of a female onto the evidence.[2] History, philosophy, politics; art and music; the social and behavioral sciences; even the biological and physical sciences give pride of place to male experience and achievements and to the societal processes thought to belong to men.

The research to which I refer reveals the place of women—or rather the absence thereof—in the theories, interpretations, and narratives constituting the disciplines of knowledge. Since the subject matter of the liberal curriculum is drawn from these disciplines, that curriculum gives pride of place to male experience and achievements and to the societal processes associated with men. In so doing, it is the bearer of bad news about women and the reproductive processes of society. Can it be doubted that when the works of women are excluded from the subject matter of the fields into which they are being initiated, students of both sexes will come to believe, or else will have their existing belief reinforced, that males are superior and females are inferior human beings? Can it be doubted that when in the course of this initiation the lives and experiences of women are scarcely mentioned, males and females will come to believe, or else believe more strongly than ever, that the ways in which women have lived and the things women have done throughout history have no value?

At campuses across the country projects are underway to incorporate the growing body of new scholarship on women into the liberal curriculum. Such efforts must be undertaken at all levels of schooling, not simply because women comprise one half the world's population, but because the exclusion of women from the subject matter of the "curriculum proper" constitutes a hidden curriculum in the validation of one gender, its associated tasks, traits, and functions, and the denigration of the other. Supporting our culture's genderized hierarchy of value even as it reflects it, this hidden curriculum must be raised to consciousness and counteracted (Ch. 8, this volume). Introduction of the new scholarship on women into the liberal curriculum proper—and for that matter into the vocational curriculum too—makes this possible, on the one hand because it allows students to understand the workings of gender and, on the other, because it provides them with the opportunity to appreciate women's traditional tasks, traits, and functions.

In a curriculum encompassing the experience of one sex, not two, questions of gender are automatically eliminated. For the value hierarchy under discussion to be understood, as it must be if it is to be abolished, its genderized roots must be exposed.

Furthermore, if intimacy and connection are to be valued as highly as independence and distance, and if emotion and feeling are to be viewed as positive rather than untrustworthy elements of personality, women must no longer be viewed as different and alien—as the Other, to use Simone de Beauvoir's expression (1961).

Thus, we need to incorporate the study of women into curricula so that females—their lives, experiences, works, and attributes—are devalued by neither sex. But simply incorporating the new scholarship on women in the curriculum does not address the alienation and loss Rodriguez describes so well. To overcome these we must seek not only a transformation of the content of curriculum proper, but an expansion of the educational realm to include the reproductive processes of society and a corresponding redefinition of what it means to become educated.

The expansion of the educational realm I propose does not entail an extension of a skill-oriented home economics education to males. Although it is important for both sexes to learn to cook and sew, I have in mind something different when I say that education must give the reproductive processes of society their due. The traits associated with women as wives and mothers—nurturance, care, compassion, connection, sensitivity to others, a willingness to put aside one's own projects, a desire to build and maintain relationships—need to be incorporated into our ideal. This does not mean that we should fill up the curriculum with courses in the three Cs of caring, concern, and connection. Given a redefinition of education, Compassion 101a need no more be listed in a school's course offerings than Objectivity 101a is now. Just as the productive processes of society have given us the general curricular goals of rationality and individual autonomy, so too the reproductive processes yield general goals. And just as rationality and autonomy are posited as goals of particular subjects, e.g., science, as well as of the curriculum as a whole, so nurturance and connection can be understood as overarching educational goals and also as the goals of particular subjects.

But now a puzzling question arises. Given that the standard subjects of the curriculum derive from the productive processes of society, must we not insert cooking and sewing and perhaps childrearing into the curriculum if we want caring, concern, and connection to be educational objectives? Science, math, history, literature, auto mechanics, refrigeration, typing: these are the subjects of the curriculum now and these derive from productive processes. If for subjects deriving from productive processes we set educational goals whose source is the reproductive processes of society, do we not distort these subjects beyond recognition? But then, ought we not to opt instead for a divided curriculum with two sets of subjects? One set might be derived from the productive processes of society and foster traits associated with those, with the other set derived from the reproductive processes of society and fostering their associated traits. Is this the only way to do justice to both sets of traits?

If possible, a replication within the curriculum of the split between the productive and reproductive processes of society is to be avoided. So long as education insists on linking nurturing capacities and the three Cs to subjects arising out of the reproductive processes, we will lose sight of their *general* moral, social, and political significance. Moreover, so long as rationality and autonomous judgment are considered to belong exclusively to the productive processes of society, the reproductive ones will continue to be devalued. Thus, unless it is essential to divide up curricular goals according to the classification of a subject as productive or reproductive, we ought not to do so. That it is not essential becomes clear once we give up our stereotypical pictures of the two kinds of societal processes.

Readers of June Goodfield's *An Imagined World* (1981) will know that feeling and emotion, intimacy and connection can be an integral part of the processes of scientific discovery.[3] Goodfield recorded the day-to-day activities of Anna, a Portuguese scientist studying lymphocytes in a cancer laboratory in New York. Anna's relationship to her colleagues *and* to the cells she studied provides quite a contrast to the rationalistic, atomistic vision of scientists and scientific discovery most of us have. To be sure, some years ago James Watson (1969) made it clear that scientists are human. But Watson portrayed scientific discovery as a race between ambitious, aggressive, highly competitive contestants while Goodfield's Anna calls it "a kind of birth." Fear, urgency, intense joy; loneliness, intimacy, and a desire to share: these are some of the emotions that motivate and shape Anna's thought even as her reasoned analysis and her objective scrutiny of evidence engender passion. Moreover, she is bound closely to her colleagues in the lab by feeling, as well as by scientific need, and she empathizes with the lymphocytes she studies as well as with the sick people she hopes will one day benefit from her work.

If scientific activity can flourish in an atmosphere of cooperation and connection, and important scientific discoveries can take place when passionate feeling motivates and shapes thought, then surely it is not necessary for science education to be directed solely toward rationalistic, atomistic goals. And if nurturant capacities and the three Cs of caring, concern, and connection can become goals of science teaching without that subject being betrayed or abandoned, surely they can become the goals of *any* subject.

By the same token, if rational thought and independent judgment are components of successful childrearing and family living, it is not necessary to design education in subjects deriving from the reproductive processes of society solely around "affective" goals. That they can and should be part and parcel of these activities was argued long ago, and very convincingly, by both Mary Wollstonecraft and Catharine Beecher (Martin, 1985) and is a basic tenet of the home economics profession today.

Thus, just as nurturance and concern can be goals of any subject, rationality and independent judgment can also be. The temptation to institute a sharp separation of goals within an expanded educational realm corresponding to a sharp separation of subjects must, then, be resisted so that the general significance of the very real virtues we associate with women and the reproductive processes of society is understood and these virtues themselves are fostered in everyone.

Conclusion

In becoming educated one does not have to travel Rodriguez's road from intimacy to isolation. His journey of alienation is a function of a definition of education, a particular ideal of the educated person, and a particular definition of excellence—all of which can be rejected. Becoming educated can be a journey of integration, not alienation. The detailed task of restructuring an ideal of the educated person to guide this new journey I leave for another occasion. The general problem to be solved is that of uniting thought and action, reason and emotion, self and other. This was the problem Dewey addressed, but his failure to understand the workings of gender made it impossible for him to solve it.

I leave the task of mapping the precise contours of a transformed curriculum for another occasion too. The general problem to be solved here is that of giving the reproductive processes of society—and the females who have traditionally been assigned responsibility for carrying them on—their due. Only then will feeling and emotion, intimacy and connection be perceived as valuable qualities so that a journey of integration is possible.

Loss, pain, isolation: It is a tragedy that these should be the results of becoming educated, the consequences of excellence. An alternative journey to Rodriguez's requires fundamental changes in both educational theory and practice. Since these changes will make it possible to diffuse throughout the population the nurturant capacities and the ethic of care that are absolutely essential to the survival of society itself, indeed, to the survival of life on earth, they should ultimately be welcomed even by those who would claim that the loss, pain, and isolation Rodriguez experienced in becoming educated did him no harm.

Notes

1. Quite clearly, Rodriguez's class background is a factor in this judgment. Notice, however, that the form his fear takes relates to gender.

2. This scholarship cannot possibly be cited here. For reviews of the literature in the various academic disciplines see past issues of *Signs: Journal of Women in Culture and Society*.

3. See also Keller (1983).

CHAPTER 12

Curriculum and the Mirror of Knowledge

During long walks over the Nantucket moors in the summer of 1987, I made my way through the contemporary rhetoric of fragmentation to images of broken glass, eventually arriving at the metaphor that, according to Richard Rorty, has for centuries dominated Western Philosophy. My title, "Curriculum and the Mirror of Knowledge," is a play on his Philosophy and the Mirror of Nature. *The essay itself, many of whose substantive ideas found their way into* The Schoolhome, *makes use of a number of my early analyses of curriculum even as it adds a new dimension to the original formulation of the epistemological fallacy. A revised version of the paper I wrote for a collection celebrating Paul Hirst's work in education over three decades, this essay served as my contribution to the April 1991 Conference on Pluralism and Responsibility at the University of Massachusetts, Boston.*

When in the 1980s commentators on American society began expressing their fears for the younger generation and for the nation itself, I was reminded of Chinua Achebe's novel *Things Fall Apart*. Chronicling the life and death of an intrepid man whose ruling passion is to become one of the lords of his fatherland, Achebe portrayed a clan and culture at the brink of destruction. "Does the white man understand our custom about land?" Okonkwo asks upon his return from a seven year exile in his motherland. A kinsman replies:

> How can he when he does not even speak our tongue? But he says that our customs are bad; and our own brothers who have taken up his religion also say that our customs are bad. How do you think we can fight when our own brothers have turned against us? The white man is very clever. He came quietly and peaceably with his religion. We were amused at his foolishness and allowed him to stay. Now he has won our brothers, and our clan can no longer act like one. He has put a knife on the things that held us together and we have fallen apart. (Achebe 1959: 162)

Forthcoming in *Defending Diversity: Philosophical Essays on Multiculturalism*, Lawrence Foster and Patricia Herzog, eds. (Amherst: University of Massachusetts Press, 1994), copyright © 1994 by The University of Massachusetts Press; also forthcoming in *Beyond Liberal Education: Essays in Honour of Paul H. Hirst*, Robin Barrow and Patricia White, eds., copyright © 1994 by Routledge, London.

At the feast Okonkwo provided during his last days in exile, one of the oldest inhabitants of the motherland rose to thank him for calling the clan together. "I fear for the younger generation, for you people," he said. "As for me, I have only a short while to live, and so have Uchendu and Unachukwu and Emefo. But I fear for you young people because you do not understand how strong is the bond of kinship. You do not know what it is to speak with one voice . . . I fear for you; I fear for the clan." (Achebe 1959:155–6).

Although the elders in our twentieth century white man's culture did not speak of kinship bonds, their rhetoric resembled the Ibo's. Just as the Ibo elders of Achebe's narrative repeatedly invoke images of breaking up and falling apart, our own invoked the image of fragmentation. Nowhere was this so evident as in discussions of American education. Imbuing the curriculum of their childhood with cohesiveness and unity, William Bennett, Allan Bloom, E.D. Hirsch, Jr., and the others characterized the current course of study as fragmented and incomplete.

It is a sign of America's fundamental optimism that even as we mourn things lost, we propose strategies for regaining them: core curricula, great books, fundamental questions, lists for cultural literacy. But if behind the rhetoric of fragmentation there lies the belief that all things shattered can be restored, the image nevertheless demands attention. The implicit claim that the curriculum of yore was an integrated, unified whole does too.

1. Broken Glass

Only certain substances fragment. Cloth and paper rip or tear, plaster cracks, wood splinters. Earthenware fragments, however, and so does glass. Do those who use the language of fragmentation imagine the pieces of the school curriculum to be the parts of a broken bowl or pot? Surely not. Do they presuppose a curriculum made of glass: a window on the world, perhaps, or a mirror of reality? A mirror definitely but one turned on knowledge not nature, else they would not be saying that the "crisis of liberal education is a reflection of the crisis at the peaks of learning" (Bloom 1986: 346).

The picture of a mirror is familiar enough by now although the application of it to curriculum is not. In *Philosophy and the Mirror of Nature*, Richard Rorty traced back through the history of Western philosophy the image of mind as a mirror turned on nature and of knowledge as the representation in that mirror. His primary objective was to discredit the mirror metaphor. Not even the minds of the best and brightest amongst us are "glassy essences," Rorty argued (Rorty 1979). Knowledge is not and never can be a mirror reflection of reality. But in calling into question the imagery of the mind as mirror, the image in the mirror was destroyed. For Rorty did not simply argue that it is a mistake to view knowledge, on the model of a mirror reflection, as a direct, undistorted representation of nature. Telling us, in effect, that if there were a mirror the knowledge we would see reflected in it would consist of free floating bits and pieces, he also challenged the idea that knowledge constitutes a unified and justified whole.

In this Rorty was not alone. When his book was published in 1979 scholars in fields as diverse as history and literature, biology and psychology had already been criticizing knowledge for being inaccurate and incomplete—in its representation of blacks, women, the poor, for example. At the same time, by denying the very possibility of the unity of knowledge and of our finding a solid foundation on which to rest even our partial perspectival theories, philosophers, historians of science, and literary critics, among others, were posing a much deeper challenge. There appears to have been, then, a double shattering: the image of a unified body of knowledge derived from first principles that our elders have claimed to see in the mirror is illusory and so is any conception of the mind as a mirror.

After Rorty traced the history of the mirror metaphor of mind in Western philosophy, Allan Bloom in *The Closing of the American Mind* outlined the history of the knowledge reflected in the mirror. His saga was not merely the tale of the growth of intellectual specialization, not simply a story of competing and apparently incommensurable theories. It was a narrative of the erosion of faith in a truth that transcends time, place, social circumstance, and individual personality and in the very possibility of a unified, justified knowledge. Rorty's book and Bloom's might be considered the two sides of a coin were it not for the fact that Rorty considered it salutary that the mirror has at long last broken whereas Bloom's purpose was unabashedly restorative: what Rorty and others have shattered, Bloom would repair.

Unfortunately for Bloom, the intellectual history he wrote in 1987 exemplified the inadequacies of the mirror metaphor he was defending. Although he wanted his readers to believe that knowledge is the outcome of a direct, unmediated meeting between mind and ideas—if not between mind and nature itself, he allowed "Nihilism, American Style," a theoretical construction of his making, to shape his representation of our past. And while he pleaded for not merely the possibility but the primacy of non-interpretive readings, he interposed his own interpretations between our glassy essences and the texts he would have us know directly.

Bloom's highly selective, interpretive reading of the history of ideas contradicts his message that individual minds directly mirror ideas. But if even Bloom's efforts to restore the mirror tend to confirm its shattering, are not our elders right to fear for our youth? If the double shattering of mind and knowledge has indeed occurred, will not curriculum inevitably be fragmented?

Criticizing the university for offering "a democracy of disciplines" that is "really an anarchy" (Bloom 1987:337), Bloom was convinced that the undergraduate arts and sciences curriculum already was fragmented. Implying that the shattering had happened relatively recently, certainly since he himself attended the University of Chicago, he insisted that it reflected "an incoherence and incompatibility among the first principles with which we interpret the world" (Bloom 1987:346). Bloom called the fragmentation of knowledge "an intellectual crisis of the greatest magnitude, which constitutes the crisis of our civilization" (Bloom 1987:346) and implied that the fragmented liberal curriculum, in turn, cannot speak to those who would develop into whole human beings.

Connecting a problem of curriculum back to a problem of knowledge and forward to a problem of our young, Bloom constructed a chain of epistemological, educational, and personal disintegration. Ignoring the questions about knowledge that intrigued Bloom, and focusing instead on the fragmentation of the American elementary and secondary curriculum, Hirsch added another link to the chain. The most effective recipe one could invent for the fragmentation of culture itself, Hirsch said in his best selling book *Cultural Literacy*, is the curricular fragmentation we are now experiencing (Hirsch 1987:21). Is it any wonder that both his voice and Bloom's reached vast audiences? In manifesting their concern about the younger generation, they at once gave voice to and tapped into the profound and largely unarticulated fear that this white man's culture is falling apart.

2. The Mirror of Curriculum

I have been speaking here as if a double shattering has occurred, yet mind is not actually a hard brittle substance, knowledge not really a reflection in a mirror. Bloom's interpretations of texts do, however, add confirmation to the already strong case against any theory that views mind as standing in direct unmediated contact with reality. And comments like Cynthia Ozick's in the *New York Times Book Review* that both science and the humanities are "multiplying, fragmented, in hot pursuit of split ends" (Ozick 1987) support Bloom's diagnosis of knowledge as disconnected and incomplete.

The theoretical question of whether the split ends of knowledge can ever be fused, the fragments pieced together into a single whole is not easily answered. This issue need not be decided for an exploration of the implications of the present reality of a disconnected, unintegrated knowledge to proceed, however. To be sure, Bloom's remark about the crisis of liberal education suggests that a fragmented curriculum is the inescapable consequence of fragmented knowledge. The implicit assumption that curriculum is a mirror turned on knowledge rests, however, on what I have elsewhere called the epistemological fallacy (Ch.9, this volume).

Remarking that if music is not knowledge it does not follow that it should not be taught, some years ago the philosopher William Frankena pointed out that in discussions of curriculum, theories of knowledge are relevant but they are never in themselves decisive (Frankena 1970:20). This point leads to the more general one that it is a fallacy to argue directly from a theory of the structure, nature, extent, or limits of knowledge to conclusions about curriculum. If music is not knowledge, it can still be included in curriculum. If how to pickpocket or swindle constitutes a kind of knowledge, curriculum space is not therefore guaranteed it. And if knowledge itself is fragmented, it does not follow that curriculum must be.

Why over the years has Frankena's warning gone unheeded? The mirror metaphor of curriculum is deeply embedded in curriculum thought. Because a mirror faithfully reflects its object, insofar as curriculum is conceived of as a glass turned on knowledge a correspondence between the structure of knowledge and of curriculum is to be expected. Why does the fragmentation of curriculum seem an inevitable result of the double shattering of the mirror of mind and the representation in it? Because a reflection of a shattered mirror image will of necessity represent that shattering, the picture of curriculum as mirror masks the fact that educators can construct their own integrated wholes.

They not only can. They do. In recent years I visited two sites of learning whose curricula, though very different, were both so integrated, so unified as to make attributions of fragmentation quite inappropriate. The curriculum of Shakespeare & Company's Workshop for Theater Professionals was divided into four subjects—voice, movement, fight and text—but, considering them conceptually interconnected the faculty had arranged so much practical carry over from one class to the next that, as a student said in my presence, "You can't even tell when one class ends and another begins. One just bleeds into the next." In contrast, the curriculum of the NEH sponsored Summer Institute on Women in Nineteenth Century American Culture held at the University of New Hampshire defied description in terms of separate subjects. Drawing its primary content from the fields of history and literature but also incorporating material from art and theater, sociology and education, its program represented another kind of unity altogether.

Neither program was designed for school or college students. Moreover, the specialized purposes of each both distinguish their curricula from the sort being charged with fragmentation and simplify the integrative project. Yet, such examples indicate that when educators set themselves to construct unified wholes, the actuality of a fragmented knowledge does not have to translate into a fragmented curriculum.

Hiding the logical lapses of those who commit the epistemological fallacy, the picture of curriculum as a shattered mirror exonerates those who might otherwise be accused of abdicating responsibility. It also misrepresents the process of curriculum construction. Whether a mirror breaks in two or into 1000 pieces, once the shattering has occurred the fragments are of necessity disconnected. The chances of restoring a shattered mirror are slight but supposing such action to be possible, there is only one right ordering of the fragments. Their edges jagged, their shapes assorted, like the pieces of a jigsaw puzzle their relationship to one another is both predetermined and unique as, of course, is their place in the mirror, itself a preformed whole.

The parts of a curriculum are not like this. Capable of being connected to one another in more than one way, they can also be integrated into more than one whole. Take philosophy and literature. We normally view them as independent subjects yet they can be conceived of as mutually illuminating a common topic, for instance the moral life; the techniques of literary analysis can be seen as applying to philosophical texts; works of literature and philosophy from a given historical period can be viewed jointly as products of their times. Take history and science. Assumed to be even more distinct than philosophy and literature, these subjects can be seen in relation to one another: science, for example, as a formative element of history; scientific theories, in turn, as historical products. Furthermore, they can be made the constituents of quite different unities. Philosophy, literature, science, history, and also mathematics, the social sciences, and the arts can be given a place in a curriculum organized around the theme of world peace as they all can in one that takes as its focus the variety of human culture and experience.[1]

By imposing on curriculum the logic of mirrors, we fail to see that subjects connect to one another in different ways and that a given subject has no fixed essence. Serving in one instance to illuminate issues of justice and the moral life and in another to raise questions about human nature and the relationship between nature and culture, philosophy, for example, will function differently in different curricular contexts, indeed will be seen differently in them. Perceived for some purposes as a way of thinking, for others it may be understood as a cluster of questions and answers, a body of great works or a route to self-understanding.

Cries of distortion often greet the claim that even the most prosaic school subject can be seen under different aspects. Students will not really be learning English literature if this autonomous subject is viewed in relation to social justice! If the sciences are brought within the orbit of world peace, students will not learn physics, chemistry, biology as they really are! But how are physics, mathematics, literature and philosophy, really? If from one point of view physics is a methodology or a set of theories, from another it is a social construction and from yet another the source of a technology that imprisons as it tries to liberate. Literature, mathematics, philosophy are also seen differently from different standpoints.

Does one point of view have privileged curricular status? Many would say that only when physics is seen through the eyes of the physicist or philosophy through the eyes of the philosopher is the one seen as physics, the other as philosophy. The two mirror imagery lends support to this claim: since the mirror of mind is turned on nature, the reflection in it will be what scientists see; since the mirror of curriculum is turned on that reflection, it in turn will reflect what is seen through their eyes.

Ignoring what is surely true, namely that the practitioners of a given field do not all see in the same way—just think of the different outlooks of a cognitive psychologist and a Freudian or of an analytic philosopher, a phenomenologist, and a neo-Marxist—this presumption in favor of the standpoint of "the" practitioner of a discipline begs the question of why only practitioners manage to see their disciplines as they "really" are. Granted, despite their differences they all view their chosen fields from the "inside." Yet as Richard Rhodes's *The Making of the Atomic Bomb* makes painfully clear, the eyes of even the keenest insider are sometimes myopic.

Speaking in November 1945 about the question of why scientists built the bomb the United States had dropped on Japan only three months earlier, Robert Oppenheimer cited the fear that Nazi Germany would build it first, the hope that the war would be shortened, and the motives of curiosity and a sense of adventure. "When you come right down to it," Rhodes reports Oppenheimer as saying, "the reason that we did this job is because it was an organic necessity. If you are a scientist you cannot stop such a thing. If you are a scientist you believe that it is good to find out how the world works; that it is good to find out what the realities are . . . " (Rhodes 1988:761).

Look at the world through the eyes of a physicist as the mirror metaphor demands, and the effects on it of the enterprise of physics are indiscernible. So are physics' interconnections with politics and government, its responsiveness to the exigencies of war, its ranking of the value of knowledge above the value of human life, all splendidly documented by Rhodes. Step outside physics and see it through the eyes of a historian, a sociologist or even an interested citizen—as the metaphor of a mirror turned on nature forbids—and these can appear to be just as much a part of the way physics "really" is as any components of the view from within.

To assign the practitioner's standpoint a privileged curricular position is to forget that the purposes of education bear on the issue of how to view the subjects of a curriculum and that those purposes are not everywhere the same. If in the education of specialists it is appropriate to teach a field from the standpoint of those who engage in it—and even here one wishes that some attention might be paid to perspectives that take into account the human, the social, and the planetary consequences of "advances" in knowledge—in general and liberal education the issue of how to view the subjects of the curriculum is by no means so clear cut. Because the two mirror metaphor denies the very possibility of our having knowledge about the disciplines of knowledge, the fact that we face such choices is often overlooked. This imagery, by placing mind outside nature peering in and picturing knowledge as a reflection of nature, conceals the existence of "external" standpoints from which physics, philosophy, economics can themselves become objects of study.

3. The Inward Gaze

Even as mirror imagery distorts the curricular enterprise by detaching it from human purposes and making invisible the many points at which choices must be made, it lends credence to a rhetoric that directs one's gaze to curriculum's inner structure. By definition, if there is a fragment there must once have been a whole. Thus, a language of fragmentation boasts a vocabulary of incompleteness. Its terminology is also one of lack of unity since necessarily a fragment was once a part of some whole; of disconnection since if something is a fragment it is a separate, distinct, unattached entity; and of meaninglessness. Instead of a mirror think for a moment about a fragile bowl. Constituting a unified whole that in its own way is both complete and integrated, its decorative as well as its utilitarian elements derive whatever meaning or significance they have from their contribution to that whole. Let the bowl break into pieces and in lieu of unity, and of the integrity, completeness, and meaning this implies, there will be disconnection, incompleteness, and an absence of meaning.

Presupposing a once existing whole into which the various subjects fit and from which they gain their meaning, the rhetoric of curricular fragmentation is at bottom accusatory. Why did our school and college curriculum fall apart? How did it happen? Who is to blame? It is also equivocal. In the language of fragmentation claims of incompleteness, disconnection, and meaninglessness pertain to an entity's inner constitution. The connectedness of the parts of the entity and their place in the whole: such are its concerns. Does the curriculum fit people's needs? Can it serve students well? Questions focusing on the entity's relationship to things outside itself cannot even be asked for this is a language of internal relationships. As such, it draws attention to defects of a curriculum's inner composition. Its external shortcomings are overlooked.

In ordinary talk about curriculum, however, the attributions of incompleteness, disconnection, lack of meaning, lack of integration and their polar opposites—completeness, connection, meaning, integration—have both an internal and external sense. Is a curriculum incomplete when it is not a unified whole or when it is not inclusive? Is it disconnected when its various subjects are unrelated to one another or when it does not connect up with student needs and purposes? Does it lack meaning when there is no unifying principle or theme to give the various subjects significance or when the subjects are not meaningful to students? Does it lack integration when the various parts are not tied together or when new knowledge and different perspectives are not incorporated in it?

Our elders' silences about external completeness, connection, meaning, and integration bespeak volumes. These were the primary issues for an earlier generation of educational critics. From the late 1960s through the 1970s the American curriculum was damned for being irrelevant, not for being fragmented. Its connection to students' lives was doubted, its remoteness from the concerns of society deplored. And when its completeness was questioned, the charge referred to the exclusion of subject matter relating to the background and experiences of students, not to a lack of unity.

It is not surprising that what occupied one wave of educational critics is ignored by the next. Yet the inward gaze of the present generation of elders should not go unnoticed for the one kind of curricular completeness, connection and meaning does not insure the other.

Curricula can certainly be constructed so that they are unified wholes whose subject matter fits together in a way that gives meaning to its parts and are also connected to people's lives and purposes so as to make them meaningful to students. The subject matter of the NEH sponsored Summer Institute on Women in Nineteenth-Century American Culture, for instance, was not only highly integrated; participants also found it extraordinarily relevant to their past experience and their ongoing lives. Indeed, members of the program described their experience to me as "a homecoming." It provided "the missing link," they told me. It gave them back their "history," they said. The enthusiasm with which students entered into the classroom exercises and activities of the Shakespeare & Company Workshop and the palpable joy they derived from them in turn testify to the fact that the meaning this curriculum succeeded in having for its participants far exceeded that of simply meeting their professional goals. Taking the fundamental problem of an interpreter of Shakespeare's plays to be that of understanding his language yet seeing acting as a pursuit that engages the whole person, the staff provided experiences for students that tapped into deep feelings and emotions while also placing each of them in close relation to some text.

Despite these happy examples, a curriculum possessing the internal properties of connection and meaning can just as easily be so remote from student experiences and concerns as to be meaningless to them. As long ago as 1983 sociologist Sara Lawrence Lightfoot reported that at the public high school in Brookline, Massachusetts, a relatively affluent suburb of Boston, 10 percent of the student body who spoke English as a second language represented fifty-five native languages originating in twenty-five countries. Thirty percent of this student body was minority, the largest proportion being Asian with that category including Chinese, Japanese, Korean, Indian, and Iranian. Twelve percent of the total was Black. In turn, at the John F. Kennedy High School outside New York City, 40 percent of the student body was Hispanic, 35 percent Black, 2 percent Asian. Equally significant, 800 students were enrolled in Spanish-speaking sections of its English as a Second Language Program, but the program also accommodated native speakers of Russian, Albanian, Chinese, Vietnamese, Korean, among other languages (Lightfoot 1983).

In 1987–1988, when Samuel Freedman, the author of *Small Victories*, entered the world of Seward Park High School in New York City, 155 freshmen required bilingual education or courses in English as a second language and nine of ten continuing students lived in non-English speaking families (Freedman 1990:26). At approximately the same time in the school in Holyoke, Massachusetts that Tracy Kidder described in *Among Schoolchildren*, 314 of 620 students were Hispanic. All told, less than 45 percent of the children were white (Kidder 1989:65). As I write, California's population is close to 40 percent nonwhite with Hispanics constituting 22 percent of inhabitants (Mydans 1990). In Massachusetts, only 23 percent of the students attending the Boston public schools are white (Ribadeneira and Hernandez 1990). And a long article on education and the changed American population in *The New York Review of Books* begins, "Each year, this country becomes less white, less 'European,' and less tightly bound by a single language" (Hacker 1990:19).

Saying nothing about the external issues of inclusiveness, relevance, and meaningfulness, our elders sing the praises of a curriculum that had no space for portraying blacks as full human beings—in American history they were seen first as slaves and then as the objects of Lincoln's Emancipation Proclamation, elsewhere they were invisible. They extol a course of study in which women were invisible in both the public world and their private homes. They seek to restore an American education that had no room reserved for American Indian cultures and no place in which the poor, whether male or female, of color or of no color, were accurately depicted.

4. The Restorative Presumption

Break a fragile object and what do you do? Piece the fragments together of course, for insofar as this can be accomplished its unity is restored and with it integrity, completeness and meaning. To be sure, you may have to sift through remains of other objects to find the fragments. Moreover, they may no longer fit neatly together. Still, if the procedure is not quite as simple as it first appears, it is nevertheless the obvious one to adopt. The obvious one in the case of something you cherish, that is. If, however, that shattered object was not in your opinion well-suited to its environment or well-fitted to its purpose, you might decide to make or buy a new one rather than restore this old one.

There can be no doubt that those who have been decrying the condition of American education cherish the curriculum of their youth. They have told us so repeatedly. They have said how well versed in the classics their generation was, how extensive its knowledge, how disciplined its minds. And they have made it quite clear that they are willing to sift through the new course offerings in order to piece together the fragments belonging to it. Interpreting the multiplication of courses in the last decades as a pandering to the baser instincts and provincial tastes of our youth, they have assured us that those new subjects were designed for lazy students with no ambition. Presenting curricular proliferation in a crass light, they have quite overlooked the fact that some of the new offerings integrate into the school curriculum for the very first time material directly related to the lives and backgrounds of a majority of the student population.

It scarcely needs saying that a more inclusive curriculum is not in every case a better one. We have all heard too many stories of subjects so banal, so trivial, so unworthy of study to be this naive. Yet in a society that is fast changing color, how rational is it to judge courses in third world philosophy frivolous? In a nation with a history of slavery and a continuing record of racial division and inequality are the study of Black history and literature, and the inclusion of slave narratives on the reading lists of American history and literature courses, really the irrelevancies they are described as? In a land in which rape is rampant, the victims of child sexual abuse are most often girls, and women are subjected to sexual harassment at home, at school, and at work, is it sensible to say that courses that represent and analyze women's history, lives, experiences are parochial and take too subjective a point of view?

This is not to say that the reports of curricular multiplicity and disconnection should be discounted. At the least they indicate the extent to which educators have abdicated responsibility for shaping the curriculum of our nation's youth. In so doing they reveal the mirror metaphor of curriculum busily at work, as it were: as knowledge proliferates so do school subjects; as it becomes ever more disconnected, so do studies. Yet if our elders' objective is curricular unity in the sense of internal integration, why do they not try to pull the split ends together in some brand new creative way? Why do they look back with longing to a curriculum that treated each separate subject as "a separate nation with its own governance, psychology, entelechy" (Ozick 1987)? And if our elders insist on looking backwards, why do they not try to integrate history, literature, philosophy, physics, biology, mathematics into a coherent whole?

Not long ago the condition that our elders have taken as a sign that knowledge is falling apart was looked upon favorably as evidence of a knowledge "explosion." Whether one calls it a fragmenting of existing knowledge or a burgeoning of new knowledge, some of those split ends constitute a problem for our elders: they have taken it upon themselves to criticize the very texts and theories of the curriculum of the past for being inaccurate and incomplete—in their representations of blacks, women, the poor, for example.

Among the new fields of inquiry that have been charged with destroying the unity at the peaks of learning are ones revealing that those products of Western culture we once thought so universal, so objective, so all embracing that we proudly constructed the curriculum of school and college around them are not. That comprehensive study of the United States' past, American history, has been shown to misrepresent, when it does not entirely neglect, the lives, works, and experiences of women and minority men. Instead of being universal as claimed, psychology's norms and its narratives of human development turn out to have been derived from studies of boys and men. The evidence for its theories of intelligence has in turn been manipulated so that white males invariably score the highest. It has also been demonstrated that biology's accounts of nature have mapped society's sex stereotypes onto the animal "kingdom," its studies of primates have consistently made the male the main actor of the troop and the linchpin of that small society, its predominant account of human cultural evolution has done likewise although there is no more evidence for the theory named Man-the-Hunter than for the one called Woman-the-Gatherer.

This list is far from exhaustive but even the most thoroughgoing survey would not do justice to the situation at the peaks of learning. The new scholarship has not simply revealed biases and gaps in the knowledge accumulated by the different disciplines. It has cast doubt on the very objectivity of the judgments by which some works of art, literature, history, science, philosophy have been included in the cultural canon and others have been put in the scrap heap. It is not just that scholars have recovered long lost works by women and by men who are not white. It is not even that recent research challenges the portrayals of both groups enshrined in science and history as well as in literature and the arts. Accepted definitions of what constitutes great art and literature and even good science have been called into question. It has been shown that the creation of works in the canon of Western Culture has rested on the exploitation of the very people misrepresented in them. And the idea of canonizing any set of works is itself debated.

Why do our elders look backwards? At an assembly Okonkwo's kinsman said: "You all know why we are here, when we ought to be building our barns or mending our huts, when we should be putting our compounds in order. My father used to say to me: 'Whenever you see a toad jumping in broad daylight, then know that something is after its life.'" (Achebe 1959:186). Our elders have seen a toad jumping in broad daylight. Just as the white man put the knife in the things that held the Ibo together, the knowledge our elders would prohibit, if they could, is putting it in the white man's creation. Revealing the incompleteness of Western Culture's theories, the partiality of its claims, the bias of its narratives, its disfiguring portraits, this research cuts through the illusion that "the" classics speak for all of us. Exposing the white man's arbitrary norms by uncovering alternate ways of seeing, thinking, feeling, acting, and being in the world, it excises the myth that the canon of great works itself is eternal and immutable.

Were culture transmitted biologically from one generation to the next, our elders would not need to look back. But it is passed down by education, not by our genes. Remember that one major function of education in our society has been to transmit "high" culture or Culture with a capital "C"—history, literature, philosophy, science, and the like—to our young, and our elders' enthusiasm for the curriculum of yore and disdain for the more inclusive one today are explained. After all is said and done, curriculum is what enables knowledge to survive. It passes along the cultural code from one generation to the next as DNA does the genetic. If the new scholarship that casts doubt on the objectivity and universality of the white man's heritage is incorporated into the curriculum to be studied by our nation's young, the fragmentation of the white man's Culture—a.k.a. Western Culture—will be perpetuated. On the other hand, if the offending knowledge can be kept out of the curriculum of our school's and colleges, the new ideas and directions it contains will have a short life.

By piecing together that earlier curriculum, our elders believe they can simultaneously pass along the white man's Culture to the next generation and erase from our cultural memory the scholarship that threatens its fragmentation. To revert to mirror imagery, one reason they seek to preserve the curriculum of their youth is that they like seeing only themselves in that reflecting surface. Let the mirror of curriculum reflect what now appears on the mirror of mind and not only will our elders see in it free floating bits and pieces of knowledge. They will see other people in that glass they think of as their very own. Pretend that knowledge has not fragmented and the image in the glass has not changed—or else somehow manage to freeze and preserve the reflection of an earlier knowledge on the mirror of mind—and what is seen in the mirror of curriculum will contain no split ends. It will also satisfy our elders' vanity. Keep the second mirror turned on that earlier representation and, as a bonus, the knowledge that has been shattered may itself be restored.

5. Curriculum Without Mirrors

In implicitly acknowledging that curriculum has power of life and death over knowledge, our elders reject the very mirror imagery they invoke to explain the multiplicity they deplore. We should not let their inconstancy distract us from the question of whether the perception that past knowledge was integrated is an optical illusion, however. Just as the curriculum of our past treated its component subjects as separate entities, was not knowledge itself composed of a number of distinct forms?

It is tempting to remark on the irony of a rhetoric that attributes unity to a curriculum and to a knowledge neither of which was integrated and to leave the matter there, implying that elders like Bloom know not of what they speak. I submit, however, that they are not mistaken. Until very recently both existing knowledge and the curriculum it was thought to reflect were governed by an integrative principle as selective as it was unseen.

What unity did knowledge and curriculum each possess? It was not the kind that would be achieved by reducing one subject or form of knowledge to another. Nor was it a function of bringing everything under a relatively small set of concepts. Rather, each school subject, like each form or field of knowledge, partook of the viewpoint of what was then said to be—and by many is still said to be—the sum total of our cultural heritage; or alternatively, that portion of our cultural heritage that should be preserved. The prose and poetry, the narratives and theories, the conceptual structures and methodologies of Western Culture that the curriculum was expected to hand down to future generations were authored by the educated white man, for the educated white man, and about the educated white man and his world or, if about other people and other worlds, from his perspective.

Does the point of view on the world which gave the curriculum of yesteryear its unity yield so complete and objective a picture that, although it originates with one set of people, it serves all of us well? In Henry James's novel *The Bostonians*, published in 1886, Basil Ransom tells Verena Tarrant that his interest is in his own sex:

> The masculine character, the ability to dare and endure, to know and yet not fear reality, to look the world in the face and take it for what it is—a very queer and partly very base mixture—that is what I want to preserve, or rather, as I may say, to recover; and I must tell you that I don't in the least care what becomes of you ladies while I make the attempt! (James 1966:290)

In attempting to preserve the primacy of the white man's point of view it sometimes seems that our elders do not in the least care what happens to either the ladies—over 50% of the school and college population today is female—or the non-white men.

No doubt some of those young people who do not find their own lives, histories, experiences, world views in their school curriculum will manage to make the white man's viewpoint their own. Unable to establish rapport with a curriculum that does not reach out to them, all too many who fail to see themselves in the norm drop out of school figuratively, if not literally, and retreat into their groups and themselves. Lapsing into a kind of cultural solipsism, they feel like—and increasing numbers are acting and living like—outsiders in their own land. The United States does not have to return to the curriculum of yesteryear to see this happen. Although the subjects of the curriculum have multiplied, the lenses with which schools fit our young are, with few exceptions, still ground by the educated white man to his specifications.

Patricia, a low income young woman in a New York City public high school told sociologist Michelle Fine, "I just can't concentrate in school, thinkin' about my mother gettin' beat up last night. He scares me too but I just don't understand why she stays" (Fine and Zane 1989:33). How ill-matched her yearning to understand the world she lives in and her school curriculum! Even the excluded women and men who are not so disaffected as to become school and culture's dropouts stand to suffer from a curriculum that assimilates all human experience and accomplishments to his. "What do you think this is lady, a delivery room?" said a 1980s Massachusetts court clerk to a pregnant attorney as she entered a full courtroom. In that same decade a court officer asked a lawyer who had won an acquittal for her client, "What are you, sleeping with the judge?" (Kennedy 1989: 6)

A curriculum based on the exclusionary principles one associates with elite clubs is a downright dangerous prescription for a multi-racial, ethnically diverse, two-sex society that is struggling to keep things from falling apart at a historical moment when the clouds of nuclear as well as ecological disaster loom large. Treating a problem of inclusion as one of exclusion, our elders worry about the intellectual purity of their subject matter as much as realtors once did about the racial and religious purity of the people to whom they sold property. Displaying the selfsame exclusionary bent in their recommendations, they equate giving curriculum space to research by and about the women and the non-white men who were members of this society from the beginning with a lowering of quality and a diminution of content. Bewailing the lack of integration in today's curriculum, they endorse restrictive policies regarding the knowledge and perspectives to be included therein. Calling curricular inclusiveness "anarchy," they try to ban the very subject matter that would enable us to acknowledge the differences of sex, race, class, ethnicity, religion without having them make a difference to such questions as who is qualified to govern, be educated, practice the professions.

Is the equation of curricular inclusiveness with chaos valid? To make the curriculum of our schools and colleges receptive to voices and perspectives that have been excluded is no more a prescription for disorder than any step toward democracy. The "democratization" of the curriculum undoubtedly introduces a degree of complexity. But complexity does not entail chaos.

Does the opening up of the American curriculum by bringing in new voices and perspectives spell the dilution of quality? No one who has read Achebe's *Things Fall Apart*, Virginia Woolf's *Three Guineas*, Zora Neal Hurston's *Their Eyes Were Watching God*, Lorraine Hansberry's *A Raisin in the Sun* can possibly think so. As for the complaint that the inclusion of these works would diminish content, the truth lies elsewhere. I, at least, know of no work on our elders' list of "the" classics that shows the white man putting a knife into clans like Okonkwo's from the standpoint of the victim, none that discusses the white man's past exclusion of the white woman from both his education and his professions, none that represents a black woman's repudiation of the roles white society has written for her, none that portrays a ghetto family's agonizing decision to move into a white neighborhood.

Making differences among people disappear by representing the white man's history, experience, and work as every man's and every woman's, our elders discount the significance for education of their existence in the nation itself. It might seem that in a democracy theirs is the best approach to diversity. Were ours a society whose history held no traces of race, religious, ethnic, and gender discrimination, curricular silence on these matters would be of little consequence. Had the white man's Culture long since incorporated the standpoint of others, our differences from him might require no comment. In our situation, however, denial promotes denigration.

Given the extraordinary shifts the United States population has already undergone, the costs of suppressing perspectives other than the white man's are high. With scholarship now revealing the limitations of his position and also making people aware, often for the first time, of the worlds he could not see, the injustice of suppressing other points of view is magnified. If we were the Ibo, exclusion might be our best alternative. But our nation was founded on diversity and has always thrived on the introduction of new ideas and viewpoints. Things will not fall apart if from an early age children look through lenses of many different hues. Quite the opposite.

"Though we see the same world, we see it with different eyes," Virginia Woolf wrote in *Three Guineas* (Woolf 1938:18). Educators who are ready to take responsibility for their actions could make this dictum the unifying principle of a curriculum premised on inclusion rather than exclusion. Once mirror imagery is abandoned, other principles will suggest themselves too, many of them far more substantive than this one derived from Woolf. The fact that internal integration is a matter of degree, not an all or nothing affair (cf. Martin 1977) will also become apparent.

6. Conclusion

Rejection of the mirror metaphor of mind does not entail the shattering of the mirror metaphor of curriculum. There can then be no two-mirror logic, but knowledge can be viewed as a human or social construction rather than a reflection of reality and curriculum still thought of as a glassy essence turned on knowledge. Does a mirrorless concept of curriculum radically sever education from the theory of knowledge? Not at all. A repudiation of the epistemological fallacy leaves open Rorty's question of the status of epistemology itself. It is also quite compatible with the thesis that there is an intimate relationship between curriculum and knowledge, for it is the assumption of a hierarchy—of a one-way causal influence flowing from knowledge to curriculum—that is rejected when mirror imagery is discarded, not all connections between the two. The presupposition that knowledge has a legitimate claim to all curriculum space is also disclaimed.

Will a mirrorless concept of curriculum turn our gaze outward? Not necessarily. But at least it allows us to ask those questions about external meaning, disconnection, incompleteness that our elders have been avoiding. In particular it lets us ask if a nation worried about falling apart does not require a *unifying* curriculum—one that develops kinship bonds among girls and boys of different races, social classes, ethnicities—far more than a *unified* one.[2] And it makes it possible for us to acknowledge that even if at some time in American history a curriculum over which the white man's perspective had a monopolistic hold fit this bill, it no longer does.

Notes

I wish to thank Ann Diller, Michael Martin, Beatrice Nelsen, Jennifer Radden, and Janet Farrell Smith for their helpful comments on this essay.

1. The analysis of the parts of curriculum presented here is based on the analysis of the parts of a single subject in Martin (1977).

2. The notion of a unifying curriculum was suggested to me by Mann's discussion of the need for a unifying discourse (1990).

CHAPTER 13

The Radical Future of Gender Enrichment

I end this volume with "The Radical Future of Gender Enrichment" because in writing it I quite consciously tried to join the ideas about curriculum that I had been developing since 1969 and my work on the education of girls and women. The immediate occasion for the paper was an invitation from Jane Gaskell and John Willinsky to contribute to a collection of essays initially called "Gender Enriches Curriculum." A play on Zillah Eisenstein's The Radical Future of Liberal Feminism, *my title was meant to reflect my belief that the verb "enrich" did not adequately capture gender's transformative potential.*

How does the study of gender enrich curriculum? Let me count the ways.

I

The androcentrism of the disciplines of knowledge is by now an established fact. Thanks to the study of gender we know, for example, that the field of history, that comprehensive study of the past, misrepresents when it does not entirely skip over the lives, works, and experiences of women.[1] We know that instead of being universal, as claimed, psychology's norms and its narratives of human development have been derived from studies of boys and men. We even know that biology's accounts of nature have mapped society's sex stereotypes onto the animal "kingdom," its studies of primates have consistently made the male the main actor of the troop and the linchpin of that small society, its predominant account of human cultural evolution has done likewise although there is no more evidence for the theory named Man-the-Hunter than for the one called Woman-the-Gatherer.

In addition, research on gender has cast doubt on the very objectivity of the judgments by which some works of art, literature, history, science, philosophy have been

This essay is forthcoming in *Gender In/Forms Curriculum: From Enrichment to Transformation,* Jane Gaskell and John Willinsky, eds., by Teachers College Press.

deemed valuable, or even great, and others have been put in the scrap heap. I do not simply mean that scholars have recovered long lost works by women and that recent research challenges the portrayals of women enshrined in science and history as well as in literature and the arts. Accepted definitions of what constitutes great art and literature and even good science have been called into question by the study of gender and so has the idea of canonizing any set of works.

Insofar as school's course of study draws its subject matter from fields such as history, literature, mathematics, the natural sciences, the human and social sciences—as of course it does to a great extent—it has repeated the distortions of these latter. But to recognize that the gender bias of the disciplines is reflected in the subject matter of school is one thing and to improve the school curriculum is another. If this end is to be achieved, more accurate representations of women's lives, works, and experiences must be incorporated into the school curriculum.

The question is, how? Even as some scholars have begun to reconstruct the intellectual disciplines, others have distinguished different stages of curricular change and have debated the pros and cons of making the study of women a separate subject as opposed to integrating subject matter about women into existing school subjects. The question is also, which women? Do we introduce into the school curriculum a few famous ones or do we attempt to bring in all women? And whichever course we adopt, do we unthinkingly cast our net so as to include only middle class, white women or do we make sure to reach out to all women?

As participants in the National S.E.E.D. Project on Inclusive Curriculum[2] and other groups attempting to transform the school curriculum well know, the task of subject matter inclusion is as challenging as any curriculum maker could wish. Yet it would be a mistake to think that the androcentrism of the school curriculum is due solely to the fact that its subject matter mirrors the gender biases of the intellectual disciplines. By alerting us to the contamination in one of curriculum's wellsprings, the study of gender allows us to shut off a major source of distortion and misrepresentation. But school's subject matter normally comes wrapped up in those neat bundles we call subjects and even a quick survey of these by one wearing gender sensitive lenses reveals another kind of bias.

II

At a time when we are continually being reminded that gender is a social construction, it is not always remembered that school subjects are constructions too (Ch. 10, this volume). Our subjects were never just "out there" in the world waiting to be brought into school's course of study. On the contrary, those bundles of subject matter that are so often treated as God-given were actually made by human beings. This does not mean that curriculum development is a capricious enterprise or that school subjects are nothing but arbitrary collections of subject matter. It does, however, signify that one of the most important decisions curriculum makers face is that of determining which of the innumerable things there are should serve as the points of departure for our school subjects.

That every school subject takes something in the world as its starting point is seldom acknowledged, perhaps because a subject usually derives its name from what, for want of a better term, I will call its *subject-entity*. Thus, the school subject Physics draws its name from the science physics, the school subject French draws its name from the language French, the school subject Reading draws its name from the activity of reading. Quite clearly, despite the sameness of name, a subject is not identical with its subject-entity. On the one hand, the subject French, for instance, has an educational function that the language French does not; on the other, the subject matter belonging to the subject French can be drawn from a whole range of sources that includes the French language but goes beyond it to, for instance, linguistics, literature, history, geography.

Now I can think of only one subject, and it is very much to the point that I am not sure what name to give it—should I be calling it Home Economics, Family Studies or something else altogether?—that clearly and unequivocally draws its subject-entity from "the world of the private house," to use Virginia Woolf's phrase (Woolf 1938, p.18). Need I say that, historically, this world has been considered women's domain? Need I add that even in the best of times this school subject tends to be situated much closer to the margins of curriculum than to the center or that when there are budget crises, the subjects on the margins are the first to go?

The devaluation of Home Economics—or Family Studies if you prefer—is not news. Study the social construction called gender, however, and one sees that the negative assessment is part of a larger pattern of discrimination against a whole class of subject-entities.

The very different treatment in the school curriculum of the strikingly similar cases of politics and education illustrates the double standard by which subject-entities are judged (Martin 1992, p.139). Activities in the real world around which institutions have grown up, education and politics would each seem well-suited to be a subject-entity of a school subject. Nevertheless, one and not the other has been welcomed into the general or liberal curriculum in this capacity. Notice that in becoming a subject-entity the activity called politics has been converted from an occupation to be undertaken into an object of study. Students are taught theory, history, research *about* politics, not politics itself. Success in the subject that sometimes goes under the name Political Science and sometimes Government is judged by the comprehension of a body of knowledge and perhaps the ability to undertake relevant inquiries, not by the efficacy of action taken in the real world. But the activity we call education can also be recast. It too has inspired its fair share of theory and research, some of it as enlightening and profound as one could wish. And despite disclaimers, education is no less interesting than politics. Indeed, from the standpoint of the survival of both the individual and society, not to mention the planet, it is surely as important a set of activities and institutions as any.

Why have curriculum makers favored politics as a subject-entity over education? Politics' advantage is that, considering it one of society's "productive" processes, North

American culture has situated it in the public world and placed it in men's care. Education's problem is that even though school has moved it out of the private home and into the public world, it is seen as a "reproductive" societal process whose "natural" practitioners are still assumed to be women (Martin 1985).

Just to recognize the unequal treatment of subject-entities drawn from society's reproductive processes or associated in our cultural consciousness with home and family is to enrich curriculum making. After all, calling attention to the unrepresentative nature of our subject-entities, and hence our subjects, is a necessary prelude to redressing the curricular imbalance. However, I do not see how the double standard can be abolished if the gap in school's goals is not filled in.

III

Don the lenses of a student of gender and one sees not only the absences and distortions in the content of today's course of study and a serious subject-entity imbalance. One notices for perhaps the first time the telling omission in the list of goals curriculum is supposed to further (Martin 1990; 1992).

It has been said that "the stated goals of education in modern democratic societies remain constant: the development of each person as (a) a worker, (b) a citizen, and (c) an individual" (Waks and Roy 1987, p. 24). A case for adding (d) a keeper of the cultural heritage can be made, but the list with this emendation seems correct. To be sure, the four goals are not given equal time in every discussion of education. Still, together they represent the full range of what education is expected to do. That these expectations fail to take account of a basic function of education in a modern or postmodern society, namely (e), the development of each person as a member of a home and family, escapes everyone's notice.

Let me make it clear that in adding (e) to the list I am not presupposing any particular type of home and family, let alone some traditional form with its gender inequalities. Lesbian families, interracial families, stepfamilies, single parent ones: whatever the type, education is needed for life therein. Yet, for example, in the spate of reports published in the 1980s on the condition of education in the United States, home and family were all but ignored. Granted, the reports did advise parents to support the teacher's authority and warn them against dereliction in their duty to monitor homework. The thought that school might be derelict in its duty to prepare young people to live in those private homes and families from which they exit each morning did not occur to the authors of these tomes. It did not occur to their many critics either.

An analysis that recognizes that institutions as well as individuals are gendered explains the gap. One major assumption underlying educational thought in the United States today, and presumably in other Western nations as well, is that the function of school in a modern democratic society is to prepare children, practically all of whom are born into the domestic environment of the home and who spend their earliest years in close contact with its ongoing reproductive processes, to take their places in the larger society—in the "public world" of politics, economics, and "high" culture. To be sure, almost all those who enter the larger world continue to live their lives in private homes as members of private families, albeit in homes and families of many different sorts. Yet my compatriots do not seem to think that the tasks and activities carried out in the latter or the personal qualities one needs in order to function well there require education. Holding onto the by now discredited perception of home and family as "natural" institutions, retaining the outmoded custom of assigning women primary responsibility for running them, and persisting in the mistaken belief that whatever knowledge and skill are needed are either innately female or will be picked up informally by girls and women as they mature, they assume that these things will take care of themselves.

The evidence suggests otherwise. Although the statistics on domestic violence in the United States vary considerably depending on which reports one reads, it seems safe to say that at least two million women are beaten by their husbands each year and that as many as 600,000 are severely assaulted by them four or more times a year. Violence in the other direction—by women toward their husbands and lovers—does occur but in comparison to these figures its incidence is negligible (Breines and Gordon 1983; Langone 1984; Reynolds 1987).

If the incidence of wife beating is staggering, so is that of child abuse. Recent studies suggest that 38 million adults were sexually abused as children and that, in all, 22 per cent of Americans are victimized, with this proportion quite possibly on the rise. Investigators are now discovering that males as well as females are victims of child sexual abuse and that women as well as men are the victimizers. There is not equal representation in the two categories, however. Female victims far outnumber males and the great majority of offenders are men. Interestingly enough, despite our ever present fear that a stranger will molest our children, the vast majority of child sexual abuse cases occur in or close to home. Nearly eight million of those victimized as children were abused by a family member. When the abuser is not a family member he or she—but far more likely he—is very probably a family friend or else a neighbor, the family physician, or someone standing in loco parentis: a baby sitter or day care worker, a teacher or coach, a foster parent or a member of the staff of an institution for abused and neglected children (Breines and Gordon 1983; Crewdson 1988).

Include in this picture the statistics on divorce and desertion and one clearly sees the folly of assuming that in American society, at least, being a person who contributes positively to home and family comes naturally.

The reasons for adding (e) to the list of educational goals and restructuring the school curriculum accordingly are many, but a nagging question remains. If education for family living is really needed, is it not home's responsibility rather than school's? School and home are indeed partners in the education of a nation's young (Martin 1992). Moreover, it is correct to say that, in the past, (e) was assigned to the hidden partner whose continuing contributions to a child's development are both relied on by school and society and refused public recognition. But home and family have been transformed in the last decades. As John Dewey pointed out almost a century ago in connection with the changes in the American household wrought by the Industrial Revolution, when conditions change radically "Only an equally radical change in education suffices" (Dewey 1956, p.12).

Dewey's answer to the question he posed in *The School and Society* of what radical change in school suffices when home changes—namely, placing the occupations of the once traditional home at the center of the school curriculum—does not address the problems created at century's end by the most recent transformation of our private homes. The issue today is not the removal of work from the household into factories but the domestic vacuum that is created when mothers as well as fathers leave home each day to go to work. To be sure, it is not just in the last decades that women have left their own homes to go to work—often in other women's homes. But in the past it was primarily the very poor who did not return home once they had children.

Let me emphasize that to acknowledge this new reality is not to blame mothers for going out to work. After all, if fathers had not already done so there would be no domestic vacuum. However, the evidence I have cited suggests that in the United States, at least, the changed and changing home is not adequately handling the assignment of teaching young children to live at home in families and preparing older ones for their future lives there. There would seem, then, to be no alternative but to respond to Dewey's challenge by adding (e) to our list of the goals of schooling.

That curriculum will thereby be enriched goes without saying. Why is so little space presently reserved in the general curriculum for subject-entities and subject matter associated with home and family? The curricular gap is explained by the gap in our goals. Why learn about home and family, why study society's reproductive processes, if school's function is to equip students to take their places as workers and citizens in the world outside the private home? Granted, education's goals do not dictate the details of curriculum. But just as the exclusion of (e) from the list accounts for the extraordinary absence in school's course of study, its inclusion will insure the presence of what has been left out. Or rather, some of what is missing, for (e) can all too easily be interpreted very narrowly. It can be construed as mandating simply that curriculum space be given over to theories and narratives about home. It is equally important, however, that boys and girls alike learn to exercise the virtues which our culture thinks of as housed in our private homes.

IV

Basic knowledge about home and family—for instance, about their histories and their different cultural forms; indeed, the fact that they have histories and take different forms—has been missing from the school curriculum because of the gap in school's goals and the prejudice against subject-entities drawn from society's reproductive processes. But that is not all. In the reports issued in the 1980s on American higher education, lower education, teacher certification, professional preparation, one finds repeated demands for proficiency in the 3Rs, for clear, logical thinking, and for higher standards of achievement in science, mathematics, history, literature, and the like. One searches in vain for discussions of love or calls for mastery of the 3Cs of care, concern, and connection.

Once again, a gender analysis explains the omission (Martin 1992, pp. 136–7). Associated in our cultural consciousness with home and with the reproductive processes housed there, and viewed as women's exclusive property, the 3Cs are thought to have no bearing on the activities of the public world. Those reports on the condition of American education testify, however, to the preoccupation of educators with life in that domain. Giving home the silent treatment, they view boys and girls as travelers to the public arena, and school as the place they stop en route in order to acquire the knowledge, skill, attitudes, and values that they will presumably need when they reach their destination.

Once children enter school they do not go home again in this unexamined scenario; not ever, not even as adults. True, the authors of the reports expected children to do something called "homework" but the term is a misnomer. Designed by teachers as part of the ongoing work of the classroom, these assignments have no more to do with the business of the home than the briefs a lawyer reads on the commuter train each evening or the papers a teacher corrects after dinner. Homework is schoolwork done after school hours. The worksite may be the private home, but the home represented in the script is a house in which the silence of school prevails and parents act as proctors for their offspring.

The reports turn school's partner in the educational enterprise into an antagonist ever ready to subvert its mission. The idea that because home has changed school might have to change did not occur to the authors of these tomes. The thought that school should take over its partner's responsibility of preparing young people to live in those homes and families from which they exit each morning first to go to school and then to go to work in the public world was the furthest thing from their minds.

Obviously, to go beyond is not necessarily to leave behind. Nevertheless, in the United States, if not in all Western societies, people tend to think of becoming educated not just as a process of acquiring new ways of thinking, feeling, and acting. They also assume that it is a matter of casting off the attitudes and values, the patterns of thought and action associated with domesticity.

Does it matter? In May 1989 a courageous sixteen-year-old wrote to the *Boston Globe* expressing concern about the rise in teen violence (Naples 1989; cf Martin 1992, pp. 44–45). He said he had gotten used to kids carrying knives, but now they were carrying guns. "There are a couple of reasons for this rise," he said, "but the main one is to be tough or respected. They feel power when they have that deadly piece of steel in their hand. Another reason is that they are so easy to get." Since he had observed this change in just six months, he wondered what the world would be like in six years. Would it turn into "a combat zone" controlled by kids with guns?

Historians have shown that when the Industrial Revolution irrevocably changed the American household by removing both work and workers from it, home—specifically the white middle and upper class home—came to be viewed as a haven in a cold, cruel, world: the place to which men retreated after spending a long day in the greedy, pugnacious, possessive, jealous public arena. Whether or not it ever actually fit this description, its presumed ethos of love and intimacy and the values of care, concern, and connection it was said to embody were thought to be conducive to the rest and renewal required by the husbands and sons who were expected to reenter the fray each morning. But home's culturally assigned task was not merely to refresh and invigorate. It was expected to play a moral role as well. Besides inducting infants into human culture and teaching young children the basics of American life, it was supposed to provide its members with an ongoing education in the very kindness and cooperation, affection and sympathy that were also considered to be the prerequisites of life in a harmonious society.

According to Dewey, before the Industrial Revolution industry, responsibility, imagination, and ingenuity were the basic elements of home's curriculum. Perhaps so, but after that cataclysmic event it was considered home's particular function to teach what Carol Gilligan has called an "ethic of care." Serving to curb the selfishness and dampen the pugnacity of men who spent their days in the public world of work and politics, the moral education extended by the home was supposed to keep society as a whole from slipping into a war of every man against every man. As the nations of nineteenth century Europe were deemed able to keep the peace so long as the balance of power among them was maintained, the individuals in a society were considered able to live together harmoniously so long as the moral equilibrium between private home and public world was preserved.

Whatever efficacy that delicate balance of home and world might once have had, the changes in both make our continued reliance on home for a curriculum in an ethic of care anachronistic. That the 3Cs are as vital to the well being of the world beyond the private home and are essential to the maintenance of life on earth makes this outdated arrangement all the more reprehensible. Yet even as research on gender exposes this curricular absence, thus paving the way for curriculum improvement, it uncovers the scorn that boys have for girls and women. For an ethic of care to be a genuine part of the curriculum of boys as well as girls, school will have to address the misogyny of its male inhabitants.

V

For four years in the 1970s Rafaela Best watched a group of elementary school children in the Central Atlantic region of the United States learn what she called the "second curriculum"—the one that teaches each sex "how to perform according to conventional gender norms" (Best 1983, p. 5). Coming to know the children intimately, she reported in *We've All Got Scars* that although most of the boys did not master this material by the end of first grade, in the next two years the majority became proficient in it. The ones who did not grasp the norms or were simply unable or unwilling to meet them were scorned by the other boys and excluded from their club. These outcasts were not necessarily shunned by the girls in the class but they were perceived as losers both by themselves and by those who had passed the various tests of masculinity with flying colors. Tracing the mastery of the second curriculum by six, seven, and eight year old boys, Best showed how closely the macho ideal to which they aspired was linked to a scorn of girls and women and a fear of feminization. The excluded boys "were regarded as being like girls and not like real men," she reported (Best 1983, p. 24; cf Martin 1992, pp. 72ff, 102ff). For a third grader to be called a sissy "was a fate worse than death" (Best 1983, p. 22). To be a cry-baby or to be oriented to one's mother or female teacher was inexcusable. Kenny, one of the "losers" in the class, liked doing housekeeping tasks in school for his teacher and enjoyed receiving her hugs in return. Jason, another loser, cried frequently. And Edward, whose behavior in school was far too perfect, was not good at games. Fighting, or at least the willingness to fight when challenged, was one essential ingredient of masculinity in the "winners" eyes. Playing well and playing rough was another. Engaging in "anti-establishment" activities ranging from throwing mudballs at houses and cars to stuffing paper in the school locks was a third. All three aspects of seven and eight year old machismo were valued in large part because their opposites betokened femininity.

Can we disregard Best's boys? In 1989 Derrick Jackson told *Boston Globe* readers about sixth graders in a public school who had been asked to tell the first word that came to mind about the other sex. The girls said: "Fine. Jerks. Conceited. Ugly. Crazy. Dressy. Sexy. Dirty minds. Boring. Rude. Cute. Stuck up. Desperate. Sexually abusive. Punks." The boys said: "Pumping ('big tits'). Nasty. Vagina. Dope bodies (big breasts and behinds). Door knob (breasts). Hooker. Skeezer (a girl who will 'do it' with 50 guys)" (Jackson 1989).

There is nothing idiosyncratic about these images. Here is what Margaret Clark, in *The Great Divide*, reported that primary school girls in Australia have to say on the subject:

> There's a group of boys in our class who always tease us and call us—you know, dogs, aids, slut, moll and that (Clark 1989, p. 25).
> This boy used to call us big-tits and period-bag and used to punch us in the breasts (Clark 1989, p. 25).
> They take things off us and drag us into the boys' toilets (Clark 1989, p. 39).
> They call us rabies, dogs, aids (Clark 1989, p. 39).
> They reckon I'm a dog. My brother gave me to them. He said, 'Oh, come here, I've got a pet for you. Do you want my dog? And he gave me to them as a pet dog.' (Clark 1989, p. 40).

According to the female teachers in Clark's report, the girls were not the boys' only targets, however:

> I've been here for four years, but at the beginning of this year the whole school blew up with some problems. Boys that I had visited at home, taught in my class and been on camp with—I thought I had a good relationship with them—put their fingers up at me and then stood there as if to say, 'What are you going to do about it?' I was horrified. I could not believe it (Clark 1989, p. 22).
> I used to spend a lot of time on the basketball court, to get the girls involved but last

year I was bullied off the court, by one of my boy students. I was in tears. He bullied me off (Clark 1989, p. 22).

Almost any day of the week I see boys using sexuality as a way of exerting power. You know boys going up to a female teacher and sticking two fingers up at her (Clark 1989, p. 23).

There's a case of a little boy in this school. Now he didn't know that I was the principal. I guess he just assumed it would be a man. He was sent to me for being obnoxious and obscene with one of the children in the playground. So I went and spoke to him, treating him fairly gently because he does have a lot of problems. He just stood there and was quite defiant. I just said to him 'now listen. I am the boss of this school.' Now that child just changed (Clark 1989, p. 24).

Female teachers are nothing to some male children (Clark 1989, p. 23).

By comparison, the experience of 16 year old Kathy, an Inner London comprehensive school student, cited by Dale Spender seems mild:

Sometimes I feel like saying that I disagree, that there are other ways of looking at it, but where would that get me? My teacher thinks I'm showing off, and the boys jeer. But if I pretend I don't understand, it's very different. The teacher is sympathetic and the boys are helpful. They really respond if they can show you how it is done, but there's nothing but 'aggro' if you give any signs of showing them how it is done (Spender 1980, p. 150).

Yet other reports cited by Spender resemble these given by Clark:

A group of year 6 students were walking across the school yard from the library to the classroom. One of the boys ran up behind one of the girls, rammed a rule between her legs and called her a slut (Clark 1989, p. 25).

Well, as the music started, without a word spoken, the girls lined up at the back and the boys all moved together and sort of faced the girls. The girls started to move and sing but the boys stood in the line and started singing very loudly and moving in a very sexual way, you know swinging their hips and their arms and legs and walking slowly towards the girls as they did it, staring at them. It was an aggressive and threatening situation. The girls immediately stopped moving, stopped singing and just looked at each other with very stunned expressions (Clark 1989, p. 42).

Studies of gender relations in classrooms leave little doubt that boys need training in the 3Cs. The reports of male violence point to the same conclusion. Yet how can we expect boys and men to appropriate for themselves traits and values that both they and their culture associate with girls and women? Why would anyone want to adopt an ethic belonging to a despised people?

Given the misogyny that stands in the way of teaching the 3Cs to boys as well as girls, it is tempting to renounce the undertaking. Yet insofar as both our private homes and public spaces are plagued by violence, the policy of excluding an ethic of care from the school curriculum or including it only in the curriculum of girls is a recipe for disaster. What can we do?

The studies cited here make it quite clear that misogyny is learned in school as well as in society at large. One response to a hidden curriculum of school or society or both is to do nothing, to act as if it does not exist (Ch. 8, this volume). But nonaction scarcely

seems defensible when the hidden curriculum at issue dehumanizes half the population. A better response than inaction to an offensive hidden curriculum is to raise it
to consciousness by bringing it into the curriculum proper as an explicit topic of study.
Besides making it possible to reduce the misogyny, this step would enrich the school
curriculum by introducing subject matter about the psychological and cultural construction of gender and even perhaps by making gender itself the subject-entity of a
school subject. Yet although it would also help to pave the way for the entrance of the
3Cs, it is not enough.

VI

If the goal of preparing young people to live in private homes as family members
does not assure space for the 3Cs in the curriculum of boys as well as girls, neither does
it guarantee that domesticity will be made the business of both sexes (Martin 1992,
pp.106–7, p. 150ff). One of Best's boys, vintage 1975, said to her, "I'll starve to death
before I'll cook" (Best 1983, p. 80). When asked how he planned to keep his house clean
and have food to eat he replied, "I'll get a wife for that." This scorn for things domestic finds an echo in Anne Machung's report on a survey of the expectations of graduating
seniors at the University of California Berkeley campus (Machung 1989). The overwhelming majority of those studied hoped to marry, have children, and pursue a career.
Of the women, nearly nine-tenths planned to acquire graduate degrees and half thought
they would earn at least as much as their husbands. Few anticipated getting divorced
or raising their youngsters alone. Each one believed she would rear two or three children and expected to interrupt her career for anywhere from six months to twelve years
to do so. While in Machung's words the women were "talking career but thinking job"
in order to be in a position to take care of the children they wanted to have, the men
were talking family but thinking career. They were willing to "help out" at home but
they did not want to be told what to do or have their contributions measured against
their wives', let alone share housework equally. As for child care, most not only believed
it to be the wife's responsibility; they could barely see themselves making day care
arrangements or missing work when the children were sick.

If Machung's college seniors sound like Best's boys grown up, they also bear a close
resemblance to the young men in the philosophy of education course I recently taught.
Like many of the women students in my class, I had started to think that American
culture was no longer in the clutches of those traditional gender stereotypes that place
women in the home and put them in charge of society's reproductive processes. Then,
in connection with our study of Rousseau, I played the song "William's Doll" from
the recording Free To Be You and Me and was forced to change my mind. Young
William wanted a baby doll to hug and hold and wash and clean and dress and feed.
As the song proceeded and William continued to ask for a doll against his father's
wishes and his friends' taunts, the young men in my class began exchanging looks. By
the time Grandma had come to William's rescue, saying that he wanted the doll so

that when he was a father he would know what to do, they were beside themselves. Why? It turned out that, to a man, they believed that if you give a small boy a doll to play with—not a GI Joe but a baby doll—he will grow up to be homosexual, in their eyes something definitely unnatural and abnormal. That he will ultimately contract AIDS seemed also to be a foregone conclusion.

Although I did not know this at the time, a decade earlier Best had played the same song for the young children she was studying and to similar effect. The boys in grades one to three did not look askance; they crawled under their desks and hid under the coats on the rack. Commenting that some years later those boys could listen to "William's Doll" "without experiencing trauma," she said that for fifth graders gender "stereotypes were no longer so urgent" (Best 1983). Quite possibly her ten year old boys were beginning to make some accommodations to girls because of her interventions in their classrooms, but the scene in my classroom attested to the staying power of the stereotypes. It also bore witness to young men's continuing resistance to domesticity.

Whatever gains women may have made in the last decades, the cultural conviction that caring and concern are womanly virtues and that domesticity in general and the nurture of children in particular are primarily, if not exclusively, women's business persists. So does the belief that the activities and tasks associated with society's reproductive processes are too trivial to command men's attention and too menial to warrant their participation.

Although boys do not learn to devalue and resist domesticity only in school, the silences about home and family in the curriculum proper constitute a hidden curriculum in anti domesticity. As gender research has long since demonstrated, the power of curricular silence is immense. The British philosopher R.S. Peters was right: whether or not what is taught in school is in fact worthwhile, in calling something "education" we place our seal of approval on it (Peters 1967, p.3). Not that education always lives up to its reputation. Peters knew that some teaching is good and some bad, that some curricula are well designed and others are not. His point was that although the content of education differs from one culture to the next, whatever it is that a culture chooses to call education will comprise the information it takes to be important for young people to know and the activities it considers worthwhile. Peters did not pursue the logic of his own argument but it is easily done. Just as the inclusion of something in the curriculum—a topic, a body of fact and theory, a perspective—signifies the value placed on it, exclusion bespeaks the culture's devaluation of it. In addition, the act of exclusion serves to reinforce that assessment.

The devaluation of domesticity is so widespread that it might seem the prudent course to forego hope of bringing it into the curriculum as everyone's business. The problem is, men's resistance to domesticity is taking its toll on society. "I've had 4,000 arrests on nonsupport, and this guy was the smoothest I've seen. All he talked about was how he loved sailing and couldn't wait to get back to it," a State Department of Revenue investigator told a news columnist (English 1989). The man's ex-wife who at one time held two jobs so as to stay off welfare said, "Now, I hope Chip can finish college. He's such a nice kid. I just do not understand how a father could leave a child like that."

What with many fathers leaving home altogether, the majority of men who remain there being unwilling to do more than a tiny fraction of home's work, and mothers as well as fathers going out to work each day, children are being left to their own devices and women are becoming "bone-weary" (Landers 1990). Gender roles have changed considerably in the last decades and our cultural construction of domesticity has not kept pace. To bring domesticity into school as the business of both sexes will not just enrich curriculum. It will help bring both the concept and the practices of domesticity into alignment with the new realities of family life. "I have a little difficulty being a househusband," an unemployed coal miner told *Time* correspondent Melissa Ludtke. "But I love being with the kids. I also believe it is good for them to see me doin' housework, so they don't keep believin' that outside work belongs only to the man and inside is the woman" (Ludtke 1988).

VII

Needless to say, if the curriculum is really to teach boys as well as girls to shoulder responsibility for the tasks and functions of the private home, our cultural construct— or perhaps I should say constructs—of domesticity and the hidden curriculum in anti-domesticity will both have to be raised to consciousness. The links between misogyny and the denigration of domesticity will also need to be addressed for, as the attitudes of Best's boys make clear, the scorn of things domestic and of females are closely linked. And, of course, school will have to take to heart the fear of feminization that lurks behind these phenomena.

Even this listing suggests that it may well be a mistake to speak of curriculum "enrichment," as I have been doing. And if the domain of the 3Cs is to be enlarged, curriculum makers will also have to take steps to counteract the stereotypical images of the private home and the public world—and of society's reproductive and productive processes—as polar opposites. Connoting mere addition—as when milk is enriched by an injection of vitamins—the term does not begin to capture the radical implications for curriculum of the study of gender. Actually, "enrichment" is doubly misleading: masking the transformative potential of research on gender, it implies that there is nothing really wrong with curriculum—that curriculum only needs a bit of fortification. Add up the misrepresentations of and silences about women in curriculum's subject matter, the double standard by which its subject-entities are judged, the gap in its goals, its failure to save space for an ethic of care and to reserve room for the tasks and responsibilities of domesticity, however, and it becomes quite clear that curriculum as it stands is failing to transmit to the next generation one half of the cultural heritage.[3] This in itself should be enough to undermine the faith that curriculum requires only minor improvement. Take into account the misogyny and anti-domesticity that are now being passed along by curriculum's silences and distortions and any lingering doubts that curriculum needs to be radically revised will surely be dispelled.

As I hope I have shown here, the study of gender is as germane to the reconstruction of curriculum as to its deconstruction. I do not want to leave the impression, however, that curricular enrichment and radical curriculum revision are incompatible: that attempts to accomplish the former will necessarily subvert the latter. On the contrary, I have become increasingly convinced that the radical reconstruction of curriculum we so badly need will come about not in one fell swoop but as the "emergent" outcome of massive doses of enrichment, each one of which may require a small act of courage.

Notes

I wish to thank Ann Diller, Susan Franzosa, Barbara Houston, Susan Laird, Michael Martin, Beatrice Nelson, Jennifer Radden, Janet Farrell Smith and members of the Gender Enrichment Conference Workshop for their helpful comments and suggestions on an early draft.

1. History and the other disciplines of knowledge also misrepresent the lives, works, and experiences of minority men. However, because my topic is gender I will not discuss this gap in the text here.

2. The Project is based at the Wellesley College Center for Research on Women in Wellesley, Massachusetts. Peggy McIntosh and Emily Style are its co-directors.

3. When one counts in the omissions relating to minorities, it turns out that it is actually transmitting much less!

REFERENCES

Achebe, C. (1959). *Things Fall Apart.* Greenwich, Conn.: Fawcett.

Archambault, R. D. (1965). *Philosophical Analysis and Education.* London: Routledge & Kegan Paul.

Bass, Alison. (1991). "Talking to Men, A Bold Woman Just Can't Win." *The Boston Globe,* 7 January: 33, 34.

Bereiter, Carl. (1973). *Must We Educate?* Englewood Cliffs, N.J.: Prentice-Hall.

Beardsley, E. (1977). "Traits and Genderization." In M. Vetterling-Braggin, F. A. Elliston, & J. English, eds., *Feminism and Philosophy,* 117–123. Totowa, NJ: Littlefield.

de Beauvoir, S. (1961). *The Second Sex.* New York: Bantam.

Beecher, Catharine M. (1829) *Suggestions Respecting Improvements in Education.* Hartford: Packard and Butler.

Best, Rafaela. (1983). *We've All Got Scars.* Bloomington: Indiana University Press.

Bloom, A. (1987). *The Closing of the American Mind.* New York: Simon & Schuster.

Blum, L. (1980). *Friendship, Altruism, and Morality.* London: Routledge & Kegan Paul.

Breines, W., & Gordon, L. (1983). "The New Scholarship on Family Violence." *Signs,* 8(3): 493–507.

Brent, Allen. (1978). *Philosophical Foundations for the Curriculum.* London: George Allen and Unwin.

Bronars, Joanne. (1970). "Tampering with Nature in Elemental School Science." In *Readings in the Philosophy of Education: A Study of Curriculum.* Jane R. Martin, ed. Boston: Allyn & Bacon.

Bruner, Jerome S. (1961). *The Process of Education.* Cambridge, MA: Harvard Univ. Press.

Chodorow, N. (1978). *The Reproduction of Mothering.* Berkeley: University of California Press.

Clark, Margaret. (1989). *The Great Divide.* Canberra: Curriculum Development Centre.

Clark, Lorenne M. G. and Lange, Lynda, eds. (1979). *The Sexism of Social and Political Theory.* Toronto: Univ. of Toronto Press.

Crewdson, John. (1988). *By Silence Betrayed: Sexual Abuse of Children in America.* Boston: Little, Brown.

Dewey, John. (1956). *The School and Society.* Chicago: The University of Chicago Press.

English, Bella. (1989). "No Support, But Nice Tan." *The Boston Globe,* 15 May.

Featherstone, Joseph. (1969). "The British Infant Schools." *Radical School Reform.* Beatrice and Ronald Gross, eds. New York: Simon and Schuster.

Fine, M. and Zane, N. (1989). "Bein' Wrapped Too Tight: When Low-Income Women Drop Out of High School." In Weis, L., Farrar, E. and Petrie, H., eds. *Dropouts from School.* Albany: SUNY Press.

Fisher, Dorothy Canfield. (1912). *A Montessori Mother.* New York: Henry Holt.

Frankena, W. (1970). "A Model for Analyzing a Philosophy of Education." In *Readings in the Philosophy of Education: A Study of Curriculum.* Jane R. Martin, ed. Boston: Allyn & Bacon.

Freedman, S. (1990). *Small Victories.* New York: Harper & Row.

Gayer, Nancy. (1970). "On Making Morality Operational." In *Readings in the Philosophy of Education: A Study of Curriculum.* Jane R. Martin, ed. Boston: Allyn & Bacon.

Gilligan, Carol. (1982). *In a Different Voice.* Cambridge: Harvard University Press.

Goodfield, J. (1981). *An Imagined World.* New York: Harper & Row.

Graubard, Allen. (1971) *Free the Children.* New York: Random House.

Gross, Beatrice, and Gross, Ronald, eds. (1969). *Radical School Reform.* New York: Simon & Schuster.

Hacker, A. (1990) "Trans-National America," *The New York Review of Books 37* (18): 19–24.

Henry, Jules. (1968). *Culture Against Man.* New York: Random House.

Herndon, James. (1968) *The Way It Spozed to Be.* New York: Simon & Schuster.

Hirsch, E.D. Jr. (1987). *Cultural Literacy.* Boston: Houghton Mifflin.

Hirst, P.H. (1974). *Knowledge and the Curriculum.* London: Routledge & Kegan Paul.

Hirst, P. H., and Peters, R.S., (1970). *The Logic of Education.* London: Routledge & Kegan Paul.

Holmes, Henry. (1912). "Introduction." *The Montessori Method.* By Maria Montessori. New York: Frederick A. Stokes.

Holt, John. (1964). *How Children Fail.* New York: Dell.

Hunt, J. McV. (1964). "Introduction." *The Montessori Method.* By Maria Montessori. New York: Schocken Books.

Illich, Ivan. (1971). *Deschooling society.* New York: Harper & Row.

Jackson, Derrick Z. (1989). "The Seeds of Violence," *The Boston Globe,* 2 June.

James, H. (1966) *The Bostonians.* New York: Penguin.

Janeway, E. (1971). *Man's World, Woman's Place.* New York: Morrow.

Johnson, A.G. (1980). "On the Prevalence of Rape in the United States." *Signs,* 6(1): 136–146.

Kaplan, A.G., & Bean, J.P., eds. (1976). *Beyond Sex-role Stereotypes.* Boston: Little, Brown.

Kaplan, A.G., & Sedney, M.A. (1980). *Psychology and Sex Roles.* Boston: Little, Brown.

Katz, Michael. B. (1971). *Class, Bureaucracy and Schools: The Illusion of Educational Change in America.* New York: Praeger.

Keller, E. F. (1983). *A Feeling for the Organism.* San Francisco: W.H. Freeman.

Kennedy, J. (1989). "Researchers Say Male Lawyers Worst at Offensive Behavior." *The Boston Globe.* 23 June: 6.

Kidder, T. (1989). *Among Schoolchildren.* Boston: Houghton Mifflin.

Kilpatrick, William Heard. (1914). *The Montessori System Examined.* Boston: Houghton Mifflin.

King, A. R., and Brownell, J. A. (1966). *The Curriculum and the Disciplines of Knowledge.* New York: John Wiley.

Kozol, Jonathan. (1967). *Death at an Early Age.* Boston: Houghton Mifflin.

Kozol, Jonathan. (1988). *Rachel and Her Children.* New York: Crown.

Landers, Ann. (1990). "A Few Survival Tips for Working Parents," *Boston Globe,* 26 February.

Lightfoot, S.L. (1983). *The Good High School.* New York: Basic.

Lott, B., Reilly, M.E. & Howard, D.R., (1982). "Sexual Assault and Harassment: A Campus Community Case Study." *Signs,* 8(2): 296–319.

Ludtke, Melissa. (1988). "Through the Eyes of Children." *Time,* 8 August.

Machung, Ann. (1989). "Talking Career, Thinking Job: Gender Difference in Career and Family Expectations of Berkeley Seniors." *Feminist Studies,* 15: 35–58.

Mann, P. (1990). "Unifying Discourse: City College as Postmodern Public Sphere." *Social Text,* 25/6: 81–102.

Martin, Jane Roland. (1977). "The Anatomy of Subjects." *Educational Theory* 27(2): 85–95.

Martin, Jane Roland. (1990). "Filling the Gap: The Goals of American Education Revised." *International Review of Education,* 36: 145–157.

Martin, Jane Roland. (1987). "Martial Virtues or Capital Vices? William James' Moral Equivalent of War Revisited." *Journal of Thought,* 22: 32–44.

Martin, Jane Roland, ed. (1970). *Readings in the Philosophy of Education: A Study of Curriculum.* Boston: Allyn & Bacon.

Martin, Jane Roland. (1985). *Reclaiming a Conversation.* New Haven: Yale University Press.

Martin, Jane Roland. (1992). *The Schoolhome: Rethinking Schools for Changing Families.* Cambridge, MA: Harvard University Press.

Martin, Jane Roland. (1982). "Two Dogmas of Curriculum." *Synthese,* 51(April): 5–20.

Martin, Jane Roland. (1976). "What Should We Do with a Hidden Curriculum When We Find One?" *Curriculum Inquiry,* 6:135–151.

Mayer, Martin. (1964). "Introduction." *The Montessori Method.* By Maria Montessori. Cambridge, MA: Robert Bentley.

Mill, John Stuart. ([1869]1970). *The Subjection of Women.* Reprint. Robert Wendell Carr, ed. Cambridge, MA: MIT Press.

Mintz, Steven and Susan Kellogg. (1988). *Domestic Revolutions: A Social History of American Family Life.* New York: The Free Press.

Montessori, Maria. (1912). *The Montessori Method.* New York: Frederick A. Stokes.

Montessori, Maria. (1964). *The Montessori Method.* New York: Schocken Books.

Montessori, Maria. 1972). *Education for Peace.* Chicago: Henry Regnery.

Montessori, Maria. (1984). *The Absorbent Mind.* New York: Dell.

Mydens, S. (1990). "A Shot at the Action for Hispanic Citizens." *The New York Times,* 10 June.

Naples, Robert. (1989). "Letter to the Editor." *The Boston Globe,* 26 May.

Nyquist, Ewald B. and Gene R. Hawes, eds. (1972). *Open Education.* New York: Bantam Books.

Okin, Susan Moller. (1979). *Women in Western Political Thought.* Princeton: Princeton Univ. Press.

Pestalozzi, Johann Heinrich. ([1781]1885). *Leonard and Gertrude.* Boston: D.C. Heath.

Peters, R.S. (1972). Education and the Educated Man. In R. E Dearden, P.H. Hirst, & R.S. Peters, eds., *A Critique of Current Educational Aims.* London: Routledge & Kegan Paul.

Peters, R.S. (1967). *Ethics and Education.* Glenview, Ill.: Scott, Foresman.

Phenix, Philip. (1964). *Realms of Meaning.* New York: McGraw-Hill.

Plato. (1974). *Republic.* G. M. A. Grube, trans. Indianapolis: Hackett.

Pursell, William. (1976). *A Conservative Alternative School: The A+ School in Cupertino.* Bloomington, Ind.: Phi Delta Kappa.

Rathbone, Charles H., ed. (1971). *Open Education.* New York: Citation Press.

Reynolds, Pamela. (1987). "Violence at Home." *The Boston Globe,* 29 March: A15, 17.

John Langone, (1984). *Violence.* Boston: Little, Brown.

Rhodes, R. (1988). *The Making of the Atomic Bomb.* New York: Simon & Schuster.

Ribadeneira, D. and Hernandez, P. (1990). "Boston Schools Steer Hispanics Down a Path to Failure." *The Boston Globe,* 10 June.

Rodriguez, R. (1982). *Hunger of Memory.* Boston: David R. Godine.

Roland, Jane. (1959). " On 'Knowing How' and 'Knowing That'." *The Philosophical Review,* LXVII.

Rorty, R. (1979). *Philosophy and the Mirror of Nature.* Princeton, N.J.: Princeton University Press.

Rosen, Charles and Henri Zerner. (1984). *Romanticism and Realism.* New York: W.W. Norton.

Rosenblum, Nancy. (1987). *Another Liberalism: Romanticism and the Reconstruction of Liberal Thought.* Cambridge: Harvard University Press.

Rousseau, Jean-Jacques. (1979). *Emile.* Allan Bloom, trans. New York: Basic Books.

Rusk, Robert R. (1965). *Doctrines of the Great Educators.* 3d ed. New York: St. Martin's Press.

Scheffler, Israel. (1966). *Philosophy and Education,* 2d ed. Boston: Allyn & Bacon.

Schell, J. (1982). *The Fate of the Earth.* New York: Avon.

Schmid, Randolph E. (1988). "Unmarried US Couples Increase, Top 2.3 Million." *The Boston Globe,* 13 May: A6.

Schrag. Peter, and Divoky, Diane. (1975). *The Myth of the Hyperactive Child.* New York: Pantheon Books.

Silber, Kate. (1965). *Pestalozzi.* New York: Schocken Books.

Silberman, Charles E. (1970). *Crisis in the Classroom.* New York: Random House.

Spender, Dale. (1980). "Talking in Class." In *Learning to Lose.* Dale Spender and Elizabeth Sarah, eds. London: Women's Press.

Stacey, Judith; Bereaud, Susan; and Daniels, Joan, eds. (1974). *And Jill Came Tumbling After: Sexism in American Education.* New York: Dell.

Stacey, Judith. (1987). "Sexism by a Subtler Name? Postindustrial Conditions and Postfeminist Consciousness in the Silicon Valley." *Socialist Review* 96: 8–28.

Vallance, Elizabeth. (1973/74). "Hiding the Hidden Curriculum: An Interpretation of the Language of Justification in Nineteenth-century Educational Reform." *Curriculum Theory Network* 4, no. 1: 5–22.

Waks, Leonard and Rustum Roy. (1987). "Learning from Technology." In Kenneth D. Benne and Steven Tozer, eds. *Society as Educator in an Age of Transition.* Eighty-sixth Yearbook of the National Society for the Study of Education. Chicago: University of Chicago Press.

Watson, J.D. (1969). *The Double Helix.* New York: New American Library.

White, Jessie. (1917). *Montessori Schools: As Seen in the Early Summer of 1913.* London: Oxford.

Wollstonecraft, Mary. (1967). *A Vindication of the Rights of Woman.* New York: Norton.

Woolf, Virginia. (1928). *A Room of One's Own.* New York: Harcourt Brace Jovanovich.

Woolf, Virginia. (1938). *Three Guineas.* New York: Harcourt, Brace & World.

INDEX